MENTOR'S GUIDE   **Capstone** Curriculum

Module 16 — Urban Mission

Doing Justice & Loving Mercy: Compassion Ministries

Let Justice Roll Down:
THE VISION *and* THEOLOGY OF THE KINGDOM

Doing Justice and Loving Mercy (1):
THE URBAN CONGREGATION

Doing Justice and Loving Mercy (2):
THE URBAN COMMUNITY *and* NEIGHBORHOOD

Doing Justice and Loving Mercy (3):
SOCIETY *and* WORLD

This curriculum is the result of thousands of hours of work by The Urban Ministry Institute (TUMI) and should not be reproduced without their express permission. TUMI supports all who wish to use these materials for the advance of God's Kingdom, and affordable licensing to reproduce them is available. Please confirm with your instructor that this book is properly licensed. For more information on TUMI and our licensing program, visit *www.tumi.org* and *www.tumi.org/license*.

Capstone Module 16: Doing Justice and Loving Mercy: Compassion Ministries Mentor's Guide

ISBN: 978-1-62932-036-6

© 2005, 2011, 2013, 2015. The Urban Ministry Institute. All Rights Reserved.
First edition 2005, Second edition 2011, Third edition 2013, Fourth edition 2015.

Copying, redistribution and/or sale of these materials, or any unauthorized transmission, except as may be expressly permitted by the 1976 Copyright Act or in writing from the publisher is prohibited. Requests for permission should be addressed in writing to: The Urban Ministry Institute, 3701 E. 13th Street, Wichita, KS 67208.

The Urban Ministry Institute is a ministry of World Impact, Inc.

All Scripture quotations, unless otherwise noted, are from The Holy Bible, English Standard Version, copyright © 2001 by Crossway Bible, a division of Good News Publishers. Used by permission. All Rights Reserved.

Contents

Course Overview
- 3   About the Instructor
- 5   Introduction to the Module
- 7   Course Requirements

13   Lesson 1
Let Justice Roll Down: The Vision and Theology of the Kingdom

57   Lesson 2
Doing Justice and Loving Mercy: The Urban Congregation

101   Lesson 3
Doing Justice and Loving Mercy: The Urban Community and Neighborhood

147   Lesson 4
Doing Justice and Loving Mercy: Society and World

191   Appendices

295   Mentoring the Capstone Curriculum

303   Lesson 1 Mentor's Notes

311   Lesson 2 Mentor's Notes

321   Lesson 3 Mentor's Notes

329   Lesson 4 Mentor's Notes

About the Instructor

Rev. Dr. Don L. Davis is the Executive Director of The Urban Ministry Institute and a Senior Vice President of World Impact. He attended Wheaton College and Wheaton Graduate School, and graduated summa cum laude in both his B.A. (1988) and M.A. (1989) degrees, in Biblical Studies and Systematic Theology, respectively. He earned his Ph.D. in Religion (Theology and Ethics) from the University of Iowa School of Religion.

As the Institute's Executive Director and World Impact's Senior Vice President, he oversees the training of urban missionaries, church planters, and city pastors, and facilitates training opportunities for urban Christian workers in evangelism, church growth, and pioneer missions. He also leads the Institute's extensive distance learning programs and facilitates leadership development efforts for organizations and denominations like Prison Fellowship, the Evangelical Free Church of America, and the Church of God in Christ.

A recipient of numerous teaching and academic awards, Dr. Davis has served as professor and faculty at a number of fine academic institutions, having lectured and taught courses in religion, theology, philosophy, and biblical studies at schools such as Wheaton College, St. Ambrose University, the Houston Graduate School of Theology, the University of Iowa School of Religion, the Robert E. Webber Institute of Worship Studies. He has authored a number of books, curricula, and study materials to equip urban leaders, including *The Capstone Curriculum*, TUMI's premiere sixteen-module distance education seminary instruction, *Sacred Roots: A Primer on Retrieving the Great Tradition*, which focuses on how urban churches can be renewed through a rediscovery of the historic orthodox faith, and *Black and Human: Rediscovering King as a Resource for Black Theology and Ethics*. Dr. Davis has participated in academic lectureships such as the Staley Lecture series, renewal conferences like the Promise Keepers rallies, and theological consortiums like the University of Virginia Lived Theology Project Series. He received the Distinguished Alumni Fellow Award from the University of Iowa College of Liberal Arts and Sciences in 2009. Dr. Davis is also a member of the Society of Biblical Literature, and the American Academy of Religion.

Introduction to the Module

Greetings, in the strong name of Jesus Christ!

As disciples of the Lord Jesus Christ, we are responsible to display in our words and deeds the life of the Kingdom to Come in the midst of our churches, and through our lifestyles and ministries of compassion to others. This module, *Doing Justice and Loving Mercy: Compassion Ministries*, highlights the ways in which we as Christian leaders both conceive and practice generosity in the body of Christ and in the world. As leaders of the church in the city, it is critical that we understand the richness of the biblical insights around this subject, as well as explore the possible ways in which we as believers and Christian ministers can demonstrate the love and justice of the Kingdom where we live.

The first lesson, ***Let Justice Roll Down: The Vision and Theology of the Kingdom***, focuses on the first word, or *prolegomena* toward an understanding of doing justice and loving mercy. We will define the structure of the world from a biblical point of view, and assess the different ways in tradition that church/world relationships have been viewed, and highlight a theology of God that can help us understand the critical role that doing justice and loving mercy plays in our kingdom testimony. We will also look carefully at the *imago Dei* (i.e., the image of God) in Scripture. We will see the uniqueness of humankind, and explore its implications for viewing all individuals, families, peoples, and nations as precious and irreplaceable.

Our second lesson, ***Doing Justice and Loving Mercy: The Urban Congregation***, explores the priority of demonstrating justice and mercy in the Church of Christ. As the people of God, we must understand the "home grown" quality of Christian love, and in this lesson we will consider the significance of God's grace in sustaining ministries of mercy and love, and the implications of experiencing God's grace in our approaches to justice and mercy. We will observe, too, the practices of justice and mercy in God's OT community as well as in the Church, God's kingdom community today. We will also observe the "two-four-six" rules of God's love and justice through the Church. We will begin by looking at the *two objects* which can receive God's justice and mercy, members of the Church and those outside. We will then consider the *four channels* through which God manifests his love: the family, the Church, care societies, and the state. We will finish our study by looking at six principles which should inform our care-giving as local congregations.

In lesson three, *Doing Justice and Loving Mercy: Urban Community and Neighborhood*, we will discuss the two critical truths underlying our understanding of serving in the world: God as creator and Jesus as Lord of all. The Church responds to the lordship of Jesus Christ, serving both as the locus (place) of God's working as well as his agent (ambassador) through whom he works. We will look at the four classic ways that church/world relations have been understood in Church history, and then look at four models which can help us understand better just how the urban church should interact with its neighborhood and community. We will here also introduce a simple yet effective approach to organize our efforts together as we seek the Lord's will to minister mercy and justice in our urban neighborhoods. Prepare, Work, and Review, (PWR) is a simple but exciting process of seeking the Lord's wisdom in ministry. And in this lesson we will provide some practical advice on how to organize in order to provide effective care to others as we address the needs of those in our community.

Finally, in lesson four, *Doing Justice and Loving Mercy: Society and World*, we will seek to expand this notion of doing justice and loving mercy to the very ends of the earth. Here we will look to comprehend our calling to live as *world Christians*, striving to think *globally* but to act *locally*. We will look critically at the issues of poverty and oppression, and the protection of the environment. After considering these weighty issues, we close this module's discussion with a focus on one of the great issues of our time, the concept of difference. We will explore the oft-misunderstood notion of diversity from a kingdom perspective. We will explore the ways in which wrong concepts of difference can fuel bigotry and hatred among people, lead to violence, war and the loss of life and destruction of property. Here we will explore three Christian approaches to mass violence and war, and end our time with a plea for us to embrace a dynamic ministry of Christian peacemaking.

In a world torn by violence, cruelty, and injustice, we desperately need representatives of the Kingdom who can demonstrate both the justice and mercy of our Lord Jesus Christ. Only the Church can reveal the righteousness, unity, and grace of the Kingdom of God in the midst of a world torn by malice, vengeance, and disunity. Only in Christ can we pursue a peace that is authentic and that will last. Until our Lord returns, we are called to display his righteousness in the earth.

May God richly bless you in every way as you refresh your memory of our call to demonstrate justice and love mercy, in the Church and in the world, to the glory of God.

- Rev. Dr. Don L. Davis

Course Requirements

Required Books and Materials

- Bible (for the purposes of this course, your Bible should be a translation [ex. NIV, NASB, RSV, KJV, NKJV, etc.], and not a paraphrase [ex. The Living Bible, The Message]).

- Each Capstone module has assigned textbooks which are read and discussed throughout the course. We encourage you to read, reflect upon, and respond to these with your professors, mentors, and fellow learners. Because of the fluid availability of the texts (e.g., books going out of print), we maintain our *official* Capstone Required Textbook list on our website. Please visit *www.tumi.org/books* to obtain the current listing of this module's texts.

- Paper and pen for taking notes and completing in-class assignments.

Suggested Readings

- McKinney, Bishop George D. *The New Slave Masters*. Colorado Springs, CO: Life Journey, 2005.

- Niebuhr, Reinhold. *Moral Man and Immoral Society*. Louisville, KY: John Knox Press, 2002.

- Phillips, Keith. *Out of Ashes*. Los Angeles: World Impact Press, 1996.

- Sider, Ronald J. *Just Generosity*. Grand Rapids: Baker Book House, 1999.

- Stott, John. *New Issues Facing Christians Today*. Grand Rapids: Zondervan, 1999.

- Yoder, John. *The Politics of Jesus*. Grand Rapids: Eerdmans Publishing Co., 1994.

Summary of Grade Categories and Weights

Attendance & Class Participation	30%	90 pts
Quizzes	10%	30 pts
Memory Verses	15%	45 pts
Exegetical Project	15%	45 pts
Ministry Project	10%	30 pts
Readings and Homework Assignments	10%	30 pts
Final Exam	10%	30 pts
Total:	100%	300 pts

Course Requirements

Grade Requirements

Attendance at each class session is a course requirement. Absences will affect your grade. If an absence cannot be avoided, please let the Mentor know in advance. If you miss a class it is your responsibility to find out the assignments you missed, and to talk with the Mentor about turning in late work. Much of the learning associated with this course takes place through discussion. Therefore, your active involvement will be sought and expected in every class session.

Attendance and Class Participation

Every class will begin with a short quiz over the basic ideas from the last lesson. The best way to prepare for the quiz is to review the Student Workbook material and class notes taken during the last lesson.

Quizzes

The memorized Word is a central priority for your life and ministry as a believer and leader in the Church of Jesus Christ. There are relatively few verses, but they are significant in their content. Each class session you will be expected to recite (orally or in writing) the assigned verses to your Mentor.

Memory Verses

The Scriptures are God's potent instrument to equip the man or woman of God for every work of ministry he calls them to (2 Tim. 3.16-17). In order to complete the requirements for this course you must select a passage and do an inductive Bible study (i.e., an exegetical study) upon it. The study will have to be five pages in length (double-spaced, typed or neatly hand written) and deal with one of the aspects highlighted in this course on the theme of justice, social ethics, and the Christian responsibility for generosity and compassion in the city. Our desire and hope is that you will be deeply convinced of Scripture's ability to change and practically affect

Exegetical Project

your life, and the lives of those to whom you minister. As you go through the course, be open to finding an extended passage (roughly 4-9 verses) on a subject you would like to study more intensely. The details of the project are covered on pages 10-11, and will be discussed in the introductory session of this course.

Ministry Project

Our expectation is that all students will apply their learning practically in their lives and in their ministry responsibilities. The student will be responsible for developing a ministry project that combines principles learned with practical ministry. The details of this project are covered on page 12, and will be discussed in the introductory session of the course.

Class and Homework Assignments

Classwork and homework of various types may be given during class by your Mentor or be written in your Student Workbook. If you have any question about what is required by these or when they are due, please ask your Mentor.

Readings

It is important that the student read the assigned readings from the text and from the Scriptures in order to be prepared for class discussion. Please turn in the "Reading Completion Sheet" from your Student Workbook on a weekly basis. There will be an option to receive extra credit for extended readings.

Take-Home Final Exam

At the end of the course, your Mentor will give you a final exam (closed book) to be completed at home. You will be asked a question that helps you reflect on what you have learned in the course and how it affects the way you think about or practice ministry. Your Mentor will give you due dates and other information when the Final Exam is handed out.

Grading

The following grades will be given in this class at the end of the session, and placed on each student's record:

A - Superior work	D - Passing work
B - Excellent work	F - Unsatisfactory work
C - Satisfactory work	I - Incomplete

Letter grades with appropriate pluses and minuses will be given for each final grade, and grade points for your grade will be factored into your overall grade point average. Unexcused late work or failure to turn in assignments will affect your grade, so please plan ahead, and communicate conflicts with your instructor.

Exegetical Project

As a part of your participation in the Capstone *Doing Justice and Loving Mercy* module of study, you will be required to do an exegesis (inductive study) on one of the following passages on the definition and practice of compassion ministries in and through the Church and urban community:

- ☐ Isaiah 1.11-17
- ☐ Isaiah 58.1-10
- ☐ Matthew 25.31-46
- ☐ James 2.14-17
- ☐ 1 John 3.15-18

Purpose

The purpose of this exegetical project is to give you an opportunity to do a detailed study of a major passage on doing justice and loving mercy, and your application of it as it applies to the urban community and the practice of Christian leadership. Using one of the passages above as your foundational text, you must think critically about the ways in which this text makes plain your duty, privilege, and responsibility to show compassion, both to members of the household of faith, as well as those who are on the outside of the Church.

As you study one of the above texts (or a text which you and your Mentor agree upon which may not be on the list), our hope is that your analysis of your selected text will make more clear to you the shape and texture of compassion ministries in the Church. We also desire that the Spirit will give you insight as to how you can relate its meaning directly to your own personal walk with God, as well as to the leadership role God has given to you currently in your local assembly, and its ministries to those who are broken and in need of Christian care.

This is a Bible study project, and, in order to do *exegesis*, you must be committed to understand the meaning of the passage in its own setting. Once you know what it meant, you can then draw out principles that apply to all of us, and then relate those principles to life. A simple three step process can guide you in your personal study of the Bible passage:

Outline and Composition

1. What was *God saying to the people in the text's original situation*?

2. What principle(s) does *the text teach that is true for all people everywhere*, including today?

3. What is *the Holy Spirit asking me to do with this principle here, today*, in my life and ministry?

Once you have answered these questions in your personal study, you are then ready to write out your insights for your *paper assignment*.

Here is a *sample outline* for your paper:

1. List out what you believe is *the main theme or idea* of the text you selected.

2. *Summarize the meaning* of the passage (you may do this in two or three paragraphs, or, if you prefer, by writing a short verse-by-verse commentary on the passage).

3. *Outline one to three key principles or insights* this text provides on doing justice and loving mercy in the context of showing compassion to others.

4. Tell how one, some, or all of the principles may relate to *one or more* of the following:

    a. Your personal spirituality and walk with Christ

    b. Your life and ministry in your local church

    c. Situations or challenges in your community and general society

As an aid or guide, please feel free to read the course texts and/or commentaries, and integrate insights from them into your work. Make sure that you give credit to whom credit is due if you borrow or build upon someone else's insights. Use in-the-text references, footnotes, or endnotes. Any way you choose to cite your references will be acceptable, as long as you 1) use only one way consistently throughout your paper, and 2) indicate where you are using someone else's ideas, and are giving them credit for it. (For more information, see *Documenting Your Work: A Guide to Help You Give Credit Where Credit Is Due* in the Appendix.)

Make certain that your exegetical project, when turned in meets the following standards:

- It is legibly written or typed.
- It is a study of one of the passages above.
- It is turned in on time (not late).
- It is 5 pages in length.
- It follows the outline given above, clearly laid out for the reader to follow.
- It shows how the passage relates to life and ministry today.

Do not let these instructions intimidate you; this is a Bible study project! All you need to show in this paper is that you *studied* the passage, *summarized* its meaning, *drew out* a few key principles from it, and *related* them to your own life and ministry.

Grading

The exegetical project is worth 45 points, and represents 15% of your overall grade, so make certain that you make your project an excellent and informative study of the Word.

Ministry Project

Purpose

The Word of God is living and active, and penetrates to the very heart of our lives and innermost thoughts (Heb. 4.12). James the Apostle emphasizes the need to be doers of the Word of God, not hearers only, deceiving ourselves. We are exhorted to apply the Word, to obey it. Neglecting this discipline, he suggests, is analogous to a person viewing our natural face in a mirror and then forgetting who we are, and are meant to be. In every case, the doer of the Word of God will be blessed in what he or she does (James 1.22-25).

Our sincere desire is that you will apply your learning practically, correlating your learning with real experiences and needs in your personal life, and in your ministry in and through your church. Therefore, a key part of completing this module will be for you to design a ministry project to help you share some of the insights you have learned from this course with others.

Planning and Summary

There are many ways that you can fulfill this requirement of your study. You may choose to conduct a brief study of your insights with an individual, or a Sunday School class, youth or adult group or Bible study, or even at some ministry opportunity. What you must do is discuss some of the insights you have learned from class with your audience. (Of course, you may choose to share insights from your Exegetical Project in this module with them.)

Feel free to be flexible in your project. Make it creative and open-ended. At the beginning of the course, you should decide on a context in which you will share your insights, and share that with your instructor. Plan ahead and avoid the last minute rush in selecting and carrying out your project.

After you have carried out your plan, write and turn in to your Mentor a one-page summary or evaluation of your time of sharing. A sample outline of your Ministry Project summary is as follows:

1. Your name

2. The place where you shared, and the audience with whom you shared

3. A brief summary of how your time went, how you felt, and how they responded

4. What you learned from the time

Grading

The Ministry Project is worth 30 points and represents 10% of your overall grade, so make certain to share your insights with confidence and make your summary clear.

DOING JUSTICE AND LOVING MERCY: COMPASSION MINISTRIES Capstone Curriculum / 13

LESSON
1

Let Justice Roll Down
The Vision and Theology of the Kingdom

page 303 📖 1

Lesson Objectives

page 305 📖 2

Welcome in the strong name of Jesus Christ! After your reading, study, discussion, and application of the materials in this lesson, you will be able to:

- Recite the elements of a valid first word, or *prolegomena*, for an understanding of doing justice and loving mercy.

- Outline and define the system of the world from a biblical point of view, and show the different ways in Church tradition that church/world relationships have been viewed.

- Highlight a biblical theology of God that can help you understand the critical role that doing justice and loving mercy plays in our kingdom testimony.

- Explain carefully and precisely the image of God and its basis in the teachings of the Bible.

- Lay out the ways in which the Scriptures portray humankind as unique and precious because of God's special gift of creation, forming human beings in his own image and likeness.

- List the reasons why we ought to view all individuals, families, peoples, and nations as precious and irreplaceable.

- Detail the theological implications of the teaching regarding the *imago Dei*, especially how this high view of humankind justifies our best and most dedicated effort at the preservation and care for human life, wherever it exists and wherever we find people in distress.

Devotion

Am I My Brother's Keeper?

page 306 📖 3

Gen. 4.1-16 - Now Adam knew Eve his wife, and she conceived and bore Cain, saying, "I have gotten a man with the help of the Lord." [2] And again, she bore his brother Abel. Now Abel was a keeper of sheep, and Cain a worker of the ground. [3] In the course of time Cain brought to the Lord an offering of the fruit of the ground, [4] and Abel also brought of the firstborn of his flock and of their fat portions. And the Lord had regard for Abel and his offering, [5] but for Cain and his offering he had no regard. So Cain was very angry, and his face fell. [6] The Lord said to Cain, "Why are you angry, and why has your face fallen? [7] If you do well, will you not be accepted? And if you do not do well, sin is crouching at the door. Its desire is for you, but you must rule over it." [8] Cain spoke to Abel his brother. And when they were in the field, Cain rose up against his brother Abel and killed him. [9] Then the Lord said to Cain, "Where is Abel your brother?" He said, "I do not know; am I my brother's keeper?" [10] And the Lord said, "What have you done? The voice of your brother's blood is crying to me from the ground. [11] And now you are cursed from the ground, which has opened its mouth to receive your brother's blood from your hand. [12] When you work the ground, it shall no longer yield to you its strength. You shall be a fugitive and a wanderer on the earth." [13] Cain said to the Lord, "My punishment is greater than I can bear. [14] Behold, you have driven me today away from the ground, and from your face I shall be hidden. I shall be a fugitive and a wanderer on the earth, and whoever finds me will kill me." [15] Then the Lord said to him, "Not so! If anyone kills Cain, vengeance shall be taken on him sevenfold." And the Lord put a mark on Cain, lest any who found him should attack him. [16] Then Cain went away from the presence of the Lord and settled in the land of Nod, east of Eden.

What is ultimately our responsibility for the well-being of others, whether they are friends, family, neighbor or stranger, alien or kinsman, enemy or beloved? It appears in all of us that there is an inclination to only love those who are "near by," those people whom we count as friends, or immediate family. Why ought we to sacrifice our precious few resources and opportunities on behalf of people we either don't know well, on those who are inclined to waste our good will or abuse our kindness, or worse yet, on those who actually and indeed hate us? Ultimately, who is the neighbor that we are called to love even as ourselves (cf. Lev. 19.18)?

Genesis 4 contains one of the great but tragic episodes of the entire Scriptures. Occurring on the heels of the great Fall of the first human pain whose voluntary and unfortunate rebellion produced the curse and death on humankind, we see tangibly one of its results. Alienation. Jealousy. Hatred and malice, which lead to violent murder and justification. While this story appears on the surface to be about the conflict between two brothers, upon a closer look we see greater meaning. In this story of conflict between Cain and Abel in fact the prophecy of Genesis 3.15 is concretely played out: the seed of the woman meets the seed of the serpent. Cain yields to the evil that crouches at the door, brutally murders his very own brother because of jealousy and malice, is cursed, and becomes the original creator of the godless city and its godless society. This way of rejecting God's will, of hating those who in fact keep it, is referred to in the New Testament as the "way of Cain" (Jude

11), or as "sin against one's brother" (1 John 3.12, 15). All in all, this story reveals the kind of profound and cancerous lack of trust and obedience to the Lord which results in a dangerous envy of God's own people. This envy is deadly, and leads to violence, murder, alienation, and finally to the very judgment of God himself.

In this text, the brothers of Cain and Abel are contrasted and played against one another, with the entire passage above contrasting them in every way. Cain is shown as a person whose work, as one commentator puts it, "lines him up with the curse," one who works the ground, (cf. Gen. 4.2; cf. 3.17). Abel, on the other hand, appears as a keeper of sheep, worships God through the sacrifice of the flock, a form of worship which foreshadows the great sacrifice of our Lord Jesus Christ. According to the Apostle John, Abel's act of offering sacrifice in worship was righteous, while Cain's works were evil (1 John 3.12). We know that the heart of the sacrifice was the offering of the gift in faith, without which it is impossible to please God (Heb. 11.6).

Instead of learning the kind of sacrifice that would please God, Cain's lack of trust in God is shown in his reaction to God's rejection of his fruit offering. Cain became angry, so much so that he refused to listen even to God's own advice (4.6-7). God's counsel was telling and specific: if in fact Cain would do what was right and therefore please God, his situation would be well. However, sin was crouching like a predatory beast ready to overcome him if he refused the counsel and surrendered to his dark discouragement. Sin desired him but he could master it.

Cain refused the good counsel of God and murdered his brother. Rather than admit any wrong, he denied his responsibility for his brother. "Am I my brother's keeper?" Here is the clear image of a heart that is dead and dark, that can hate his brother so much that he rejects all responsibility for his welfare, and even kill him, and feel no remorse for it. Here, in bold relief, is the modern problem—that rebellion against God creates an inevitable alienation with our brothers, and ultimately, if left unchecked, can lead to murder and curse. God is gracious even in judgment, protecting Cain in his banishment with a mark or sign that would deter those seeking to avenge Abel's murder. Even in this, the rebellious Cain defies God's punishment of wandering and instead builds the first city in the land of Nod (meaning "wandering"), east of Eden (v. 16).

The lessons for us are clear as we begin our module study. Our relationship to God and relationship to others are deeply interconnected and affecting; no one can claim a deep walk with God and hate their brother (1 John 4.20-21), and if we do love God, we will sacrifice on behalf of our brothers and sisters (1 John 3.14ff.). We are in fact our brothers (and our sisters!) keepers, called to care for one another, and not consume one another in our comparisons, jealousies, hatreds, and violence. To be intimate with the God and Father of our Lord Jesus Christ is to care deeply for others, for God is love. The one claiming to know God who does not love, does not know God at all (1 John 4.7-8).

For those of us serving Christ in the city we must embrace this truth with all our hearts. A vital, growing, intimate walk with God will always express itself in specific, particular, and consistent acts of love and mercy to our brothers and sisters, our neighbors, and even our enemies. Are we our brother's keeper? Certainly, yes, if in fact we have been redeemed in the blood of Jesus Christ. Listen to the Apostle John's commentary on Cain and Abel:

> 1 John 3.11-15 - For this is the message that you have heard from the beginning, that we should love one another. [12] We should not be like Cain, who was of the evil one and murdered his brother. And why did he murder him? Because his own deeds were evil and his brother's righteous. [13] Do not be surprised, brothers, that the world hates you. [14] We know that we have passed out of death into life, because we love the brothers. Whoever does not love abides in death. [15] Everyone who hates his brother is a murderer, and you know that no murderer has eternal life abiding in him.

Let us embrace the new commandment of our Lord, to love one another. Indeed, we are truly our brother's keeper.

Nicene Creed and Prayer

After reciting and/or singing the Nicene Creed (located in the Appendix), pray the following prayer:

> *Holy God, you confound the world's wisdom in giving your kingdom to the lowly and the pure in heart. Give us such a hunger and thirst for justice and perseverance in striving for peace, that by our words and deeds the world may see the promise of your kingdom, revealed in Jesus Christ our Lord, who lives and reigns with you in the unity of the Holy Spirit, one God, forever and ever. Amen.*
>
> ~ Presbyterian Church (U.S.A.) and Cumberland Presbyterian Church. The Theology and Worship Ministry Unit. **Book of Common Worship**. Louisville, Ky.: Westminster/John Knox Press, 1993. p. 209

Quiz	No quiz this lesson
Scripture Memorization Review	No Scripture memorization this lesson
Assignments Due	No assignments due this lesson

Family First, Always

page 307

In a discussion in an adult Sunday School class, several students are discussing the "order of loves" that the Christian is called to represent. Are we to love our marriages and family members first, in a way that is different, prior to, and better than the other loves that we have. Some argued that the love commandment implies that we are to love all people sacrificially, even our enemies. Others read the text to suggest that we are to do good to all people, but *especially* to the members of the household of God (cf. Gal. 6.10). What is your understanding of the various orders of love the disciple of Jesus is called to demonstrate to others? Are we to love different people in different degrees, or are we called to love everyone the same?

Humanism Is a Bad Word

In the late twentieth century a number of Christian scholars began to discuss the idea of *Christian humanism*, an idea that human beings, all of them, are made in the image of God and therefore are deserving of basic human rights that we must protect and defend. While some evangelical Christian leaders embraced this vision, many others rejected it as both compromise and a kind of first step toward universalism. Humanists, they argued, center their thinking and explanation of the highest of creation on *human life*, as if it were the end of all things. This is patently unchristian; God almighty, his sovereign purpose and will, are in fact the end of all things. On the other side, Christian humanists contend that salvation proves the uniqueness and wonder of human life to God; he gave his only Son to redeem his creation, especially his human creation. What do you think of the validity of the concept of Christian humanism? Is it actually possible to be both a *Christian* and a *humanist*?

Human Life Begins at Creation, not the Fall

Many lament the fact that a number of Protestant theologies on human life seem to put all of their emphasis on the Fall, that tragic event of the voluntary rebellion against the will of God committed by Adam and Eve which spiraled the creation into curse and chaos. The first statements of humankind, however, do not begin with the Fall, but with creation, where God made humankind in his own image, beautiful, creative, and free. What difference does it make if you base your fundamental thinking about humankind on the *creation of humankind* rather than on the *fall of humankind*? How ought we, in our theological discussions, to understand the importance of both of these foundational realities when describing the nature and purpose of humanity in the world?

Let Justice Roll Down: The Vision and Theology of the Kingdom

Segment 1: Toward a Theology of Justice and Mercy

Rev. Dr. Don L. Davis

As creator and maker of the earth, our God is concerned about the world and those who live within it. Traditionally, Christian communities have taken various positions to the world, including withdrawal from it, living in tension with it, or accepting responsibility to transform it. The Church is both the locus and agent of the Kingdom of God *in the world but not of it*. As such, the Church affirms that God is the God of all nature as well as the God of salvation, the God of creation as well as the God of covenant, and the God of justice as well as the God of justification. In its own ministry as the representative of the Kingdom of God, the Church is called to display and announce freedom to the world, to express God's wholeness in the world, and to stand for God's justice throughout the world.

Our objective for this segment, *Toward a Theology of Justice and Mercy*, is to enable you to see that:

- In order to understand the Christian's responsibility to do justice and love mercy in the world, we must carefully define the relationship of the Church to the world, and both of these to the Kingdom of God.

- As creator and maker of the earth, our God is concerned about the world and those who live within it.

- The word most commonly used in the NT to refer to the world system is *kosmos*, meaning "order, arrangement, ornament, adornment." It speaks of structure and orderly arrangement of its belief and conduct systems.

- Traditionally, Christian communities have taken various positions to the world, including withdrawal from it, living in tension with it, or accepting responsibility to transform it.

- The Church is both the locus and agent of the Kingdom of God *in the world but not of it*. As such, the Church affirms that God is the God of all nature as well as the God of salvation, the God of creation as well as the God of covenant, and the God of justice as well as the God of justification.

- In its own ministry as the representative of the Kingdom of God, the Church is called to display and announce freedom to the world, to express God's wholeness in the world, and to stand for God's justice throughout the world.

Video Segment 1 Outline

I. **Prolegomena to Justice and Compassion: Are We Our Brother's Keeper? Or Should We Be Concerned about the "World" and Those in the World?**

Amos 5.20-24 - Is not the day of the Lord darkness, and not light, and gloom with no brightness in it? [21] I hate, I despise your feasts, and I take no delight in your solemn assemblies. [22] Even though you offer me your burnt offerings and grain offerings, I will not accept them; and the peace offerings of your fattened animals, I will not look upon them. [23] Take away from me the noise of your songs; to the melody of your harps I will not listen. [24] But let justice roll down like waters, and righteousness like an ever-flowing stream.

A. The world in the biblical languages and worldview

1. *Kosmos* - word most commonly used to refer to the world system; means "order, arrangement, ornament, adornment"

a. Used in regards to the "earth," Matt. 13.35; John 21.25; Acts 17.24

b. Used in regards to the universe, Rom. 1.20

c. Used in regards to the "human race, humankind," Matt. 5.19; John 1.9

2. The use of *kosmos* in opposition to God and the Church: present condition of human affairs alienated from God, his Kingdom, and his people

a. John 7.7

b. John 8.23

c. John 14.30

d. 1 Cor. 2.12

e. Gal. 6.14

f. Col. 2.8

g. 1 John 5.19

B. Different responses in Christian history in church-world relationships

1. The tradition of *withdrawal*: avoiding the error and lies of the world by maintaining a safe distance between ourselves and the world, 2 Cor. 6.15-18

2. The tradition of *tension*: we live within the world but exist in a strong tension with it, 1 John 2.15-17.

3. The tradition of *transformation*: we are to take dominion over the structures of the world, because Jesus is Lord, we as believers are called to not only engage the world but conform its structures and orders to the Kingdom of God, John 17.9-16.

C. Should we strive to become *Christian humanists* (J. I. Packer); the case against:

1. "Dirt rubs off; clean never does:" engaging the world opens us up to the possibility of conforming to it, Rom. 12.1-2.

2. In trying to care too much for the world, you may wind up becoming friends with it, James 4.4.

3. Social activity, friendship without regeneration is a waste of time in light of the Lord's imminent return.

    a. Isa. 40.6-8

b. 1 John 2.17

c. 1 Cor. 7.31

4. The risk is simply too great: we face the danger of losing our convictions for the sake of making changes that, in the long run, won't last anyway, Matt. 16.24-26.

D. A biblical alternative: *the Church in the world as agent of the Kingdom of God*

1. The God and Father of our Lord Jesus Christ is the maker of the entire universe, including all beings and persons and things, Ps. 24.1-2.

2. The world, which was made good, was cursed as a result of the voluntary rebellion of the devil and the first human pair.

    a. Placed under bondage to sin and its effects: the *loss of freedom*

    b. Exposed to the corruption of decay and death: the *loss of wholeness*

    c. Thrown into the grips of cruelty, alienation, and greed: the *loss of justice*

3. In Jesus Christ, the reign of God has been reasserted, Mark 1.14-15.

    a. His incarnation is the inauguration of the Kingdom of God.

Mic. 6.8
He has told you, O man, what is good; and what does the Lord require of you but to do justice, and to love kindness, and to walk humbly with your God?

b. His life and ministry represents the overthrow of the devil and his reign of darkness.

c. Through his incarnation, death, and resurrection, the curse has been rescinded, sin has been judged, and the devil defeated.

d. The Church is the kingdom community, indwelt by the Holy Spirit, given the task to be the locus and agent of the Kingdom to Come in this present time.

   (1) T*he **locus** of the Kingdom*: the place where God's presence, covenant, kingdom blessings, forgiveness, and people dwell

   (2) *The **agent** of the Kingdom*: the means by which God announces his kingdom reign to the world and demonstrates its freedom, wholeness, and justice

II. Prolegomena: A Biblical Theology for Doing Justice and Loving Mercy

We must rediscover how a biblical view of God and humanity can provide us with the biblical ground for doing justice and loving mercy (adapted from John Stott).

A. God is the God of all *nature* as well as the God of *salvation*.

   1. God is the God of the *secular* domain as well as the sacred.

   2. Biblical testimony is clear and numerous.

      a. Ps. 24.1-2

      b. Deut. 10.14

c. 1 Chron. 29.11

d. Job 41.11

e. Ps. 50.12

3. The physical universe is the handiwork of God, who sustains and exercises authority over it, Gen. 1.31; 1 Tim. 4.4.

4. The structures and categories ingredient in the creation mandate of God (cf. Gen. 1.26-27) are the good gifts of a gracious Lord.

    a. Sex, marriage, and family

    b. Beauty and order of the natural world

    c. Work and leisure

    d. Friendships and community

    e. Music and the creative arts

5. Respect (or the lack thereof!) for God's creation and the life in it reflects one's spiritual understanding of God's place as the maker and creator of the entire universe, Jer. 10.11-13

B. God is the God of *creation* as well as the God of the *covenant*.

1. God is the God of the gentiles as well as the God of Israel, Rom. 3.29.

2. God's Word begins with God's relationship to *Adam* (as representative of humankind) not *Abraham* (representative of the covenant people of the Lord) with his rule over creation before his detail of the covenant.

3. The purpose of the Abrahamic covenant: the blessing of all the families of the earth, Gen. 12.1-3

   a. The call of God on Abraham to make him a great nation

   b. The corresponding blessing and curse of God on those who blessed or cursed Abraham

   c. In him "*all the families of the earth shall be blessed*": God's universal call to all peoples through Abraham

4. The parochial problem of God's people: God's love and mercy extends to us alone and to no others!

   a. Ps. 33.12

   b. Acts 17.24

C. God is the God of *justice* as well as the God of *justification*.

1. God's concern for the broken, the poor, the oppressed, the abused of humankind lies at the heart of the ministry of the Messiah, Luke 4.18-19, cf. Isa. 61.1-4.

2. The same God of salvation is the God of justice, Ps. 146.5.

3. God hates inhumanity to human beings anywhere and everywhere it manifests itself, cf. Amos 2.4-8.

III. Implications of God's Majesty in Kingdom Expression

A. Because God is a God of all nature, his kingdom rule in Christ must be expressed in *a call to freedom*.

1. All creation is under the curse: *universal slavery and bondage*, Rom. 8.19-23

2. Jesus' incarnation and passion: freedom over the law, over sin, over the devil, and over death, 1 John 3.8

3. The Church expresses its freedom: experiencing God's freedom and prophesying deliverance to the captives, Gal. 5.1; John 8.31-32

B. Because God is a God of creation, his kingdom rule in Christ must be demonstrated in an *expression of wholeness (shalom)*.

1. The creation is subject to corruption under the curse: *generational and chronic sickness*, Rom. 8.19-23

2. Jesus' incarnation and passion: elimination of disease and its effects, overcoming of the curse, introducing of the fullness of God's goodness and blessing, Luke 4.18-19

3. The Church expresses the *shalom* of God: the people of God serve the world as a locus and agent of wholeness and blessing, Matt. 5.14-16.

C. Because God is a God of justice, his kingdom rule in Christ must be revealed through our *acts of justice*.

1. The creation has been alienated in its relationships and actions under the curse: *alienation and intrinsic selfishness*, Eph. 4.17-19

2. Jesus' incarnation and passion: breaking of the flesh, of alienation and injustice, opening up to reconciliation and peace, Eph. 2.14-16

3. The Church expresses its justice: experiencing justice in the midst of God's community, and working to display justice in all of its relationships and undertakings, Acts 2.42-47

Conclusion

» The first word, or *prolegomena* for understanding our call to do justice and love mercy is based on a theology of God that sees our role as kingdom agents.

» We strive to do justice and love mercy because the God and Father of our Lord Jesus Christ is a God of nature as well as salvation, creation as well as covenant, and justice as well as a God of justification.

Please take as much time as you have available to answer these and other questions that the video brought out. The God and Father of our Lord Jesus Christ is the creator, the maker of all heaven and earth. He did not abandon his creation, even after the fall of humankind, but has through his own work of providence and salvation expressed his love and concern for the world and its inhabitants. As believers, we must understand the various positions Christian communities have taken throughout history regarding the Church's relationship and responsibility to the world system. As Christian leaders, we must also grapple with our own views of both God and the world so we can know how best to represent the Kingdom of God in the world today. Review the questions below as they help to refresh your own memory regarding the Word of God we considered in our first segment. Be clear and concise in your answers, and where possible, support with Scripture!

Segue 1

Student Questions and Response

page 307 5

1. Why is it important to develop a careful and clear understanding of God, the world, and the Church before we seek to understand the Christian's responsibility to do justice and love mercy in the world? Explain your answer.

2. Why is it so significant that God, who is both *creator* and *sustainer* of the earth, also decided to *save his creation*? What significance does God's concern for the world play for us as believers in Christ today–what ought to be our attitude toward those who live in the world?

3. What is the meaning of the NT term referring to the world system, *kosmos*? What is the difference between the *kosmos* and the physical earth itself? What are some of the NT meanings given to God's understanding of and commitment to the *kosmos*?

4. What are three of the traditional and historical models that Christian communities have taken in regard to the Church's relations to the world? Which one is most convincing to you? Which is least valid?

5. What does the statement mean that says "the Church is both the locus and agent of the Kingdom of God *in the world but not of it.*"

6. How has the life, death, resurrection, and ascension of Jesus Christ affected our understanding of the world and the Kingdom of God? In what ways is the Church called now to reflect Jesus' rule in the world today. Be specific.

7. What does it mean to say that the Father is the God of all nature and the God of salvation? Why is this important for doing justice in the world today?

8. In the same way, what does it mean to say that the God of creation is also the God of covenant? Again, why is this important for doing justice in the world today?

9. Finally, what does it mean to say that the God of justification is also the God of justice? How does this influence our call to reflect justice and mercy in the world, in our very lives and communities, today?

Let Justice Roll Down: The Vision and Theology of the Kingdom

Segment 2: The Image of God as Basis for Social Concern and Action

Rev. Dr. Don L. Davis

Summary of Segment 2

page 307

The ground for doing justice and loving mercy among the poor in the city is the affirmation of the *imago Dei* in every boy, girl, woman, and man. Every person is worthy of care because they share in God's unmatched, unique, and irreplaceable *imago Dei*. Because all are made in God's image, all humankind is unique and precious. This image constitutes the reason why we ought to do justice and love mercy among all individuals, families, peoples, and nations on earth. Each of them as bearers of the *imago Dei* are to be considered as precious and irreplaceable.

Our objective for this segment, *The Image of God as Basis for Social Concern and Action*, is to enable you to see that:

- A good working definition of the *imago Dei* (i.e., image of God) in Scripture, is "The unique condition of all human beings that they are made like God and therefore are worthy of our respect, protection, and care."

- The affirmation of humankind being created in the image of God is a *unique affirmation*, no other creature or angels are said to have been created in the image of God.

- While the precise manner in which humankind is created in God's image is not explicitly stated in Scripture, evidence exists to suggest that human beings share in corresponding traits of God's own person, namely, our personality, our reason, our ability to choose, and our moral capacity.

- The fact that humankind was made in the *imago Dei* suggests that all human beings share this image; all human beings, regardless of their individual or communal state, are therefore unique, precious, and priceless *in and of themselves*.

- The biblical implications of the *imago Dei* in humankind transforms our understanding of human persons. They are created in God's own image, crowned with glory and honor, are fearfully and wonderfully made, and are providentially nourished by God. As such, human beings have been made the objects of God's unmerited, unconditional favor and grace, and he identifies with the struggles, needs, and burdens of even the most vulnerable human beings on earth.

- Human beings, regardless of their background, can be so transformed and renewed as to become partakers of the divine nature through faith in Jesus Christ. While those who reject Christ do not share in this renewal of the image of God, they still share God's likeness *as human beings*.

- The ground for doing justice and loving mercy among the poor in the city is the affirmation of the *imago Dei* in every boy, girl, woman, and man. Every person is worthy of care because they share in God's unmatched, unique, and irreplaceable *imago Dei*.

I. The *Imago Dei*: Humankind Shares in the Likeness of God.

Video Segment 2 Outline

A. Definition of the *imago Dei*

1. "The unique condition of all human beings that they are made like God and therefore are worthy of our respect, protection, and care"

2. Genesis 1.26-28 as the seminal text dealing with humankind sharing God's image and likeness

    Gen. 1.26-28 - Then God said, "Let us make man in our image, after our likeness. And let them have dominion over the fish of the sea and over the birds of the heavens and over the livestock and over all the earth and over every creeping thing that creeps on the earth." [27] So God created man in his own image, in the image of God He created him; male and female He created them. [28] And God blessed them. And God said to them, "Be fruitful and multiply and fill the earth and subdue it and have dominion over the fish of the sea and over the birds of the heavens and over every living thing that moves on the earth."

   a. A *unique* affirmation: no other living creatures are said to have been created in God's image.

   b. Some argue that *angels* share in this image (because of their participation in *moral righteousness*).

   c. No Scripture supports this view of angels being made in the *imago Dei*.

   d. Creatures have their being *from* God, human beings have their being *in* God (cf. Acts 17.28-29).

3. Humankind became a living being: Gen. 2.7.

   a. A previous living creature did not *become* one who came to share God's image.

   b. The image of God did not *evolve* from a lower form of life.

   c. The moment, the instant man and woman became human beings, they were the image of God, both male and female, Gen. 1.27.

B. Biblical usage of the term *image of God*

1. Biblical references

    a. Gen. 5.1

    b. Gen. 9.6

    c. 1 Cor. 11.7

    d. James 3.9

2. References regarding our *recreation*

    a. Eph. 4.24

    b. Col. 3.10

C. What precisely is the *image of God* in humankind?

1. Humankind made from *the dust of the ground*: our kinship with the earth, Gen. 2.7

    a. We have a kinship with *the products and resources of the earth*: we need air, water, and food in order to survive.

b. Our constitutions and functions are *similar to other creatures which depend on the earth* for their lives and existence.

c. The image of God *is not* rooted in our physical nature and kinship with the earth.

2. The image of God viewed from the perspective of our *personality and spirituality*

   a. Our *personality*: we share with God a sense of our own self-consciousness.

   b. Our *rationality*: we share with God self-consciousness and reason.

   c. Our *will*: we share with God the ability to choose.

   d. Our *moral capacity*: we share with God a moral sensibility.

D. The preciousness of humankind: all human beings share in the *imago Dei*.

   1. All humankind shares in this image: there are no distinctions among human beings regarding the image of God, Acts 17.26.

   2. This image is foundational to understanding God's relationship to humankind, and human beings response to each other, James 3.9.

   3. We are bad off because of the curse, but human beings are unique and precious, because of creation.

II. The Implications of the *Imago Dei* in Humankind: the Remarkable Workmanship of Human Beings

A. Human beings are created in *the image of God*.

Gen. 1. 26-28 - Then God said, "Let us make man in our image, after our likeness. And let them have dominion over the fish of the sea and over the birds of the heavens and over the livestock and over all the earth and over every creeping thing that creeps on the earth." [27] So God created man in his own image, in the image of God he created him; male and female he created them. [28] And God blessed them. And God said to them, "Be fruitful and multiply and fill the earth and subdue it and have dominion over the fish of the sea and over the birds of the heavens and over every living thing that moves on the earth."

1. Made in the very image of God (all other beings made by God but not in his own image)

2. Granted dominion over all creation

3. Exalted status and position given to humankind as they were created male and female

4. Given the mandate to be fruitful and multiply

5. Implication: *Every human being, despite their social status or condition, is created in the image of God, a reflection of the divine mind and person, an instance of God's own magnificent imagination and creative power.*

B. Human beings are crowned with glory and honor.

Ps. 8.3-7 - When I look at your heavens, the work of your fingers, the moon and the stars, which you have set in place, [4] what is man that you are mindful of him, and the son of man that you care for him? [5] Yet you have made him a little lower than the heavenly beings and crowned him with glory and honor. [6] You have given him dominion over the works of your hands; you have put all things under his feet, [7] all sheep and oxen, and also the beasts of the field.

1. Made a *little lower than the angels*

2. Crowned with glory and honor

3. Granted dominion over the works of the Lord's hands

4. All things placed under humankind's feet

5. This is an allusion to the dominion of Messiah Jesus, cf. Ps. 110.1; 1 Cor. 15.24-28; Eph. 1.22; Heb. 2.8

6. Implication: *All human beings, regardless of their histories or behaviors, have been created just a little lower than the angels, crowned by God with glory, honor, and dominion.*

C. Human beings are fearfully and wonderfully made.

Ps. 139.13-16 - For you formed my inward parts; you knitted me together in my mother's womb. [14] I praise you, for I am fearfully and wonderfully made. Wonderful are your works; my soul knows it very well. [15] My frame was not hidden from you, when I was being made in secret, intricately woven in the depths of the earth. [16] Your eyes saw my unformed substance; in your book were written, every one of them, the days that were formed for me, when as yet there were none of them.

1. Formed in every way (physically and spiritually) by the genius and brilliance of Almighty God

2. Crafted by God's own special craftsmanship and care

3. From cradle to casket: God's personal design lies upon every human life.

4. God's sovereignty touches and impacts the days of every human being.

5. Implication: *Every human being is the product of God's divine genius and workmanship, fearfully and wonderfully created by him as a unique and infinitely precious being.*

D. Human life is abundantly nourished and providentially supplied by God.

Ps. 104.13-24 - From your lofty abode you water the mountains; the earth is satisfied with the fruit of your work. [14] You cause the grass to grow for the livestock and plants for man to cultivate, that he may bring forth food from the earth [15] and wine to gladden the heart of man, oil to make his face shine and bread to strengthen man's heart. [16] The trees of the LORD are watered abundantly, the cedars of Lebanon that he planted. [17] In them the birds build their nests; the stork has her home in the fir trees. [18] The high mountains are for the wild goats; the rocks are a refuge for the rock badgers. [19] He made the moon to mark the seasons; the sun knows its time for setting. [20] You make darkness, and it is night, when all the beasts of the forest creep about. [21] The young lions roar for their prey, seeking their food from God. [22] When the sun rises, they steal away and lie down in their dens. [23] Man goes out to his work and to his labor until the evening. [24] O LORD, how manifold are your works! In wisdom have you made them all; the earth is full of your creatures.

1. The abundance of the earth is provided for through God's generous providential care.

2. God is the operative cause of every good and perfect gift enjoyed by human beings everywhere, James 1.17.

3. The earth and its supply is resourced by God's hands for all the inhabitants on the earth.

4. The earth is the Lord's, and is full of his possessions.

5. Implications: *All of the bounty and nutrients that sustains human life everywhere is given by God without respect of persons or favor*, Matt. 5.44-45.

E. Human beings are the objects of God's unmerited, unconditional favor and grace.

John 3.16-17 - For God so loved the world, that he gave his only Son, that whoever believes in him should not perish but have eternal life. [17] For God did not send his Son into the world to condemn the world, but in order that the world might be saved through him.

1. God loved without qualification or partiality everyone in the entire world, living, dead, and yet unborn.

a. 2 Cor. 5.19

b. 1 John 4.9-10

c. Luke 12.7

2. The value of God's love is shown in the sacrifice of his only Son for each and every single soul, Matt. 18.14.

3. God did not send his Son to condemn, but to save all those in the world.

4. Implication: *God's unlimited and unbounded favor rests on every human being, though they may be unaware of it.*

F. God identifies with the struggles, needs, and burdens of the most vulnerable and hurting among us.

Ps. 146.5-9 - Blessed is he whose help is the God of Jacob, whose hope is in the Lord his God, [6] who made heaven and earth, the sea, and all that is in them, who keeps faith forever; [7] who executes justice for the oppressed, who gives food to the hungry. The Lord sets the prisoners free; [8] the Lord opens the eyes of the blind. The Lord lifts up those who are bowed down; the Lord loves the righteous. [9] The Lord watches over the sojourners; he upholds the widow and the fatherless, but the way of the wicked he brings to ruin.

1. God is burdened for human beings everywhere who are oppressed, hungry, and abused.

2. The Lord actively involves himself in the justice of those who are hurting, i.e., those who are blind and bowed down.

3. The Lord is aware of the cause of all those who are refugees, widows, orphans, and powerless.

4. Religion in its purest practice before God involves caring for the needs of those most vulnerable and least able to defend and protect themselves among us, James 1.27.

5. Implication: *The God of Jacob is fundamentally a God who identifies with the hurting, the poor, and the oppressed.*

G. Human beings can be so transformed and renewed as to become partakers of the divine nature.

2 Pet. 1.2-4 - May grace and peace be multiplied to you in the knowledge of God and of Jesus our Lord. [3] His divine power has granted to us all things that pertain to life and godliness, through the knowledge of him who called us to his own glory and excellence, [4] by which he has granted to us his precious and very great promises, so that through them you may become partakers of the divine nature, having escaped from the corruption that is in the world because of sinful desire.

1. Through Christ, believers have been given all things that pertain to life and godliness, 2 Pet. 1.3.

2. God has called the saved to his glory and virtue.

3. Through God's exceedingly great and precious promises, we may become partakers of God's very own nature.

4. The believing have escaped the corruption that is resident in the world, which is activated by lust.

   a. Gal. 1.3-4

   b. 1 John 5.4-5

   c. 1 John 5.19-20

5. When Christ returns for his own, we who believe will come to share in his very own glory and image.

   a. 1 John 3.2

   b. Ps. 17.15

   c. Rom. 8.29

   d. 1 Cor. 15.49

   e. Phil. 3.21

6. Implication: *Humankind, once redeemed, is capable of the unimaginable: we can actually partake of the divine nature, indwelt by God himself, sharing in his life and glory.*

III. The Implications of the *Imago Dei* for Urban Ministry

A. Through faith in Jesus Christ, we are re-created in the image of God.

1. Biblical citations

   a. Eph. 4.24

   b. Col. 3.10

2. We are created in righteousness and true holiness, destined to be conformed to the image of Jesus Christ, Rom. 8.29.

3. As the fall affected the image of God in humankind in a way of corruption and death, so salvation results in renewal of the image after the likeness of Jesus Christ himself.

   a. Jesus is the one who shares uniquely in God's image, 2 Cor. 4.4; Col. 1.15; Heb. 1.3.

   b. Jesus is the last Adam, the pattern of a new humanity to come, Rom. 8.29.

   c. The image of Jesus Christ is being formed in the Christian by the Holy Spirit, 2 Cor. 3.18; cf. Eph. 4.24; Col. 3.10.

B. Though unbelievers do not share in this renewal of the image of God, they still share in the very likeness of God.

1. Human life is therefore unique, irreplaceable, and precious.

2. Doing justice and loving mercy, even toward those who do not know Christ, is both mandated and necessary.

3. Each human being is priceless and worthy to be loved, protected, and cared for.

C. The *imago Dei* in every human being is the ground of our doing justice and loving mercy.

1. *Refuse to endorse, therefore,* any escapist or conformist notions of the world, asking God to give you grace to re-engage the world as being one who is in it, but not of it.

2. *Affirm the uniqueness and preciousness of human life*, at all levels, unborn, infants and children, the elderly.

3. *Allow the biblical view* of God as creator and humankind made in the image of God to reinterpret your "theological anthropology" (i.e., the doctrine of humanity) to conform you to the Bible's high and wondrous view of human beings.

4. *Reject any conflicts* between social justice, loving mercy, and evangelization.

a. Recognize their common source and goal.

b. Understand how they both affirm God as *creator* and *ruler* of the world.

c. *Refuse to dichotomize* (to split and separate, to create a conflict between) evangelism and social justice; they are both required to provide a full understanding of God and his Gospel.

5. See every person and every opportunity to care for them through the lens of each person sharing in God's unmatched, unique, and irreplaceable *imago Dei*.

    a. To see a human being is to see something infinitely precious.

    b. To see a broken human being is to see the Lord Jesus himself, Matt. 25.34-40.

Conclusion

» A biblical understanding of the *imago Dei* in human beings grounds and informs our commitment to love, cherish, and protect human beings, wherever we find them and whatever their lot.

» Every person is worthy of care because they share in God's unmatched, unique, and irreplaceable *imago Dei*.

The following questions were designed to help you review the material in the second video segment. In that segment we saw how the ground and basis for our executing justice and demonstrating mercy among the poor in the city is our commitment to the biblical affirmation of the *imago Dei* in every boy, girl, woman, and man. Every human being, regardless or race, background, or culture, is worthy of our care because they share in God's unmatched, unique, and irreplaceable *imago Dei*. Each human person and all human groups are unique and precious. Each are bearers of the *imago Dei* and are to be considered as precious and irreplaceable. Explore these concepts through the questions below, and support your own arguments with Scripture.

Segue 2

Student Questions and Response

1. What is the definition of the "image of God" (*imago Dei*) given in the last segment. In what ways is this affirmation of the image of God in human beings both a *unique* affirmation as well as a *special* one?

2. Do the Scriptures offer us an explicit definition of the image of God mentioned in Genesis 1 in humankind? What are some of the traits mentioned of God that we know human beings to also share?

3. How does the biblical teaching express the fact that *all humankind* was made in the *imago Dei*? Are there any human beings who, for some reason, no longer share this image? Do even the most rebellious and irreligious human beings, regardless of their individual or communal state, share in the *imago Dei*? What is the biblical evidence for your answer?

4. In light of the *imago Dei*, what are some of the ways in which the Word of God describes the implications of the *imago Dei* in humankind? How ought these various implications transform our understanding of human persons, even those we find distasteful or obnoxious?

5. How do the Scriptures describe God's inclinations and feelings toward those who are poor, oppressed, and broken? What are the implications for this in understanding the poor as *special* objects of God's unmerited, unconditional favor and grace? Explain your answer with Scripture.

6. What is the significance of the fact that human beings, regardless of their background, can be so transformed and renewed as to become partakers of the divine nature through faith in Jesus Christ? Can all human beings come to share this new nature?

7. What can be said of those who reject the offer of God's grace in Christ–do they still share God's likeness as human beings? Explain.

8. In light of the insights above, what would you consider to be the fundamental ground for doing justice and loving mercy among the poor in the city? How does this ground inform us of the worthiness of each person in the city, regardless of the character of their lives and histories?

Summary of Key Concepts

page 309 7

This lesson focuses upon the theology and vision of the Kingdom, both in terms of God as our creator who is concerned about the world and those who live within it. We also considered the power of the image of God in every person, and how that image serves as the ground for doing justice and loving mercy among the poor in the city. Although Christians have traditionally taken differing positions in regards to the Church's relationship to the world, we must engage it. The Church is both the locus and agent of the Kingdom of God *in the world but not of it*. The God and Father of our Lord Jesus is a God of nature, creation, and justice, as well as a God of salvation, covenant, and justification. In addition, we saw in this lesson how the ground for doing justice and loving mercy among the poor in the city is the affirmation of the *imago Dei* in every boy, girl, woman, and man. Every person is worthy of care because they share in God's unmatched, unique, and irreplaceable *imago Dei*. Review these and related concepts in their listing below.

- In order to understand the Christian's responsibility to do justice and love mercy in the world, we must carefully define the relationship of the Church to the world, and both of their relationship to the Kingdom of God. As the Creator and Maker of the heavens and the earth, our God is concerned about the world and those who live within it.

- The word most commonly used in the NT to refer to the world system is *kosmos*, meaning "order, arrangement, ornament, adornment." It speaks of structure and orderly arrangement of its belief and conduct systems.

- Traditionally, Christian communities have taken various positions to the world. These have included the idea of *withdrawal* from it, *living in tension with it*, or accepting responsibility to *transform* it.

- The Church is both the locus and agent of the Kingdom of God *in the world but not of it*. As such, the Church affirms that God is the God of all nature as well as the God of salvation, the God of creation as well as the God of covenant, and the God of justice as well as the God of justification.

- In its own ministry as the representative of the Kingdom of God, the Church is called to display and announce freedom to the world, to express God's wholeness in the world, and to stand for God's justice throughout the world.

- A good working definition of the *imago Dei* (i.e., image of God) in Scripture is "The unique condition of all human beings that they are made like God and therefore are worthy of our respect, protection, and care."

- The affirmation of humankind being created in the image of God is a *unique affirmation*, no other creatures or angels are said to have been created in the image of God.

- While the precise manner in which humankind is created in God's image is not explicitly stated in Scripture, evidence exists to suggest that human beings share in corresponding traits of God's own person, namely, our personality, our reason, our ability to choose, and our moral capacity.

- The fact that humankind was made in the *imago Dei* suggests that all human beings share this image; all human beings, regardless of their individual or communal state, are therefore unique, precious, and priceless *in and of themselves*.

- The biblical implications of the *imago Dei* in humankind transforms our understanding of human persons. They are created in God's own image, crowned with glory and honor, are fearfully and wonderfully made, and are providentially nourished by God. As such, human beings have been made the objects of God's unmerited, unconditional favor and grace, and he identifies with the struggles, needs, and burdens of even the most vulnerable human beings on earth.

- Human beings, regardless of their background, can be so transformed and renewed as to become partakers of the divine nature through faith in Jesus Christ. While those who reject Christ do not share in this renewal of the image of God, they still share God's likeness *as human beings*.

- The ground for doing justice and loving mercy among the poor in the city is the affirmation of the *imago Dei* in every boy, girl, woman, and man. Every person is worthy of care because they share in God's unmatched, unique, and irreplaceable *imago Dei*.

Student Application and Implications

page 309 📖 *8*

Now is the time for you to discuss with your fellow students your questions about the theology of doing justice and loving mercy, and getting to the heart of the meaning of the *imago Dei* for doing ministry in the city. It is clear that we must lay a proper theological foundation before we can truly explore the various dimensions and elements of compassion ministries in the Church. As a disciple of Jesus and an emerging Christian leader, you need to master these ideas, and explore the implications of them for your own life and ministry. Here is your opportunity to consider with your fellow students your own particular questions regarding the theology of justice and *imago Dei* ideas covered in the segments. The questions below may help you explore your own, more specific questions about the material.

* Is it possible to believe that God is both *creator* and *maker* of the heavens and the earth and not also believe that God is concerned about the world and those who live within it? Explain your answer.

* Is the concept of world as *kosmos* a negative or positive concept in Scripture, or both (cf. John 3.16 with 1 John 2.15-17)? How do we know that God loves the inhabitants of the world but that he is against the world system?

* Of all the views covered in the lesson about the relationship of the Church to the world, which one makes the most sense to you so far in your studies?

* Does a serious theological problem exist if we view *the Church* as the agent of the Kingdom and not the *Holy Spirit* as the agent? What is the role of the Holy Spirit in the Church as the people of God represent the Kingdom in the world?

* Does it weaken what we believe if we try to correct our theology by saying that God is the God of all nature as well as the God of salvation, the God of creation as well as the God of covenant, and the God of justice as well as the God of justification? Explain.

* We defined the *imago Dei* (i.e., image of God) in Scripture as "the unique condition of all human beings that they are made like God and therefore

worthy of our respect, protection, and care." Are even the most vicious, cruel, and hurtful people made in God's image, too?

* Doesn't it go against what we know about God to say that he has a special concern for the poor and oppressed? If that is so, how are we to understand passages like Matthew 25 and the "least of these, my brethren" our Lord spoke of?

* If all human beings are made in the *imago Dei*, how can we dare to put any human beings to death, whether in capital punishment or criminal justice or war? Does the *imago Dei* suggest that no human life ought ever to be taken under any circumstances? Explain your answer.

* Why do you think that many Christians advocate positions about people which seem to go against the biblical implications of the *imago Dei* in humankind? Under what circumstances (if any) can we justify treating other human beings as *our enemies*? Explain.

* What if I have grown up *disliking a particular race or group*. Is it possible to tolerate any prejudice or bigotry and still claim to be partakers of the divine nature through faith in Jesus Christ?

* How might affirming the *imago Dei* in every boy, girl, woman, and man in a group you do not appreciate transform your ideas and feelings toward them? What if affirming the truth about them doesn't lead to changed feelings about them–what next?

Taking These Matters a Little Too Far

A huge discussion now rages in the church on a recent elder's decision to start a Men's Home focused on ex-prisoners, and helping them matriculate back into society. One of the members of the church with the vision, burden, and expertise to start such a ministry, shared his burden with the elders, and over nine months they researched his burden and determined it to be valid and within the mission of the church. A growing group in the church, however, were skeptical of the validity of this idea from the start. How would they be able to guarantee the safety of many of the church members with these men now so visible in the services and activities of the church? Some of the men had sex-offender backgrounds, and many young families have expressed their dismay and concern about the presence of such individuals in the church body. Others argued strongly that the grace of God can transform, and that all human beings, regardless of background, can be changed by the grace of God in Christ. The prospect of starting this ministry has created rumors about wholesale departure from the church if they continue on with the idea. If you were senior pastor in such a congregation, how would you approach this ministry, especially in light of the insights covered in this lesson on the church, the *imago Dei*, and the church as the locus and agent of the Kingdom of God? Explain your answer.

Studying War No More

In light of the many skirmishes, battles, armed conflicts, and all out combats being waged in many parts of the world today, we as Christians must come to understand our view regarding war and violence. If God is a God of justification by faith and justice, too, then, it may be possible to talk about wars and conflicts that are justified. Throughout Church history, godly, sincere, and biblical Christians have disagreed on the validity of war to settle disputes, of Christians serving in war, even of Christians in the military. The lines are typically drawn very clearly. One side argues unequivocally that Christians are forbidden to kill others, since human beings, *all of them*, are precious in the sight of God, made in his image. Others argue, that the powers that exist do so by the authority of God, and numerous texts exhort the Christian to honor the king, submit to the reigning powers, and serve the governing institutions with deference and honor. How far are we as believers to take this teaching about the *imago Dei* when it comes to serving in a branch of armed services in a country? Can we affirm the *imago Dei* and still serve in the military, in a capacity that will require you to take human life?

The *Imago Dei* and Capital Punishment

One of the living controversies among many Christian communities is the issue of capital punishment. Many believers hold the position today that since all human beings are made in the *imago Dei*, we are forbidden to put any human being to death, even if that person has been proven to be guilty of the capital crime that brought the punishment of death upon them. Others, quoting the same texts, believe that for the state to deter evil and institute justice, capital punishment is both necessary and helpful. They claim that it not only inflicts justice on the perpetrator of the crime, it also serves as a reminder for others of the consequences of similar criminal behavior. What do you say regarding the legitimacy of the capital punishment, and the affirmation that all human beings (even guilty ones) are made in the *imago Dei*? Should it make a difference in what we think about capital punishment?

Give Me Time, I'm Still Growing

While few would contest the clear biblical injunction to love others as Christ loved us as the identifying sign of all true discipleship (John 13.34-35), many do argue about the *ways in which* that love ought to be shown, as well as *when it needs to be shown*. A new Christian who had been socialized his entire life to hate people of a particular race was not strictly exhorted to change his feelings and ideas towards them. His conversion and faith in Jesus Christ seemed in every way to be both sincere and authentic, but his ongoing suspicion, hatred, and distrust of others of another race lingered on for months, and the new convert did not hide his disdain and disgust for "those people." While some believed that his lingering attitude was a sign of his failure to convert, others viewed the residue of his past as merely an area for him to grow. All newborn babes in Christ, they argued will have areas in their lives that require time to put off the old man, be renewed in the spirit of their minds, and put on the new man created after God in the image of true holiness and righteousness (cf. Eph. 4.20ff.). What do you think of this situation–is failure to love in this case a situation of normal Christian growth, or a sign of a failure to repent? How might the leaders in such a situation find out which one it really was?

As *creator* and *maker* of the earth, our God is concerned about the world and those who live within it. Traditionally, Christian communities have taken various positions to the world, including withdrawal from it, living in tension with it, or accepting responsibility to transform it. The Church is both the locus and agent of the Kingdom of God *in the world but not of it*. As such, the Church affirms that God is the God of all nature as well as the God of salvation, the God of creation as well as the God of covenant, and the God of justice as well as the God of justification. In its own ministry as the representative of the Kingdom of God, the Church is called to display and announce freedom to the world, called to express God's wholeness in the world, and stand for God's justice throughout the world.

Restatement of the Lesson's Thesis

The ground for doing justice and loving mercy among the poor in the city is the affirmation of the *imago Dei* in every boy, girl, woman, and man. Every person is worthy of care because they share in God's unmatched, unique, and irreplaceable *imago Dei*. Because all are made in God's image, all humankind is unique and precious. This image constitutes the reason why we ought to do justice and love mercy among all individuals, families, peoples, and nations on earth. Each of them as bearers of the *imago Dei* are to be considered as precious and irreplaceable.

Resources and Bibliographies

If you are interested in pursuing some of the ideas of *Let Justice Roll Down: The Vision and Theology of the Kingdom*, you might want to give these books a try:

> Cone, James. *The God of The Oppressed*. New York: Seabury Press, 1975.
>
> Conn, Harvie. *Evangelism: Doing Justice and Preaching Grace*. Grand Rapids: Zondervan, 1982.
>
> Fletcher, William M. *The Second Greatest Commandment: A Call to A Personal and Corporate Life of Caring*. Colorado Springs: NavPress, 1983.
>
> Kirk, Andrew. *The Good News of the Kingdom Coming: The Marriage of Evangelism and Social Responsibility*. Downers Grove, IL: InterVarsity Press, 1983.

Ministry Connections

This section is a specific opportunity for you to seek the leading of the Holy Spirit as to your own particular application of the material in the module lesson. This ability to listen and follow the prompting of the Holy Spirit is significant in all study, dialogue, and submission. Here now is your chance to discover through meditation and prayer a correlation of this high theology to a real practical ministry connection in your life. The scope of this application could be today, this week, this month, or even throughout the year. All of this depends on what you need to know and what the Holy Spirit *wants you to apply in your life and ministry*.

Therefore, take some time to wait before the Lord and listen to the Holy Spirit in open prayer. What does he seem to be suggesting to you regarding your own understanding of the importance of justice and mercy in your life, in your preaching and teaching, in your ministry at church, with your neighbors? Does the Lord bring a particular person, situation, or encounter to mind that he wants you to respond to him in light of the teaching in this lesson? Does the Holy Spirit seem to be moving you to change something in your life and ministry, or perhaps begin or initiate something? The promise is sure from the Word of God: the blessing comes to the person who simply does not hear the Word, but does it (James 1.22-25). Be open to the Spirit as you explore the various implications of this teaching for your own life and ministry.

The power of prayer is critical to our development as disciples of Christ and leaders of the Church. Learning to share requests with your fellow students and leaders will enhance every phase of your growth in Christ. Of course, no one can read your mind; you will need to be open and transparent about the ways in which you will be seeking the Lord's grace to apply and relate these truths to your own walk and ministry. Moreover, your instructors are more than willing to provide you with counsel, advice, and insight into particular issues and circumstances that you may be facing. Be open to receive the counsel of your leaders as you address the various challenges you are facing today, and be sure to ask your fellow students to lift you up in prayer as seek to make the truths you mined in this lesson your very own treasure.

Remember the words of our Lord when he instructs on the power of prayer:

> Matt. 7.7-11 - Ask, and it will be given to you; seek, and you will find; knock, and it will be opened to you. [8] For everyone who asks receives, and the one who seeks finds, and to the one who knocks it will be opened. [9] Or which one of you, if his son asks him for bread, will give him a stone? [10] Or if he asks for a fish, will give him a serpent? [11] If you then, who are evil, know how to give good gifts to your children, how much more will your Father who is in heaven give good things to those who ask him!

With this encouragement in mind, ask the Lord to provide you with keen insight into the meaning of the truths here, as well as opportunity and energy to respond promptly and obediently to the Word of God for your own life. Share requests with your fellow students, and pray for one another. The prayer of the righteous is a powerful thing, indeed (James 5.16)!

Counseling and Prayer

ASSIGNMENTS

Amos 5.20-24

Scripture Memory

To prepare for class, please visit *www.tumi.org/books* to find next week's reading assignment, or ask your mentor.

Reading Assignment

Other Assignments

page 310 📖 9

In order to obtain the maximum effect from your study, you must be challenged to truly master the ideas, not merely cover them in class. In order to aid your retention of the key concepts and principles covered in this week's lesson, you will be quizzed in your next class session on the content of *video presentation*. In order to prepare for this quiz, it will be necessary for you to spend ample and uninterrupted time covering your notes, focusing especially on the main ideas of the lesson.

On a related assignment, make certain that you take the time to read in your textbooks all of the pages listed in preparation for the next lesson's assigned reading. Please summarize each the readings with no more than a paragraph or two for each, and in this summary please give your best understanding of what you think was the main point in each of the readings. Do not be overly concerned about giving detail; simply write out what you consider to be the main point discussed in that section of the book. Please bring these summaries to class next week. (Please see the "Reading Completion Sheet" at the end of this lesson.)

Looking Forward to the Next Lesson

This lesson focused upon God's character and its relationship to the world, the Church, and the Kingdom of God. As creator and maker of the earth, our God is concerned about the world and those who live within it. The Church is both the locus and agent of the Kingdom of God in the world but not of it. As such, the Church affirms that God is the God of all nature as well as the God of salvation, the God of creation as well as the God of covenant, and the God of justice as well as the God of justification. In its own ministry as the representative of the Kingdom of God, the Church is called to display and announce freedom to the world, to express God's wholeness in the world, and to stand for God's justice throughout the world.

We also saw in this lesson how the ground for doing justice and loving mercy among the poor in the city is the affirmation of the *imago Dei* in all of humankind. Every human being is worthy of care because they share in God's unmatched, unique, and irreplaceable *imago Dei*. Because all are made in God's image, all humankind is unique and precious. This image constitutes the reason why we ought to do justice and love mercy among all individuals, families, peoples, and nations on earth.

In our next lesson we will explore the lived priority of justice and mercy in the Church of Christ. As a people given over to the responsibility of demonstrating God's justice and mercy in the world today, the Church is called to create and sustain ministries of mercy and love. This ingenuity in caring is rooted in the practices of justice and mercy in Israel, God's OT community, and carries over to the Church as God's kingdom community today. We will look at caring for those both inside and outside the community, and how God has outfitted the family, the Church, care societies and the state with abundant opportunities to demonstrate God's justice and mercy in our urban communities today.

Capstone Curriculum

Module 16: Doing Justice and Loving Mercy
Reading Completion Sheet

Name _____

Date _____

For each assigned reading, write a brief summary (one or two paragraphs) of the author's main point. (For additional readings, use the back of this sheet.)

Reading 1

Title and Author: _____ Pages _____

Reading 2

Title and Author: _____ Pages _____

Doing Justice and Loving Mercy (1)
The Urban Congregation

LESSON 2

page 311

Lesson Objectives

Welcome in the strong name of Jesus Christ! After your reading, study, discussion, and application of the materials in this lesson, you will be able to:

- Outline the priority of justice and mercy for the ministry and work of the Church of Christ.

- Show from Scripture how the Church has been granted the sober responsibility of demonstrating God's justice and mercy in the world today, called to demonstrate this first to its own members, in a kind of "home grown" quality of Christian love.

- Recite how the grace of God underpins and shapes our theologies of justice, mercy, and love, and lay out the implications of experiencing God's grace in our approaches to justice and mercy.

- List the basic elements involved in the rationale and practices of justice and mercy in the life of Israel, God's OT community.

- Give the basic theological rationale for the Church as God's kingdom community, and its call to justice and mercy in this age, and specifically for the urban church.

- Give evidence of the significance of the two objects of God's justice and mercy, i.e., the members of the Church and those outside.

- Discuss the four channels through which God manifests his love: the family, the Church, care societies, and the state.

- Recount the six key principles which should inform our care-giving as local congregations as we seek to demonstrate God's justice and mercy in our urban communities.

Devotion

page 313

Created for Good Works

Eph. 2.1-10 - And you were dead in the trespasses and sins [2] in which you once walked, following the course of this world, following the prince of the power of the air, the spirit that is now at work in the sons of disobedience— [3] among whom we all once lived in the passions of our flesh, carrying out the desires of the body and the mind, and were by nature children of wrath, like the rest of mankind. [4] But God, being rich in mercy, because of the great love with which he loved us, [5] even when we were dead in our trespasses, made us alive together with Christ— by grace you have been saved— [6] and raised us up with him and seated us with him in the heavenly places in Christ Jesus, [7] so that in the coming ages he might show the immeasurable riches of his grace in kindness toward us in Christ Jesus. [8] For by grace you have been saved through faith. And this is not your own doing; it is the gift of God, [9] not a result of works, so that no one may boast. [10] For we are his workmanship, created in Christ Jesus for good works, which God prepared beforehand, that we should walk in them.

The story of our personal redemption is a story of transformation. Paul here tells the Ephesians the time line of their own new life in Christ, from their own tragic death in trespasses and sins, and enslavement to the tyranny of the devil to release, freedom, and good works in Christ. This story of transformation is the same for all true believers in Christ. Christian deliverance is movement, from the moment of the invasion of the Spirit into our worlds with his grace and salvation, to the full circle of our own good works and compassion that expresses a redeemed life. At the heart of all of this is the mercy of God, as Paul argues brilliantly, the "great love with which he loved us, even when we were dead in our trespasses, made us alive together with Christ." It was mercy and love in the heart of God that motivated our great God and Father to send his own Son into the world on our behalf, and mercy and love in the heart of the Messiah that allowed him to die such a vicious and unjust death on our behalf. All of this momentous work was by grace, God's undeserved favor which redeemed, infused the life of God into us, raised us up with Christ and seated us with him in the heavenly places. Now, through the ages to come God will use us as trophies of his matchless and indescribable goodness revealed in the person of Messiah Jesus, and all of this, amazingly, is through God's grace.

Now, in light of such a wonderful and gracious salvation, what is the most appropriate expression that God's people can extend? What is the inevitable manifestation of hearts made alive through the mercy, love, and grace of the eternal God in the death of his Son? How should we now then live?

Paul is clear. In Ephesians 2.8-10 he lays out the truth regarding our salvation and its effects in our lives: "For by grace you have been saved through faith. And this is not your own doing; it is the gift of God, not a result of works, so that no one may boast. For we are his workmanship, created in Christ Jesus for good works, which God prepared beforehand, that we should walk in them." We have been delivered from the wrath to come through the undeserved grace of God as we placed our trust in Christ as our Savior and Lord. This had nothing to do with our own works of righteousness, and therefore all our boasting is excluded. Rather, we were recreated in Christ as God's workmanship for the purpose of demonstrating good works, even those which the Father prepared for us beforehand that we should express. "For we are his workmanship, created in Christ Jesus for good works." This focus on good works is emphasized not only here, but throughout the entire NT. Here is a sampling of this salient and important fact of our calling to be "do gooders:"

> Matt. 5.16 - In the same way, let your light shine before others, so that they may see your good works and give glory to your Father who is in heaven.
>
> 2 Cor. 9.8 - And God is able to make all grace abound to you, so that having all sufficiency in all things at all times, you may abound in every good work.
>
> Col. 1.10 - . . . so as to walk in a manner worthy of the Lord, fully pleasing to him, bearing fruit in every good work and increasing in the knowledge of God.
>
> 2 Thess. 2.16-17 - Now may our Lord Jesus Christ himself, and God our Father, who loved us and gave us eternal comfort and good hope through grace, [17] comfort your hearts and establish them in every good work and word.
>
> 1 Tim. 6.18 - They are to do good, to be rich in good works, to be generous and ready to share.
>
> 2 Tim. 2.21 - Therefore, if anyone cleanses himself from what is dishonorable, he will be a vessel for honorable use, set apart as holy, useful to the master of the house, ready for every good work.
>
> 2 Tim. 3.17 - . . . that the man of God may be competent, equipped for every good work.
>
> Titus 2.7 - Show yourself in all respects to be a model of good works, and in your teaching show integrity, dignity.
>
> Titus 2.14 - . . . who gave himself for us to redeem us from all lawlessness and to purify for himself a people for his own possession who are zealous for good works.
>
> Titus 3.1 - Remind them to be submissive to rulers and authorities, to be obedient, to be ready for every good work.

> Titus 3.8 - The saying is trustworthy, and I want you to insist on these things, so that those who have believed in God may be careful to devote themselves to good works. These things are excellent and profitable for people.
>
> Titus 3.14 - And let our people learn to devote themselves to good works, so as to help cases of urgent need, and not be unfruitful.
>
> Heb. 10.24 - And let us consider how to stir up one another to love and good works.
>
> 1 Pet. 2.12 - Keep your conduct among the Gentiles honorable, so that when they speak against you as evil doers, they may see your good deeds and glorify God on the day of visitation.

Yes, we as believers have nothing to boast about before God. He saved us, cleansed us, empowers us, encourages us. We have been set free to help others be released. We have been redeemed in order that we might be redemptive. We have been lifted up that we might strengthen the lives of others.

Have you embraced your call before God, to be the workmanship of God in Christ Jesus in order that you might exhibit the very works of Christ in your family, on your street, at your job, in your ministry? This is the way to demonstrate your gratitude to God, who gave all for you in order that you might now demonstrate your love for others.

> *2 Cor. 8.9 - For you know the grace of our Lord Jesus Christ, that though he was rich, yet for your sake he became poor, so that you by his poverty might become rich.*

Nicene Creed and Prayer

After reciting and/or singing the Nicene Creed (located in the Appendix), pray the following prayer:

> *Holy God, source of all love, on the night of his betrayal Jesus gave his disciples a new commandment, to love one another as he loved them. Write this commandment in our hearts; give us the will to serve others as he was the servant of all, who gave his life and died for us, yet is alive and reigns with you and the Holy Spirit, one God, now and forever. Amen.*
>
> ~ Presbyterian Church (U.S.A.) and Cumberland Presbyterian Church. The Theology and Worship Ministry Unit. **Book of Common Worship**. Louisville: Westminster/John Knox Press, 1993. p. 270.

DOING JUSTICE AND LOVING MERCY: COMPASSION MINISTRIES Capstone Curriculum / 6 1

| Quiz | Put away your notes, gather up your thoughts and reflections, and take the quiz for Lesson 1, *Let Justice Roll Down: The Vision and Theology of the Kingdom*. |

| Scripture Memorization Review | Review with a partner, write out and/or recite the text for last class session's assigned memory verses: Amos 5.20-24. |

| Assignments Due | Turn in your summary of the reading assignment for last week, that is, your brief response and explanation of the main points that the authors were seeking to make in the assigned reading (Reading Completion Sheet). |

God's Social Network

At a time when so many nations are struggling to provide even the basic needs for their own citizens, more and more churches are experimenting with ways in which they can provide ongoing care for their members. In every way from shared insurance plans to coops for food and goods, churches are finding ways to take care of their own members' basic physical needs as well as the spiritual needs of the body. In your opinion, what is the responsibility of the local church to care for and meet the basic physical needs for its own members? Ought the church experiment in finding new ways to not only meet the spiritual needs of the people of God but also the tangible needs of the each individual and family, including health care, employment, even retirement?

The State as Sinister Structure or as God's Minister?

Throughout the history of the Church, believers have debated the role of the state. Is the state an evil institution that in its godless and often times reckless way oppressed its citizenry and mowed down those seeking to change it? Or rather, is the state an institution ordained by God to punish evil doers and recognize those who do good, God's very own minister to serve the most vulnerable and guarantee the oppressed their basic human rights? What do you believe about the role of the state in executing justice and demonstrating mercy to its own citizens, and to its allies?

What's the Difference between Them?

In the wake of so many natural disasters in our country and around the world (e.g., Hurricanes Katrina and Rita, the earthquake in Pakistan, etc.) many nations, organizations, and individuals have poured out their goods and services to care for the victims of these situations. Millions of dollars has been raised and tens of thousands of hours have been given by relief organizations and government agencies to relieve the suffering of families and individuals who have experienced death, loss, and ill health. Apparently, this sacrifice and aid appears to be motivated by good will and genuine care for human sufferers. In your opinion, is there a difference between the kind of care and concern offered to sufferers by unbelievers and that which is given by Christians? Do you think God discriminates between love shown to victims by pagan or unbelieving individuals and that offered by believers in Jesus Christ? Explain your answer.

Doing Justice and Loving Mercy: The Urban Congregation

Segment 1: Charity Begins at Home

Rev. Dr. Don L. Davis

The motivation for enduring justice and mercy is the experience of the grace of God through the Gospel of Christ. We in fact demonstrate to others the same grace and mercy we have received as members of the body of Christ, and do so in the power of the Holy Spirit. The effect of the grace of God on the believing community is to produce unconditional surrender to the lordship of Christ, and an aggressive commitment to show generosity and hospitality to the underserved and vulnerable among us. In the Old Testament, God's covenant people Israel were called to live as a sign of his rulership and Kingdom. As such, God demanded that they demonstrate justice and mercy within their ranks, that they denounce the oppression of the poor, and treat the vulnerable and hurting with great grace and care. Today, the Church of Jesus Christ is God's kingdom community, called to reveal God's justice and mercy through its good works and advocacy of the poor and the oppressed.

Our objective for this segment, *Charity Begins at Home,* is to enable you to see that:

- The motivation for enduring justice and mercy is the experience of the grace of God through the Gospel of Christ. We, in fact, demonstrate to others the same grace and mercy we have received as members of the body of Christ.

Summary of Segment 1

- The effect of the grace of God on the believing community is to produce unconditional surrender to the lordship of Christ, and an aggressive commitment to show generosity and hospitality to the underserved and vulnerable among us.

- The Holy Spirit indwelling the Christian and the Church is the *coordinator* and *instigator* of the acts of mercy, love, and justice expressed in the good works of the Church.

- In the Old Testament, God's covenant people Israel were called to live as a sign of his rulership and Kingdom. As such, God demanded that they demonstrate justice and mercy within their ranks, that they denounce the oppression of the poor, and treat the vulnerable and hurting with great grace and care.

- In this age, the Church of Jesus Christ is God's kingdom community, called to reveal God's justice and mercy through its good works and advocacy of the poor and the oppressed.

- The ethic of the Kingdom of God is summarized in the Great Commandment, to love God with all the heart, mind, soul, and strength, and the "second commandment," to love one's neighbor as oneself (cf. Deut. 6.4ff. and Lev. 19.18). Messiah Jesus has given us the "New Commandment," an intensification of the second, which is to love one another even as he has loved us (John 13.34-35).

- The urban church, as a representative of God's covenant people in the city, is called to demonstrate care to its own members, as well as generosity and hospitality to those who are outside. The local church, as an outpost of the Kingdom of God, is called to be the place where the charity of God is to begin, and from which it is to flow.

Video Segment 1 Outline

I. **Charity Begins at Home: Justice and Mercy in the Church**

A. The motivation for enduring justice and mercy: an experience of the grace of God through the Gospel of Christ

1. We have been saved by grace through faith.

    a. Eph. 2.10

    b. Jer. 31.33

    c. Jer. 32.39-40

    d. 2 Cor. 5.5

    e. 2 Cor. 5.17

    f. Phil. 1.6

    g. Phil. 2.13

2. We were (and are!) fully undeserving of the grace and mercy that we received.

    a. Rom. 5.7-8

    b. Isa. 53.6

    c. 1 Pet. 3.18

    d. 1 John 4.10

> *The only true and enduring motivation for the ministry of mercy is an experience and grasp of the grace of God in the gospel. If we know we are sinners saved by grace alone, we will be both open and generous to the outcast and the unlovely.*
> ~ Timothy J. Keller. *The Ministries of Mercy*. Phillipsburg, NJ: P & R Publishing, Company, 1997. p. 58.

3. Although he was rich, Jesus became poor in order that we who were poor might become rich.

    a. 2 Cor. 8.9

    b. John 1.14

    c. 2 Cor. 13.14

    d. Eph. 3.19

4. The heart of the Good News is that it is more blessed to give than to receive, shown in the willingness of Jesus to lay down his life for us, John 10, 15; cf. Acts 20.35.

5. No one can boast or brag regarding the mercy that God lavished upon us.

    a. 1 Cor. 1.29-31

    b. 2 Tim. 1.9

    c. Titus 3.3-5

B. Effects of the grace of God upon the believing

1. Love for the Lord demonstrated in unconditional surrender of ourselves to him as a living sacrifice, Rom. 12.1-2

2. Love for those who belong to the Lord, 1 John 4.7-8

3. Generosity and hospitality toward those who are equally underserved and unlovely

    a. Matt. 5.43-45

    b. Prov. 25.21-22

C. Implications for the ministries of mercy in and through the Church

1. The person (or church) unwilling to demonstrate love to others is either carnal or unchristian, 1 John 4.20.

2. No one can sustain a ministry of mercy and love toward others unless they have experienced the love of God personally through faith in Jesus Christ, John 15.4-5.

3. The ground of all Christian generosity, hospitality, and care giving is the experience of salvation by grace through faith in Jesus Christ.

    a. Christian love is anchored in unmerited favor, not in those who show a "worthiness to be cared for."

b. Love is the litmus test and undeniable indicator of authentic experience of forgiveness and communion with God, 1 John 4.8.

4. The Holy Spirit indwelling the Christian and the Church is the *coordinator* and *instigator* of acts of mercy, love, and justice in the Church, Gal. 5.22-23.

II. Who Is My Neighbor? OT Understandings of Care Giving

A. God's covenant people as a sign of God's rulership and his Kingdom

1. An intimate connection exists between the blessing of God and the demonstration of justice and mercy among the members of the community, Deut. 7.12-16.

2. The blessing of God upon his people was to mandate among them a ministry of care, Deut. 15.7-8.

3. The family was to provide relief for the needs of relatives, Lev. 25.25.

4. Tithes were collected for distribution among the poor, Deut. 14.28-29.

B. God demanded justice and mercy from his people.

1. God commands his people to show kindness to the poor, Prov. 14.21.

2. Fair treatment and respect to foreigners in their midst

    a. Exod. 22.21-24

    b. Exod. 23.9

    c. Exod. 23.12

3. Respect is to be given to the old, to fellow Israelites, and those sojourning through the land, Lev. 19.32-34.

4. God's verdict for his people regarding justice and mercy, Ps. 82.1-5.

C. God denounces wealth gained by oppression and abuse.

1. God is aware of the unjust oppression of brother-to-brother among his covenant people, Job 22.5-9.

2. Those whose wealth made them proud made them mock and ignore their brethren, Ps. 123.3-4.

3. God promised to punish those who spent their wealth on themselves, plundering the needy, Isa. 3.13-25, cf. Isa. 3.13-15.

D. God demands justice and mercy: he punished those who trampled the poor and the hurting.

1. God's anger was unloosed on those who abused the poor among the covenant people, Ezek. 22.23-31.

2. God promised not to forget the deeds done against the powerless in the nation, Amos 8.4-7.

3. The inhabitants of Jerusalem are admonished because they failed to share with the needy, Mal. 3.5.

E. Implications

1. God's people were to reflect the reality that they were a special kingdom people demonstrating his justice to the nations, Exod. 19.5-6.

2. The vulnerable and hurting were to be cared for with great grace, since God ransomed Israel from great hurt and abuse, Lev. 19.34.

3. God would not let oppression within the covenant community go unpunished, Job 5.11-16.

III. The Church as God's Kingdom Community: Revealing Justice and Mercy

A. A new identity: the Church as God's covenant/kingdom people

1. The Church is a chosen nation, to *bear God's name as a sign for the world to see*, Matt. 5.14-16.

2. The Church is a pilgrim people, *sojourning through the world together as God's pilgrim community*, 1 Pet. 1.17.

3. The Church is a witnessing community, *giving witness through its words and deeds of the Kingdom already here but not yet fully consummated*, Acts 2.42-47.

B. A new ethic: the Church as the primary place of mercy and justice

Deut. 15.8-10 - . . . but you shall open your hand to him and lend him sufficient for his need, whatever it may be. [9] Take care lest there be an unworthy thought in your heart and you say, "The seventh year, the year of release is near," and your eye look grudgingly on your poor brother, and you give him nothing, and he cry to the Lord against you, and you be guilty of sin. [10] You shall give to him freely, and your heart shall not be grudging when you give to him, because for this the Lord your God will bless you in all your work and in all that you undertake.

1. We are to do good to all, but especially among the members of the household of faith, Gal. 6.10.

2. Manifestations of the Holy Spirit's outpouring were accompanied by distribution of goods among believers to the elimination of need, Acts 2.42-47; Acts 4.31-32.

3. The provision for the Hellenist widows, Acts 6.1-6

4. The Great Commandment of Jesus Christ, John 13.34-35

5. The demonstration of authentic faith is displayed in regard to how one responds to a *brother or sister's need*.

   a. James 2.15-17

   b. 1 John 3.16-18

6. The needs of poor widows were mandated by apostolic authority, 1 Tim. 5.3-5.

7. Offerings were collected among affluent congregations to meet the needs among suffering believers elsewhere, 2 Cor. 8-9; Acts 11.27-30.

C. The commands of love: God's perfect law

1. The ethic of the Kingdom: the Great Commandment, Matt. 22.35-40

   a. A combination of two texts: Deuteronomy 6.4-6 and Leviticus 19.18

   b. Summarizes and grounds all of God's ethical demands for the covenant community

   c. All of God's moral will connected to one's relationship with God and with others

2. Messiah's intensification of the Love Commandment: the New Commandment, John 13.34-35

   a. Jesus speaks of it as a new commandment.

   b. Jesus as the benchmark of authentic kingdom lifestyle: love one another *just as I have loved you.*

   c. Love as the sign and condition of authentic discipleship: *by this all people will know that you are my disciples.*

D. The concentric nature of Christian love and mercy

   1. Love to one's own family, Col. 3.18-21

   2. Love to one's kindred

      a. 1 Tim. 5.4

      b. 1 Tim. 5.8

   3. Love to the body of believers, 1 John 4.7-8

   4. Love to strangers, cf. the Good Samaritan, Luke 10.29-37

   5. Love to one's enemies, Luke 6.27-28

6. Love to all, Gal. 6.10

E. The importance of love within the Christian family

1. As sign of one's salvation, 1 John 4.10

2. As proof of one's discipleship, John 13.35

3. As evidence of one's communion with God, 1 John 4.20

F. Implications for the urban church

1. As the covenant people of God, we are to begin our responsibility for justice and mercy among the members of the Church, Gal. 6.10.

2. While family is given a large responsibility to care for its own members, the local church is also a primary channel of love and grace to meet the needs of those hurting in our midst, 1 Tim. 5.3-5.

3. Membership is critical as to be able to discern those who belong to us, and therefore who are eligible for our first (not only!) acts of mercy and justice, 1 John 2.19.

4. Benevolence ministries are not merely a footnote on the page of the Church; how we care for our members is the sign of our relationship with God, 1 John 3.

5. The local church is the place for charity to begin.

   a. The place to organize for change and distribution

   b. The place to discern needs and offer support to hurting members

   c. The place where the gifts, talents, and resources of the body can be coordinated to meet the member's needs

   d. The place to congregate to renew our commitments to God, one another, and our families together

Conclusion

» Because of the grace of God we have received through the Gospel, the Church of Jesus Christ is called to demonstrate his own justice and mercy within God's kingdom community and to the world.

» As a people called to live forth the rule of God in the city, our first responsibility in showing God's justice and mercy is in the midst of our churches, charity must begin at home.

Please take as much time as you have available to answer these and other questions that the video brought out. We saw how the primary motivation for displaying justice and mercy in the Church and world is the experience of the grace of God through the Gospel of Christ. In the Holy Spirit, we demonstrate the same grace and mercy God gave us as believers in Jesus. The effect of this grace produces discipleship in Christ and generosity and hospitality to others. Review these critical themes covered in your first segment through the questions offered below.

1. According to what Scripture in the Bible, what is the motive behind the Christian impulse to demonstrate justice and mercy to others? From a Christian standpoint, is it possible to truly offer God-honoring service to

Segue 1

Student Questions and Response

page 315 3

others if we have not yet experienced the grace of God through the Gospel of Christ? Explain your answer.

2. What is the relationship of the kind of care we as believers offer to others and the grace that we ourselves have received as members of the body of Christ?

3. The grace of God empowers the believing community in both its relationship to God and to others. How exactly does the grace of God influence believers and the Church to do good works in their relationship to God, to the lost, and to the body of Christ?

4. What is the role of the Holy Spirit in the creation of good works, i.e., those acts of mercy, love, and justice expressed in the good works of the Church?

5. How did the Old Testament outline the responsibility of Israel to be a sign of God's rulership and Kingdom? What specific ways were they to demonstrate justice and mercy within their ranks, to the rich and poor, to the vulnerable (i.e., the fatherless, orphan, widow), and to others in need?

6. In what way has now the Church of Jesus Christ become God's kingdom community in this age, and to what is she called regarding God's justice and mercy?

7. Describe the relationship between the Great and Second Commandments, and the new commandment given to us by our Lord Jesus Christ. How do these relate to each other, as well as to the call of the Church for justice and mercy?

8. How ought urban churches, as a representatives of God's covenant people in the city, manifest these understandings of the Kingdom in the communities where they live and serve?

Doing Justice and Loving Mercy: The Urban Congregation

Segment 2: The Objects, Channels, and Principles of Fleshing Out God's Justice and Mercy

Rev. Dr. Don L. Davis

The Church demonstrates the justice and mercy of God to two interrelated objects of his care: the members of his own covenant community, and those who are outsiders. This includes those in our own marriages and families, as well as those counted as neighbors, strangers, foreigners, and even our enemies. Through individuals and families, local congregations, care communities and organizations, and governmental institutions and agencies God reveals his love and justice in the world. The local church plays a unique role in communicating God's mercy and love to others. God empowers his people, the Church, to represent the values of his reign (i.e., justice, love, and mercy) and has called them to demonstrate good works for his glory.

Our objective for this segment, *The Objects, Channels, and Principles of Fleshing Out God's Justice and Mercy,* is to enable you to see that:

- The Church seeks to demonstrate the justice and mercy of God to two interrelated objects of his care: the members of his own covenant community, and those who are outsiders.

- Believers are called to care for members of their own marriages, families, and extended families, as well as all the members of God's assembly. We are also called to serve those who do not believe, including those counted as neighbors, strangers, foreigners, and even our enemies.

- Through the provident leading of God, we see that four channels of God's divine justice and mercy are operating today. Individuals and families, local congregations, care communities and organizations, and governmental institutions and agencies all are used by God to display his generosity, justice, and mercy to those in need.

- As the outpost of the Kingdom of God in a particular locale, the local church plays a unique role in communicating God's mercy and love to others. Six principles can inform this care. Each local assembly is called to do good to all people, but especially to those of the household of faith. Each is called to follow the example of Jesus in selfless service, to equip its members for the work of the ministry, to show love and mercy with

Summary of Segment 2

wisdom and grace, in both word and deed, and to work to eliminate the problems altogether, and not merely their symptoms.

- God empowers his people, the Church, to represent the values of his reign (i.e., justice, love, and mercy) and has called them to demonstrate good works for his glory.

Video Segment 2 Outline

I. **Two Objects of Justice and Mercy: The People of God and Outsiders**

 A. Two objects of justice and mercy

 1. Ministering mercy and care are *intrinsic* (basic) to the Christian life in every way: no love, no redemption, John 13.34-35.

 2. Group one: the members of God's covenant community

 a. Family members

 (1) Prov. 13.22

 (2) 2 Cor. 12.14

 b. Relatives or extended family, 1 Tim. 5.8

 c. Fellow members of God's assembly, Acts 2.22-27; cf. Acts 2.42-45.

 3. Group two: those who are outside of God's covenant community

 a. Gal. 6.10

b. Rom. 12.13

c. 1 Thess. 5.15

d. Titus 3.2

e. 1 Pet. 2.17

B. Biblical descriptions of the kinds of outsiders

1. Neighbors, Luke 10.29-37; cf. Luke 10.36-37

2. Strangers

   a. Matt. 25.35

   b. 3 John 1.5-8

3. Foreigners, Heb. 13.1-3

4. Enemies

   a. Matt. 5.43-48

   b. Luke 6.34-35

c. Rom. 12.14

d. 1 Pet. 3.9

II. **Four Channels of God's Divine Justice and Mercy**

A. Individuals and the family: *individual disciples and family units can become ministers of justice and mercy by beginning in their own web of influence.*

1. The family is a ministry base, a foundation for generosity and hospitality.

    a. Lev. 25.25

    b. 1 Tim. 5.8

2. In gleaning its fields, families were to leave crops for the needy to have. Families are the "frontlines" of demonstrating the mercy of God to those who are needy and hurting (Keller, *Ministries of Mercy*, p.125).

3. Families can practice hospitality in an urban community with the members of *their extended family*, especially if they make themselves available to serve others.

B. The local congregation: *each congregation can develop outreaches, programs, and projects designed to mobilize and coordinate its members to meet the needs of others.*

1. The local body of believers is responsible to meet the needs of those who are family with them.

    a. Acts 2.42-47

    b. Acts 4.32-37

2. A church that views itself as a congregation of ministers who desire to demonstrate mercy and justice to those in its neighborhoods will recognize many people who require care.

    a. Single parents and divorced people

    b. Those with disabilities and chronic health problems

    c. Families struck with terminally ill members

    d. Substance abuse victims

    e. Unwed mothers

    f. Abused children

    g. Juvenile delinquents and prisoners

C. The association or mission society: *various groups exist to address and target specific needs of vulnerable and hurting groups within society.*

1. God can use any means, secular or sacred, to do whatever he wills.

    a. Prov. 16.4

    b. Rom. 11.36

2. God uses vessels (men and women, institutions, groups, etc.) to accomplish his purposes: Cyrus

    a. Isa. 44.28

    b. 2 Chron. 36.22-23

3. God can raise up and use both Christian and secular agencies to demonstrate his goodness and accomplish his will for his glory.

    a. Hospitals

    b. Orphanages

    c. International agencies of care (Red Cross, United Way, etc.)

D. The state and government

1. Both Hebrew and pagan kings were moved by the Lord to demonstrate justice on behalf of the poor.

    a. Pagan kings

        (1) Nebuchadnezzar, Dan. 4.26-28

        (2) Prov. 16.12

        (3) Prov. 29.4

    b. Hebrew kings

        (1) 2 Sam. 8.15

        (2) Ps. 72.1-2

        (3) Ps. 99.4

        (4) Prov. 29.14

2. The state is used of God to punish evil doers and recognize those who do good, Rom. 13.1-4.

3. God's people can serve as civil servants and impact thousands through their just service: Joseph, Gen. 47.13-17.

III. Six Principles of Ministry in a Local Church Setting

A. Do good to all people, but especially to those of the household of faith.

Gal. 6.10
So then, as we have opportunity, let us do good to everyone, and especially to those who are of the household of faith.

1. Our primary responsibility for demonstrating mercy and grace is with members of the Christian community, but we ought to never limit our love only to the saved.

2. We are to cherish the saint and sinner both, Isa. 58.10.

3. Remember that we ought to give as we would have others give unto us.

4. No roadmap exists to know how precisely to care with limited resources; there is absolutely no substitute for the leading and filling of the Holy Spirit.

Heb. 10.23-25
Let us hold fast the confession of our hope without wavering, for he who promised is faithful. [24] And let us consider how to stir up one another to love and good works, [25] not neglecting to meet together, as is the habit of some, but encouraging one another, and all the more as you see the Day drawing near.

B. Expect Christians to spontaneously give and serve, but exhort them to follow the example of Christ in selfless sacrifice.

1. Every one that loves is born of God and knows God, 1 John 4.7-8.

2. We are equally charged to provoke one another to good works and deeds.

3. The Holy Spirit will lead individuals to give and serve purely from the burdens and promptings from within believer's hearts, Gal. 5.16.

4. We are to challenge believers to give and serve with zeal and passion, to fulfill the good works God has called them to do, Eph. 2.10; Titus 2.14.

C. Every member is a minister, and every pastor/teacher is an equipper for the work of the ministry.

1. The entire assembly should be involved in the ministries of mercy, not just the leaders or the burdened.

2. Regardless of the size of the burden to be borne, every believer can demonstrate concrete acts of care for others.

   a. Prayer, James 5.16

   b. Giving

      (1) Rom. 12.8

      (2) 1 Cor. 16.1-2

      (3) 2 Cor. 8.1-4

      (4) 2 Cor. 9.12

      (5) Heb. 13.16

   c. Personal time and attention, 2 Cor. 8.3-5

3. Encourage sacrifice and cooperation for meeting mutual needs.

D. We must allow for works of love and mercy to be done both conditionally and unconditionally.

Eph. 5.15-18 - Look carefully then how you walk, not as unwise but as wise, [16] making the best use of the time, because the days are evil. [17] Therefore do not be foolish, but understand what the will of the Lord is. [18] And do not get drunk with wine, for that is debauchery, but be filled with the Spirit.

Eph. 4.11-13
And he gave the apostles, the prophets, the evangelists, the pastors and teachers, [12] to equip the saints for the work of ministry, for building up the body of Christ, [13] until we all attain to the unity of the faith and of the knowledge of the Son of God, to mature manhood, to the measure of the stature of the fullness of Christ.

1. Unconditionally: done purely because the person is in need, Isa. 58.7-8

   a. Spurn any tendency to turn your works of mercy into "acts of merit."

   b. Sin on the side of compassion; human beings are penultimately *ends in themselves*.

   c. To be "perfect" in our acts of mercy we must recognize that the Father makes it to rain on *the just and the unjust*.

2. Conditionally: dependent upon the effort and cooperation of the person receiving the care, 2 Thess. 3.6-12

   a. Do not reward laziness or sinful behavior, but publicly acknowledge service on behalf of the body.

   b. Avoid hoarding and stinginess as you strive to avoid making members dependent.

   c. Some giving will demand that individuals take the steps toward the resolution of their situation: 2 Thess. 3.10.

E. Ministry should occur in both word of proclamation as well as deeds of demonstration.

James 2.14-26 - What good is it, my brothers, if someone says he has faith but does not have works? Can that faith save him? [15] If a brother or sister is poorly clothed and lacking in daily food, [16] and one of you says to them, "Go in peace, be warmed and filled," without giving them the things needed for the body, what good is that? [17] So also faith by itself, if it does not have works, is dead. [18] But someone will say, "You have faith and I have works." Show me your faith apart from your works, and I will show you my faith by my works. [19] You believe that God is one; you do well. Even the demons believe—and shudder! [20] Do you want to be shown, you foolish person, that faith apart from works is useless? [21] Was not Abraham our father justified by works when he offered up his son Isaac on the altar? [22] You see that faith was active along with his works, and faith was completed by his works; [23] and the Scripture was fulfilled that says, "Abraham believed God, and it was counted to him as righteousness"— and he was called a friend of God. [24] You see that a person is justified by works and not by faith alone. [25] And in the same way was not also Rahab the prostitute justified by works when she received the messengers and sent them out by another way? [26] For as the body apart from the spirit is dead, so also faith apart from works is dead.

1. Words of proclamation: we must never be ashamed of the Gospel of Christ, and do all our works in the name of the risen Lord, Rom. 1.16-17.

2. Deeds of demonstration: we must always express the reality of the Gospel in concrete demonstrations of love, justice, and kindness.

    a. James 2.15-16

    b. 1 John 3.18

    c. 1 Cor. 13.4-7

3. Our zeal for good works weaves together with our testimony regarding the Lord, Titus 2.11-14.

F. Be willing to deal with symptoms as you seek to address the root causes of the needs.

Matt. 7.17 - So, every healthy tree bears good fruit, but the diseased tree bears bad fruit.

2 Cor. 5.17 - Therefore, if anyone is in Christ, he is a new creation. The old has passed away; behold, the new has come.

2 Cor. 7.1 - Since we have these promises, beloved, let us cleanse ourselves from every defilement of body and spirit, bringing holiness to completion in the fear of God.

1 Tim. 1.5 - The aim of our charge is love that issues from a pure heart and a good conscience and a sincere faith.

1. Not every situation can be solved by us; we must recognize our place in the healing and blessing of others, 1 Cor. 3.5-9.

2. Be above reproach in all dealings with one another: neither coercion or pussy-footing, 2 Cor. 4.2.

3. Teach stewardship while giving bread: do not allow your ministries of mercy to be dichotomized into unnecessary "either/or" splits, Gal. 6.7-9.

    a. Provide food *and* help people to find employment.

    b. Pay utility bills *and* work with people to be responsible for their liabilities and debts.

    c. Repair housing needs *and* train people to purchase their own homes.

4. Rule of thumb: *do all the good that you can given your limits and the person's needs.*

    a. Ps. 37.3

    b. Titus 3.8

    c. Heb. 13.16

    d. 3 John 1.11

Conclusion

» God's love and justice is revealed to two objects of his concern and care, his own covenant community, the Church, and those who are outsiders.

» Through the family, the body of Christ, care societies, and the state, God channels his mercy and justice in the world.

The following questions were designed to help you review the material in the second video segment. Here we saw the two interrelated objects of God's care, the members of his own covenant community, and those who are outsiders. As the sovereign God of all, our Lord can elect to use anyone and anything to demonstrate his love and justice. We also saw from Scripture his election of individuals and families, local congregations, care communities and organizations, and governmental institutions and agencies to reveal his love and justice in the world. We also saw the critical role that the local church plays, a unique role, in communicating God's mercy and love to others. It is significant for you to understand the ways in which God has elected to display the reality of his Kingdom, and the following questions are designed to help you revisit these truths. Be clear and concise in your answers, and where possible, support with Scripture!

Segue 2

Student Questions and Response

page 315 4

1. What is the relationship between the Church's call to demonstrate God's love and mercy to its own members, and those who stand outside the Church? What practical difference ought this to make when we confront need, whether inside or outside the Church?

2. What is the responsibility of believers to care for the members of their own marriages, families, and extended families? How does the Bible instruct us about caring for the other members of the Church?

3. Briefly describe what the Scriptures say about our responsibility as kingdom people to care for our neighbors, for strangers and foreigners, and even our enemies.

4. What role does the doctrine of God's sovereignty play in understanding God's choice to use various entities and agencies as channels of his care and mercy? Describe briefly the roles and limits of how God uses individuals and families, local congregations, care communities and organizations, and governmental institutions and agencies to display his kingdom life to others.

5. In what way does the local church play a unique role in communicating God's mercy and love to others? Explain your answer with Scripture.

6. Give your understanding of the biblical injunction for believers to do good to all people, but especially those of the household of faith. Is this a form of legitimized favoritism? Explain your answer.

7. How does the example of Jesus in selfless service inform all forms of Christian care-giving?

8. In what ways are Christian leaders called to equip the members of the church for the work of the ministry? In what sense, therefore, ought we to consider all Christians as *ministers* and Christian leaders as *equippers for the work of the ministry*?

9. Why is it important to love others with wisdom, and even sometimes based on their willingness to work? In what way ought we in helping others seek to eliminate the *underlying cause* of the problems and not merely the *symptoms of the problems*? Explain.

10. What role does the sharing of the good news of salvation relate to our efforts to offer generosity and hospitality to those in need of help? Is it valid to offer aid without offering too the good news of Christ? If so, under what circumstances?

Summary of Key Concepts

This lesson focuses upon the specific role of the local congregation in demonstrating the justice and mercy of God. In the urban community, the local church is the very outpost of the Kingdom of God, called to represent the interests and government of God in the midst of the community. The following concepts offer a full summary of the critical concepts covered in this lesson related to these important perspectives.

- The motivation for enduring justice and mercy is the experience of the grace of God through the Gospel of Christ. We, in fact, demonstrate to others the same grace and mercy we have received as members of the body of Christ.

- The effect of the grace of God on the believing community is to produce unconditional surrender to the lordship of Christ, and an aggressive commitment to show generosity and hospitality to the underserved and vulnerable among us.

- The Holy Spirit indwelling the Christian and the Church is the *coordinator* and *instigator* of the acts of mercy, love, and justice expressed in the good works of the Church.

- In the Old Testament, God's covenant people Israel were called to live as a sign of his rulership and Kingdom. As such, God demanded that they demonstrate justice and mercy within their ranks, that they denounce the oppression of the poor, and treat the vulnerable and hurting with great grace and care.

- In this age, the Church of Jesus Christ is God's kingdom community, called to reveal God's justice and mercy through its good works and advocacy of the poor and the oppressed.

- The ethic of the Kingdom of God is summarized in the Great Commandment, to love God with all the heart, mind, soul, and strength, and the "second commandment," to love one's neighbor as oneself (cf. Deut. 6.4ff. and Lev. 19.18). Messiah Jesus has given us the "New Commandment," an intensification of the second, which is to love one another even as he has loved us (John 13.34-35).

- The urban church, as a representative of God's covenant people in the city, is called to demonstrate care to its own members, as well as generosity and hospitality to those who are outside. The local church, as an outpost of the Kingdom of God, is called to be the place where the charity of God is to begin, and from which it is to flow.

- The Church seeks to demonstrate the justice and mercy of God to two interrelated objects of his care: the members of his own covenant community, and those who are outsiders.

- Believers are called to care for members of their own marriages, families, and extended families, as well as all the members of God's assembly. We are also called to serve those who do not believe, including those counted as neighbors, strangers, foreigners, and even our enemies.

- Through the provident leading of God, we see that four channels of God's divine justice and mercy are operating today. Individuals and families, local congregations, care communities and organizations, and governmental institutions and agencies all are used by God to display his generosity, justice, and mercy on those in need.

- As the outpost of the Kingdom of God in a particular locale, the local church plays a unique role in communicating God's mercy and love to others. Six principles can inform this care. Each local assembly is called to do good to all people, but especially those of the household of faith. Each is called to follow the example of Jesus in selfless service, to equip its members for the work of the ministry, to show love and mercy with wisdom and grace, in both word and deed, and to work to eliminate the problems altogether, and not merely their symptoms.

- God empowers his people, the Church, to represent the values of his reign (i.e., justice, love, and mercy) and has called them to demonstrate good works for his glory.

Student Application and Implications

Now is the time for you to discuss with your fellow students your questions about your own ministry in the local congregation, and its responsibility to show forth the justice and mercy of God in its own given situation. You are a disciple of Jesus in a church in the city, and your local church is called to represent Jesus in the midst of your community. As you have meditated upon these truths, what are the kinds questions that have come to mind about your own particular understanding of them? What issues do you still want to explore in light of the material you have just studied? Use the questions below to trigger some of your own critical questions about these concerns.

* In what ways have you experienced the grace of God through the Gospel of Christ, and how has that experience affected your desire to show others the same grace and mercy that you received?

* Answer the following question: "the three key ways in which the grace of God has influenced me so far in my walk of discipleship are . . ."

* How would you describe your daily relationship to the Holy Spirit's leading, and your readiness to obey him as he prompts you to engage in acts of mercy, love, and justice?

* Are you a member of a local church, and how do you use your gifts and resources to support its efforts to display good works to its members and to those whom it serves?

* What is your understanding of the Bible's teaching about the poor and oppressed? Can you defend the arguments of Scripture regarding the demand to demonstrate justice and mercy within their ranks, to denounce the oppression of the poor, and to treat the vulnerable and hurting with great grace and care?

* How do you fulfill the ethic of the Kingdom in your personal life, that is, to love God with all the heart, mind, soul, and strength, and the "second commandment," to love one's neighbor as oneself (cf. Deut. 6.4ff. and Lev. 19.18), and to love other disciples even as Jesus loved us (John 13.34-35)? Be specific.

* What is your attitude toward caring for those who are outside the Church? Do you make a distinction between those who are poor and deserve help, and those who are needy and don't? Explain.

* Who are the some of the "neighbors, strangers, foreigners, and enemies" in your life that God the Spirit is calling you to love? Be specific.

* What is your opinion about the role of governmental institutions and agencies to care for the needs of the hurting and needy?

* Do you agree with the idea that some need to be loved conditionally and others unconditionally? How does this line up with the Bible's teaching about love of neighbor and brother and sister?

* Do you feel equipped to serve as a servant and care-giver in your local church situation, whether in leadership or not? What kinds of skills and

insights do you need in order to become better able to represent the Lord Jesus where you are, both in your life and ministry?

What's the Problem, Exactly?

page 316 5

One of the most difficult phenomena to understand is how so many churches which preach the Gospel of Jesus Christ, and the grace of God associated with that Gospel but take oppositional stances toward others. Many today believe that Christianity is that religion that breeds bigotry and hatred toward those who are different than they are. Most of the issues that are championed either for or against usually are connected with those whose lifestyles do not line up with the teaching of Scripture, i.e., homosexuals, pornographers, abortionists, etc. What is usually heard is only our contempt for those whose behaviors that do not line up kingdom values, but never God's love for all human beings, even those who are sinners. As a result, many reject Christ not because of his offer of grace *for sinners* but on account of what they perceive in Christians as a mean-spirited narrowness that loves only those who conform to our view of all things political and social. How would you suggest we remedy this problem: is it one of perceptions about us, or something more serious?

Too Many Standards

The notion of "tough love" is one which has circulated through the Christian community for sometime. In summary, this principle suggests that we ought to care for those in need, but not necessarily without qualification. We must make certain that our love actually is helping the person solve the underlying problems that continue to place them in a position of need. This would mean that we would neither give money nor aid without standards, and that we would always follow up on the results of our care to see if in fact it actually aided the situation or not. Others argue that such an approach involves too much attention to details which interfere with our ability to care for others freely. They would suggest that our role is to care for those whom we find in need, period, and leave the sorting out between the "deserving poor" and "undeserving poor" to the Lord. What do you think of these positions–might there be another view which takes into account the insights of both views?

Insiders Need not Apply

(Based on a true story). A young family whose bread winner, husband, and father had a chronic drug abuse problem found itself without money or support. Because of the waste of the father, and the depletion of all funds and monies, the young mother and her three children found themselves without food, aid, or prospect of paying for rent or necessities. Desperate, the young mother came to a Christian care agency asking for support. During the interview, it was learned that she was an active member of a wealthy mega-church with over a dozen ministers on its pastoral staff. While she had mentioned her predicament to her small group leader at the church, she had neither received any aid from the church, nor had she informed any of its leaders of her need. Part out of shame, and part of the belief that the church would do nothing for her, she in desperation had come to the Christian missions organization for aid. In your judgment, what is the responsibility of the various characters in this drama of care giving, i.e., that of the church to this dear Christian sister, the responsibility of the missions agency, and the responsibility of the young mother and her family during this struggle for aid? Be specific in your answers.

The Work Simply Never Ends

Anyone who has ever served the needy and the hurting in the city knows that the sheer volume of the problems, the vast numbers of hurting and confused people and families, and the deep complexity of the situations that brought them to their need is overwhelming. Many stories could be told of bright-eyed Christian workers who come to a needy urban environment with ideas of immediate and dramatic change, who left later both cynical and discouraged. The needs are so great and numerous that they were overwhelmed, and all their confidence in changing the city was washed away in a flood of difficulty, despair, and in some cases, even the deaths of those whom they have befriended and served. What are the truths covered in this lesson which might offer hope and encouragement to those urban Christian leaders and workers who are on the verge of giving up because of the lack of change they have seen for all their labor? Give Scripture in your "word of encouragement."

Restatement of the Lesson's Thesis

page 316 📖 6

The motivation behind our impulse to demonstrate God's justice and mercy to others is our own experience of the grace of God through the Gospel of Christ. We in fact demonstrate to others the same grace and mercy we have received as members of the body of Christ, and do so in the power of the Holy Spirit. The effect of the grace of God on the believing community is to produce unconditional surrender to the lordship of Christ, and an aggressive commitment to show generosity and hospitality to the underserved and vulnerable among us. In the Old Testament, God's covenant people Israel were called to live as a sign of his rulership and Kingdom. As such, God demanded that they demonstrate justice and mercy within their ranks, that they denounce the oppression of the poor, and treat the vulnerable and hurting with great grace and care. Today, the Church of Jesus Christ is God's kingdom community, called to reveal God's justice and mercy through its good works and advocacy of the poor and the oppressed.

The Church demonstrates the justice and mercy of God to two interrelated objects of his care: the members of his own covenant community, and those who are outsiders. This includes those in our own marriages and families, as well as those counted as neighbors, strangers, foreigners, and even our enemies. Through individuals and families, local congregations, care communities and organizations, and governmental institutions and agencies God reveals his love and justice to the world. The local church plays a unique role in communicating God's mercy and love to others. God empowers his people, the Church, to represent the values of his reign (i.e., justice, love, and mercy) and has called them to demonstrate good works for his glory.

Resources and Bibliographies

If you are interested in pursuing some of the ideas of *Doing Justice and Loving Mercy: The Urban Congregation*, you might want to give these books a try:

   Perkins, John, ed. *Restoring At-Risk Communities*. Grand Rapids: Baker Books, 1995.

   Phillips, Keith. *Out of Ashes*. Los Angeles: World Impact Press, 1996.

   Sider, Ronald J. *Cry Justice: The Bible Speaks on Hunger and Poverty*. Downers Grove, IL: InterVarsity Press, 1980.

   Wallis, Jim. *Faith Works: Lessons From an Activist Preacher*. New York: Random House, 2000.

Ministry Connections

In reviewing the material in this lesson, you may observe that many intersections can be made with its content and your own ministry. The key to transformation is both the renewal of your mind with the truth of God (Rom. 12.1-2), and your faithful application of the Word of God in your own very practical ministry connections (James 1.22-25). Much of ministry growth is *application and experimentation*; informed by the principles we have learned, we design particular projects of application where we go and *test our theory in real life situations* regarding our learning. As we said in our previous lesson, the Holy Spirit plays a significant role in this application and experimentation. As you meditate upon these truths, what has the Spirit been suggesting to you about your own life and ministry? Are there specific areas of concern which have continued to come to mind throughout your study of this lesson, concerns which you want to explore further, thinking and praying about them throughout this upcoming week? Pin down a few key concerns that you will choose to meditate upon this next week, and ask the Holy Spirit to lead you in regards to your own specific application of these truths for your life and ministry today.

Counseling and Prayer

page 318 7

Share with your mentor and fellow students some key areas of concern that you need the Lord's leading and blessing in, in order to apply these truths fully to your own situation. Are there individuals that you want others to pray for, specific issues and needs that require the Lord's intervention, or even upcoming events or encounters that God must direct you in light of the insights gained in your study this week. Be specific in your requests, and be open to hearing the concerns and needs of your fellow students as you set aside time this week to intercede for them.

ASSIGNMENTS

Scripture Memory

Ephesians 2.8-10

Reading Assignment

To prepare for class, please visit *www.tumi.org/books* to find next week's reading assignment, or ask your mentor.

Other Assignments

As mentioned before, perhaps the most significant element in your own successful course of study is your ability to discipline yourself to prepare yourself for the dialogue and investigation that takes place in class. In light of this, you must schedule your time well in order to give your best and most rigorous thinking to the assignments for the upcoming week.

Please read carefully the assignments above, and as last week, write a brief summary for them and bring these summaries to class next week (please see the "Reading Completion Sheet" at the end of this lesson). Also, now is the time in your study of this module to begin to think about the specific character of your *ministry project*. Also, you will want to select one of the passages listed in the course requirements for your passage in the *exegetical project*. Both of these assignments demand clear preparation and forethought. Don't procrastinate in determining either your ministry or exegetical project. The sooner you select, the more time you will have to prepare!

Looking Forward to the Next Lesson

In this lesson we explored the central truths surrounding the impulse behind our call to demonstrate God's justice and mercy to others is our own experience of the grace of God through the Gospel of Christ. Through the power of the Holy Spirit, the believing community surrenders to Christ, and shows in all of its good works the life of the Kingdom, expressed in our generosity and hospitality to the underserved and vulnerable among us.

In our next lesson, we will expand our study to consider the role of the urban church in serving the world. We will reaffirm the two critical truths underlying that service: that the God and Father of our Lord Jesus Christ is the Creator, and that our risen and ascended Lord Jesus is Lord of all. We will explore the ways in ways the Church has sought to respond to that lordship in the world, and will introduce a simple yet effective approach to organize our efforts together as we seek the Lord's will to minister mercy and justice in our urban neighborhoods.

Capstone Curriculum

Module 16: Doing Justice and Loving Mercy
Reading Completion Sheet

Name _____

Date _____

For each assigned reading, write a brief summary (one or two paragraphs) of the author's main point. (For additional readings, use the back of this sheet.)

Reading 1

Title and Author: _____ Pages _____

Reading 2

Title and Author: _____ Pages _____

Doing Justice and Loving Mercy (2)
The Urban Community and Neighborhood

page 321  *1*

Lesson Objectives

Welcome in the strong name of Jesus Christ! After your reading, study, discussion, and application of the materials in this lesson, you will be able to:

- Reaffirm the two critical truths in the Nicene Creed that underlie our understanding of serving in the world: God as *creator* and Jesus Christ as Lord of all.

- Acknowledge the primary ways in which Scripture acknowledges how the Church responds to the lordship of Jesus Christ, serving both as the *locus* (place) of God's working as well as his *agent* (ambassador) through whom he works.

- Recite the four different and classic ways in Church history that Christians have understood the Church's relationship to the world: to withdraw from the world and its affairs, to transform the world through direct oversight, to live in tension with the world, being in it but not of it, and finally to live as prophetic witness to the world in our model and proclamations.

- Outline four of the biblical models of the Church which have immediate bearing on church/world relationships for urban life: we are called to be neighbors, the salt of the earth, the light of the world, and a royal priesthood of God in the city.

- Detail the specific elements of ministry management to maximize opportunities in urban Christian outreach and justice: Prepare, Work, and Review or PWR.

- Lay out in Scripture the foundation of all solid ministry management, i.e., the theology of God's purpose and wisdom, and identify and refute the major barriers and objections that some might raise to planning ministry processes.

- Give clearly and persuasively the key benefits to adopting a flexible but disciplined approach to urban ministry management.

- Know how to mobilize gifted available team members for ministry using the specific items of the PWR process, highlighting the kinds of attitudes and actions necessary for aggressive and credible outreach in urban communities.

- Identify some of the key problems and challenges associated with outreach in urban neighborhoods, and provide practical advice on how to handle these issues as you engage in proclaiming the Good News and doing good works in the city.

Why Fool Around? Go to the Source

Devotion

Prov. 2.1-9 - My son, if you receive my words and treasure up my commandments with you, [2] making your ear attentive to wisdom and inclining your heart to understanding; [3] yes, if you call out for insight and raise your voice for understanding, [4] if you seek it like silver and search for it as for hidden treasures, [5] then you will understand the fear of the Lord and find the knowledge of God. [6] For the Lord gives wisdom; from his mouth come knowledge and understanding; [7] he stores up sound wisdom for the upright; he is a shield to those who walk in integrity, [8] guarding the paths of justice and watching over the way of his saints. [9] Then you will understand righteousness and justice and equity, every good path.

page 323

In a world that places great confidence upon one's level of education and IQ (i.e., intellectual quotient), it is refreshing to rediscover the ground of authentic wisdom in Scripture. The Bible is unequivocal and clear regarding the source of true wisdom. Amazingly, the Bible seems to have no hesitation about the source of true wisdom, or what it means to really live a life dedicated to the telling, displaying, and fleshing out of the truth. Oddly to us moderns, authentic wisdom does not come from scientific method or personal genius or matriculating from a great Ivy League school. Nor does wisdom come from genetics and physical lineage. Real wisdom comes from the Lord and the Lord alone. He is the wise God who provides wisdom for those who are upright, and whose way when obeyed and followed provides a keen understanding into the nature of righteousness, justice, equity, and every good path. This text above shows that real wisdom has a fundamental *spiritual root and foundation*. Accordingly, those who would pretend to be wise and operate their affairs in wisdom while simultaneously avoiding and ignoring their relationship to the Father through Jesus Christ are deceived.

Even a cursory read of the Scripture reveals the ability of God to lead us into the treasure houses of his wisdom and understanding. The following texts represent a limited sample of the abundant biblical evidence of God as the source of our wisdom.

> Isa. 54.13 - All your children shall be taught by the Lord, and great shall be the peace of your children.
>
> Dan. 2.20-22 - Daniel answered and said: "Blessed be the name of God forever and ever, to whom belong wisdom and might. [21] He changes times and seasons; he removes kings and sets up kings; he gives wisdom to the wise and knowledge to those who have understanding; [22] he reveals deep and hidden things; he knows what is in the darkness, and the light dwells with him."
>
> Job 12.13 - With God are wisdom and might; he has counsel and understanding.
>
> Ps. 147.5 - Great is our Lord, and abundant in power; his understanding is beyond measure.
>
> Rom. 11.33 - Oh, the depth of the riches and wisdom and knowledge of God! How unsearchable are his judgments and how inscrutable his ways!
>
> Rom. 16.27 - . . . to the only wise God be glory forevermore through Jesus Christ! Amen.
>
> Col. 2.1-3 - For I want you to know how great a struggle I have for you and for those at Laodicea and for all who have not seen me face to face, [2] that their hearts may be encouraged, being knit together in love, to reach all the riches of full assurance of understanding and the knowledge of God's mystery, which is Christ, [3] in whom are hidden all the treasures of wisdom and knowledge.

Wisdom belongs to God; one may be "sharp" or "smart" or "clever" or "keen" or even "brilliant." None of these, however, are the same as the wisdom of God, which includes this spiritual dimension of simply not only *knowing about* but *seeing into*. God has unlimited insight to the true nature of the world and its affairs, and sees things in perfect relation to everything, including the end from the beginning, and acts on this perfect knowledge with the most appropriate and timely action. Wisdom is not merely data or concepts or ideas, but authentic insight into the nature of a thing, and how we ought to function in relationship to it. According to Scripture, God himself is the only source for this kind of deep insight and plan of action. He is the *only* wise God.

Amazingly, God has promised to give wisdom to those who ask him for it in faith. James makes this clear in his epistle: "If any of you lacks wisdom, let him ask God, who gives generously to all without reproach, and it will be given him. But let him ask in faith, with no doubting, for the one who doubts is like a wave of the sea that is driven and tossed by the wind. For that person must not suppose that he will receive anything from the Lord; he is a double-minded man, unstable in all his ways (James 1.5-8). If we expect to represent God with honor and integrity in the city, we must go to the source, ask the Lord for wisdom, and follow his instructions after he provides it. Herein is the key to effective ministry: only through daily reliance upon the wisdom of God in Christ will we be able to represent his interests in the places where he has called us.

Have you gone to the source lately?

After reciting and/or singing the Nicene Creed (located in the Appendix), pray the following prayer: | **Nicene Creed and Prayer**

> *O God, in the folly of the cross you reveal the great distance between your wisdom and human understanding. Open our minds to the simplicity of the gospel, that, fervent in faith and tireless in love, we may become light and salt for the world, for the sake of Jesus Christ, your Son, who lives and reigns with you in the unity of the Holy Spirit, one God, forever and ever. Amen.*
>
> ~ Presbyterian Church (U.S.A.) and Cumberland Presbyterian Church. The Theology and Worship Ministry Unit. **Book of Common Worship**. Louisville, KY: Westminister/John Knox Press, 1993. p. 210

Put away your notes, gather up your thoughts and reflections, and take the quiz for Lesson 2, *Doing Justice and Loving Mercy: The Urban Congregation*. | **Quiz**

Review with a partner, write out and/or recite the text for last class session's assigned memory verse: Ephesians 2.8-10. | **Scripture Memorization Review**

Turn in your summary of the reading assignment for last week, that is, your brief response and explanation of the main points that the authors were seeking to make in the assigned reading (Reading Completion Sheet). | **Assignments Due**

You're Quenching the Spirit

1. Many godly and sincere ministers of the Gospel believe that management interferes with the leading and prompting of the Holy Spirit. This is not believed without cause or evidence; who cannot provide anecdotal evidence of some minister or ministry which lost perspective on the nature of their business by focusing overmuch on the need for planning and administration? Indeed, many have interfered with God's leading because of a kind of strained and inflexible commitment to their plan, without cultivating a deep and spiritual sense of the Spirit's leading and desire? Do you believe that planning inherently interferes with the filling and direction of the Holy Spirit? What kind of planning might not necessarily undermine the word and direction of the Spirit in regards to ministry management?

Business Blazes the Way?

2. In many churches today, business leaders and models of business success are taken without criticism as the answer for churches which desire to be fruitful. Business success and ministry fruitfulness are often seen as "kissing cousins," essentially employing the same kinds of skills, attitudes, and directions. No attempt is made to critically evaluate whether or not business and the life of the Church connect or overlap; business is seen as the credible answer, blazing the way for progressive ministries. Look at the boards of many churches today; many assume without question that one of the staples for a "good board" are people who have proven success in business. The reason is such that: "Good business is good business, whether it is in industry, medicine, sports or the church." In light of Jesus' instruction in Luke 16.8 that the "sons of this world are more shrewd in dealing with their own generation than the sons of light," how much focus or understanding ought we to give to business as the model and trailblazer for the Church and its call to declare the Gospel to the world?

The Nature of the Beast

3. Some have convincingly argued that the very nature of the present world system is fueled by a passion for profit and greed, and that this passion for more is the fuel for the world's planning system. On the basis of this argument, some have claimed that anyone who becomes involved with the "Saul's armor" of business management

will of necessity place focus on those resources and processes that do not depend on God: our resources, our activities, our efforts, our ideas. What do you think about this claim; is it or is it not the nature of planning to lead the planner astray from the resources and blessings of the Lord. Can one obey the good word of Proverbs 3.5 "Trust in the Lord with all your heart, and do not lean on your own understanding" and be committed to a discipline of ongoing planning? What would it mean to *both* not lean on one's own understanding, and yet still be involved in setting goals, drafting priorities, making plans, and acting on them? Isn't this process *in and of itself* prone to have you dependent on your own strength and ability?

Doing Justice and Loving Mercy: Urban Community and Neighborhood

Segment 1: The Urban Church in the Urban World

Rev. Dr. Don L. Davis

The Nicene Creed provides two critical insights that underlie our understanding of serving in the world: God as *creator* and Jesus Christ as Lord of all. The Church of Jesus Christ responds to the his lordship serving both as the *locus (*place) of God's working as well as his *agent* (ambassador) through whom he works. Throughout Church history, the Church has responded in four classic ways to its relationship to the world: to withdraw from the world and its affairs, to transform the world through direct oversight, to live in tension with the world, being in it but not of it, and finally to live as prophetic witness to the world in our model and proclamations. In responding to the world, the Church fulfills its biblical call to be neighbors, the salt of the earth, the light of the world, and a royal priesthood of God in the city.

Our objective for this segment, *The Urban Church in the Urban World*, is to enable you to see that:

- The Nicene Creed provides critical insights that underlie our understanding of social justice: God is the creator of the heavens and the earth, and Jesus Christ is Lord of the Church.

- As representatives of the Kingdom of God, the Church responds to the lordship of Jesus Christ, serving both as the *locus* (place) of God's working as well as his *agent* (ambassador), that entity through whom he works.

Summary of Segment 1

page 324 3

- The Word of God teaches that there is a foundational and fundamental conflict and tension between the Church and the world, both having different sources of authority, power, and purposes.

- Throughout Church history, the Church has taken various positions in its relationship to the world. One model is to withdraw from the world and its affairs, another is to transform the world, still another is to live in tension with the world. Finally, the Church has also taken the position to be a prophetic witness in and yet not of the world.

- In connection to urban communities, four models of the Church in the world have special significance for urban outreach and ministry. The urban church is called to be a neighbor, serving the well being for those who live in the city, and called to be the salt of the earth, preserving and enriching all facets of urban life. Additionally, the urban church is called to be the light of the world, making plain the claims and life of the Kingdom of God to the city, and finally, to be a royal priesthood, interceding on behalf of those most vulnerable and voiceless in the city.

Video Segment 1 Outline

I. **The Nicene Creed and Social Justice: God the Creator and Jesus Christ Is Lord**

A. God is *creator* of the earth: humankind is a steward of the resources of God.

1. Article one of the Nicene Creed: We believe in one God, the Father Almighty, *maker* of heaven and earth and of all things visible and invisible.

2. Justice and mercy to those outside the community of faith is rooted in two important theological concepts.

a. God is the God of nature, creation, and justice: the earth and world belong to him and we are called to be stewards of God's creation.

(1) Ps. 24.1-2

(2) 1 Chron. 29.11

b. All human beings are created in the image of God, and therefore are unique, irreplaceable, and worthy of respect, honor, and care.

(1) Ps. 8.3-6

(2) Gen. 1.26-27

3. The Church acknowledges the God and Father of our Lord Jesus Christ as the true God, the Lord of all, 1 Cor. 10.26.

B. Jesus Christ is Lord: the Church is under the authority of Christ.

1. We believe in one Lord Jesus Christ: the second article of the Nicene Creed

2. Messiah Jesus is exalted as head over all things to the Church.

a. Eph. 1.20-23

b. Col. 2.19

3. Ascended to the Father's right hand and must reign until all enemies are placed under his feet, 1 Cor. 15.25

4. Pouring out gifts, empowerment, and grace on his Church through the power of the Holy Spirit, Eph. 4.7-8

II. The Church Is the Locus and Agent of the Kingdom.

A. As *locus*, the Church is the focal point of God's redemptive activity.

1. A foretaste of the Kingdom of God: an *eschatological community*, 1 Cor. 10.11

    a. Obedience to all the commands of Jesus

       (1) Matt. 7.24-27

       (2) Matt. 28.19-20

    b. Experience of the powers of the Kingdom to come in the here-and-now, Heb. 2.3-4

    c. Presence of the future Kingdom in the present evil age, Eph. 1.13-14

2. Foundational conflict and tension between the Church and the world

    a. Different sources of authority: Christ versus the devil, 1 Pet. 5.8-9

    b. Different sources of power: the Holy Spirit versus fleshly lust and greed, Acts 1.8; 1 John 2.15–17

    c. Different ends and purposes: the glory of God versus the fulfillment of personal lust, Eph. 1.5-6 - . . . he predestined us for adoption through Jesus Christ, according to the purpose of his will, [6] to the praise of his glorious grace, with which he has blessed us in the Beloved (cf. 1 John 2.17).

3. *The Church will always experience tension with the world by virtue of its allegiance and obedience to the lordship of Jesus Christ.*

B. As *agent*, the Church is a witness of the reality of God's kingdom rule in every neighborhood where they gather.

1. Boldly witnessing to the good news of the Gospel: preaching and teaching, Col. 1.27-28

2. Clearly confirming the Word of God with signs following: a demonstration of the truth of the Gospel in signs, wonders, and power in the Spirit, Heb. 2.3-4

3. Accompanying the proclamation and demonstration of the Gospel with good works: ministries of mercy and justice

    a. Eph. 2.10

    b. Col. 1.10

    c. Titus 2.14

    d. 1 Pet. 2.12

III. The Church in the World: Different Ways of Understanding our Discipleship on the Journey

A. The Church is to *withdraw from the world and its affairs*: the Church in opposition to the world

1. Biblical argument: the world is evil and contact with it should be avoided at all costs.

    a. 1 John 2.15-17

    b. 2 Cor. 6.14-18

2. Strength: takes seriously the ability of the world to wrongly influence the Church, and believes that moral evil can rub off on the Church

    a. 1 Cor. 15.33

    b. 1 Cor. 5.6

3. Problem: can ignore the Church's responsibility to be salt and light in the midst of an evil generation, Phil. 2.14-16

B. The Church is to *transform the world*: the Church is to rule over the world and its affairs.

1. Biblical argument: Christ has won the victory over the world, and the Church has gained the victory in him.

a. Phil. 2.9-11

b. Acts 2.32-33

c. Rom. 14.9

2. Strength: acknowledges the high place of Jesus now at the Father's right hand, 1 Cor. 15.25

3. Problem: ignores that in this present world the devil still exercises sizable authority over those he controls

a. 1 Pet. 5.8

b. 1 John 5.19

C. The Church is *in tension with the world*: the Church is in the world but not of the world.

1. Biblical argument: God has placed the Church in the world to lead in matters of spiritual truth, and the state to govern the affairs of the secular rule.

a. Rom. 13.1-4

b. 1 Pet. 2.13-14

2. Strength: recognizes the legitimacy of secular authority in the midst of the world, and the Church's unique role as representing Christ and his Kingdom, 2 Cor. 5.20

3. Problem: can easily accept any action that the state takes as God's will, Acts 5.28-29

D. The Church is *a prophetic witness* in and toward the world: the Church is to be both locus and agent of the Kingdom of God in the world.

1. Biblical argument: the Church as a representative of the Kingdom of God is in the world but does not in any way belong to it; it confronts the world with its kingdom righteousness and gospel proclamation.

    a. John 17.14-17

    b. Ps. 121.7

    c. Matt. 6.13

    d. Gal. 1.4

    e. 2 Thess. 3.3

    f. 1 John 5.18

2. Strength: fulfills the prophetic engagement aspect of the Church in the world; recognizes that confrontation will be the norm with the world, John 15.18-19

3. Problem: can tend to view nothing in the world system as redemptive or helpful in communicating God's will to the lost

E. Implications of these church/world models

1. Regardless of which model seems to be most persuasive to you, remember that Jesus Christ is Lord of all and head of the Church.

   a. 1 Cor. 11.3

   b. Eph. 4.15-16

2. Because Jesus is Lord, no amount of loyalty to the state or its structures is able to have final say over the Lord's own word, Matt. 28.18-20.

IV. Biblical Models of Church in the World for Urban Communities

A. We are called to be *neighbors*: we serve the well-being and care for all those with whom we live in our urban neighborhoods.

1. Biblical model: the Good Samaritan, Luke 10.29-37

2. In the urban condition, diversity and difference cause great violence, animosity, and alienation between groups, cultures, races, and ethnicities.

3. As the neighbor of the Lord in the midst of those who live in alienation, estrangement, and hatred, the Church's response must be to demonstrate a new level of reconciliation, service and care to all those in need around us.

4. The challenge: *refuse to let ethnocentric bigotries interfere with our charge to love our neighbors as ourselves (including our enemies!)*, Matt. 5.44-45.

B. We are called to be *the salt of the earth*: as those living an alternative lifestyle in the midst of the city, we preserve and enrich all that is just and good in the midst of our neighborhoods.

1. Biblical model: salt of the earth, Matt. 5.13-15

2. As an alternative community in the midst of the urban scene, the local congregation is called to reflect the very lifestyle and reality of the Kingdom of God in the midst of the urban neighborhood.

    a. Phil. 2.14-16

    b. 1 Pet. 2.9

3. As the salt of the earth, the Church's response is to so reflect the Kingdom that its life and goodness may enrich and preserve all the cultural institutions of the community (e.g., economics, politics, family, social rules, etc.).

4. The challenge: *don't allow worldliness and distraction to rob our salt of its saltiness*, James 4.4-6.

C. We are *the light of the world*: we shine the glory of God, making the way clear for those wishing to discover God's rule in Christ, simultaneously exposing the corruption that is in the world through its pride and lust.

1. Biblical model: the light of the world, Matt. 5.14-16

2. The urban condition is affected by unfruitful works of darkness and unrighteousness, which causes many to stumble and know neither God's kingdom promise or the harmfulness of the devil's ways.

   a. Eph. 5.8-14

   b. Phil. 2.15

   c. 1 Thess. 5.5

3. As the light of the world, the Church's response is to so shine forth through our good deeds the reality of the Kingdom that people see our good works and glorify God the Father.

4. The challenge: *don't set our light under a bushel so no one can see their way clearer as a result of our shining.*

D. We are *the priesthood of God*: as a holy priesthood, we intercede on behalf of our urban neighbors, standing in the gap for those who are vulnerable and voiceless, defending the rights of the poor and the oppressed.

1. Biblical model: holy and royal priesthood

    a. 1 Pet. 2.9-10

    b. Rev. 1.6

2. The condition of the urban scene is that many people whose lives are oppressed and broken have no advocate or defense, no one to represent their interests and needs before the powers, and no one who can stand in the gap on behalf of the people of the land.

    a. Ezek. 22.30-31

    b. Ezek. 13.5

    c. Ps. 106.23

3. As the priesthood of the Lord, the Church's response must be to defend the voiceless and vulnerable, to stand in the gap, in the breach, defending, advocating, pleading on their behalf, serving as their helper and friend.

4. The challenge: *don't ignore the vulnerable and broken around us, allowing the enemy and the circumstances to have their way with them.*

Conclusion

» The God and Father of our Lord Jesus Christ is the *creator* of all things, and his Son our Savior Jesus is Lord, and these truths reinforce our understanding of the need for us to serve our urban communities in justice and mercy.

» As the *locus* and *agent* of the Kingdom, the urban church serves its community, striving to be a good neighbor, the salt of the earth, the light of the world, and the priesthood of the Lord.

» The Church of Jesus Christ is called to organize itself for the purpose of making a difference in the urban community.

Please take as much time as you have available to answer these and other questions that the video brought out. In this segment we saw the way in which the Nicene Creed provides theological foundations for understanding the call for social justice. In the fact of God as *creator* and Jesus Christ as Lord of all we have the basis of all social justice: this is our *Father's world*, and *Jesus is Lord*. As his body in the world, the Church serves as the *locus* (place) of God's working as well as his *agent* (ambassador) through whom he works. Understanding how the Church has viewed its relationship to the world will help you greatly as you seek to understand your own response to injustice where you live and minister. Make certain that you grasp the basic facts and claims before you proceed to the next segment. Be sure to back up your arguments and commentary with the Word.

Segue 1

Student Questions and Response

page 326 📖 4

page 326 📖 5

1. How does the teaching of the Nicene Creed regarding God as *creator* and the lordship of Jesus Christ provide us with foundational insight on the nature of social justice in the world today? Why must we begin all discussions of justice and mercy with the truth of God as *maker* and Christ as King?

2. In what sense can we say that all the heavens and the earth *belongs to God*? Because Jesus is the Lord of the Church, why is it then important for the Church to follow *strictly his commandment and vision about the world and its needs*?

3. In what sense can we say that the Church is the *locus* or focal point of God's redemptive activity in the world? What does it mean to suggest that the Church is an *eschatological community*?

4. Describe the nature of the conflict between the Church and the world as mentioned in the Word of God. In what ways do these two entities share different sources of *authority, power, and purpose*?

5. In what way has God specially called the Church to be a witness of God's kingdom rule in every community where Christians worship and gather? What are the areas in which the Church is called to bear witness of the Kingdom's coming in Jesus Christ, in other words, how is the Church to demonstrate its witness to Christ?

6. Describe the model of the Church *withdrawing from the world and its affairs*. What are the arguments in favor of and those opposed to this view? What is your opinion about its validity?

7. Describe the model of the Church *transforming the world through direct oversight*. What are the arguments in favor of and those opposed to this view? What is your opinion about its validity?

8. Describe the model of the Church *living in tension with world*. What are the arguments in favor of and those opposed to this view? What is your opinion about its validity?

9. Describe the model of the Church *living in the world as a prophetic witness to the world of the Kingdom's coming*. What are the arguments in favor of and those opposed to this view? What is your opinion about its validity?

10. Of these four models, which one do you find most convincing, which do you find least convincing?

11. Which of the four models of the Church in the world mentioned above have special significance for urban congregations seeking to do justice and love mercy in their communities?

Doing Justice and Loving Mercy: Urban Community and Neighborhood

Segment 2: PWR: A Process for Ministry Development

Rev. Dr. Don L. Davis

In order to be good stewards of the precious resources of God entrusted to us, we must seek out a philosophy of ministry management that maximizes opportunities in urban Christian outreach and justice. One such strategy is the *Prepare, Work, and Review* approach, or PWR. All solid ministry management is founded upon a theology of God's purpose and wisdom, a theology that can face and refute the major objections raised about planning and valid spiritual ministry.

Our objective for this segment, *PWR: A Process for Ministry Development*, is to enable you to see that:

- *Prepare, Work, Review* (PWR) is the name given to a simple but effective approach to manage our efforts to do justice and love mercy in urban neighborhoods.

- All efforts toward ministry and work are rooted in God's character and work, in both his being a God of purpose in accomplishing his will in the world, and as a God of wisdom, who carries out that purpose with perfect understanding, timing, and approaches.

- Although leaders and churches may plan in such a way as to undermine the leading of the Spirit, it is also possible to plan in such a way that is open to God, flexible to circumstances, and responsive to the moving of the Spirit. PWR rightly organized can be such a disciplined, flexible approach.

- *Preparing* members of a team involves the discipline of concerted prayer for his wisdom and leading, clarifying your identity and mission, seeking God's face about ways in which he wants you to meet these needs and challenges, and making plans and assignments to help the team accomplish their tasks.

- *Working* involves mobilizing the members of the team in such a way that they both identify and use their gifts in an organized way. Team members work the plan, which is monitored during the phase of implementation.

- *Reviewing* our work includes our task to evaluate the results of our efforts in order to determine the next steps of God's leading. This involves a critical analysis of our effort, checking its fruits, and using the information to ask

Summary of Segment 2

God what he might be suggesting about our current effort, ascertaining what the Lord wants us to do next.

- The urban scene presents leaders and churches with unique problems and challenges which make outreach in urban neighborhoods especially difficult. In order to address these challenges, we must saturate all we do with prayer, be led by the Holy Spirit during every phase of the work, expect opposition, and persevere in light of God's call and commission.

Video Segment 2 Outline

I. **PWR: Understanding the Need for a Dynamic Approach to Doing Justice and Loving Mercy**

   A. God is a God of purpose.

      1. In creating the world, 1 Chron. 29.11

      2. In sending forth his people to make disciples of all nations, Matt. 28.18-20

      3. In providing the Church with power to accomplish its mission in the world, Acts 1.8

      4. In accomplishing his own purposes in his own time and manner, Rom. 11.33-36

   B. God is a God of wisdom.

      1. The Lord alone is the giver of wisdom.

a. Prov. 2.6-8

b. James 1.17

c. James 3.17

d. James 1.5

2. Wisdom is the key to any endeavor, Prov. 24.3-6.

3. We are to approach our ministries of mercies and justice with wisdom, Eph. 5.15-17.

C. Barriers to careful planning and preparation are not real.

1. *"We've never done it this way before."* Just because we have done something often does not mean that it is what we should be doing, 2 Cor. 5.17.

2. *"We're doing just fine the way we've always done it."* The challenge of Christian ministry is not mere activity but fruitfulness.

a. John 15.16

b. John 15.8

c. 1 Cor. 3.6-7

3. *"We don't want to interfere with the leading of the Holy Spirit by getting so involved with all kinds of planning stuff."* The apostles planned out various outreaches, but also listened to the Holy Spirit's signals and promptings.

   a. Acts 15.36

   b. Acts 16.8-10

4. *"We should simply do what we can now, and deal with issues later."* We are to walk with wisdom as stewards seeking to redeem all the time and resources that we can, Eph. 5.15-17.

D. A simple but effective process: PWR

   1. An acrostic: Prepare, Work, and Review

   2. A means to organize and engage in ministry

   3. An effective tool to plan, organize, and implement ministries of mercy and justice in the urban church

   4. Benefits of a flexible yet disciplined approach

      a. God can lead us beyond our plan and use our efforts as we listen to him.

         (1) Prov. 16.9

         (2) Ps. 37.23

(3) Prov. 16.1

(4) Prov. 20.24

(5) Prov. 21.30

b. Allows us to engage our task with unity and clarity

c. Eliminates waste of time and overlap of effort

d. Helps us approach new initiatives with confidence and openness

(1) 2 Tim. 1.7

(2) Acts 20.24

(3) Rom. 8.15

(4) 1 John 4.18

II. *Prepare*: Prepare Your Members for the Work Ahead.

A. Pray to the Lord, asking him to set for you your work and your context: *where do we stand right now in our community?*

1. Seek wisdom from the Lord, James 1.5.

2. Review your call and your history, Phil. 3.13-15.

3. Act out of knowledge, pay attention to *where you've come from*, and precisely *where the Lord has brought you right now.*

a. Prov. 13.16

b. Matt. 10.16

c. 1 Cor. 14.20

d. Eph. 5.17

B. Clarify your identity and mission.

1. What has God called us to do: what is *our purpose* here in this community, *our mission*?

2. Based on God's call, what is *the vision* he has provided us as a congregation?

   a. Prov. 29.18

   b. Hos. 4.6

   c. Amos 8.11-12

   d. Matt. 9.36

3. *What values* should inform all the work we do? 2 Cor. 4.2

4. Find out the critical unmet needs in your community.

    a. What *critical needs* exist (survey, polling, library research)?

    b. *Who* is currently seeking to meet some of these needs?

    c. *Which needs frequently get ignored or left out*: what needs remain unmet?

C. Seek God's face about what he would have you do to meet these needs.

    1. Dream: create a list of things your congregation might do to address these needs.

        a. Eph. 3.20-21

        b. Jer. 32.17

        c. Jer. 32.27

        d. Heb. 7.25

        e. Heb. 13.20-21

        f. Jude 1.24

2. Set your priorities (you can't do everything; be decisive).

D. Make plans and assign responsibilities.

1. Don't be arrogant in your thinking; be humble as you let the Lord lead you, Prov. 16.5.

2. Set clear goals that can be communicated to everyone involved.

3. Communicate a clear plan and way of approach to your team members, Rom. 12.4-6.

4. Give everyone their assignments and offer support if they need it.

III. *Work*: Mobilize Your Members for the Ministry.

A. Understand "*every-member*" ministry.

1. All believers have gifts that can be used in ministry.

    a. 1 Pet. 4.10-11

    b. 1 Cor. 12.4-7

2. Leaders equip the members of the body for the work of the ministry, Eph. 4.11-12.

3. Help believers identify their gifts in a setting of freedom, love, and support.

   a. Expose people to needs inside and outside the Church.

   b. Keller: the five invitational questions, Keller, p. 16ff.

      (1) Is there a particular need I vibrate to?

      (2) What personal, emotional, and spiritual resources do I have to meet the need?

      (3) Are there two or three others in the body I can share my burden to meet this need with?

      (4) Is there really an opening to start this ministry?

      (5) Have I really counted the cost?

B. Help your people identify and use their spiritual gifts.

   1. Create a spirit of experimentation and creative expression.

   2. Allow people to try things out (with supervision and help).

C. Organize task forces for outreach and ministry.

D. Recruit others to join the effort.

E. Don't quench the Spirit, 1 Thess. 5.19-22.

1. God can call whom he will: Cornelius, Acts 10-11.

2. God can generate ministry from the most unlikely folk: Paul, Acts 9.

3. Don't talk back to the Lord about his choice: Ananias, Acts 9.13-15.

IV. *Review*: **Evaluate Your Effort and Use the Feedback to Determine the Next Steps.**

A. Take time to evaluate the effectiveness of your effort.

1. Be wise in all you do, Eph. 5.15-17.

2. Listen to the Holy Spirit, Isa. 30.20-21.

B. Check the fruit.

1. The goal of ministry is not *activity*, but *transformation* (a new creation).

a. Gal. 6.15-16

b. 2 Cor. 5.17

c. Eph. 2.10

d. Col. 3.10-11

2. Don't be too anxious about fruit; real fruit takes time.

   a. 1 Cor. 3.6-7

   b. 2 Cor. 3.4-5

C. Use the information to ask what God might be saying about the current effort; ascertain what the Lord, the Spirit, is saying to you all.

   1. *Stop* the effort: end the activity for now.

   2. *Change* the effort: adapt some of the things you're doing.

   3. *Increase* the effort: keep doing what you are doing, and increase it.

   4. *Delegate* the effort: turn over your work to somebody else.

D. Begin the cycle again.

V. Problems and Challenges

A. Problems with neighborhood outreach

   1. Discouragement at little response

2. Running out of resources

3. Abandonment by the workers

4. Misread of the situation

5. Poor guidance and leadership

6. Intimidation by the enemy

7. Conflict among the workers

B. Handling the issues

1. Saturate all with prayer, Matt. 7.7-8.

2. Be flexible: be led by the Holy Spirit, Eph. 5.18; Gal. 5.16.

3. Expect opposition, 1 Pet. 5.8-9.

4. Be faithful: trust God for the results, Prov. 3.5-6.

Conclusion

» The PWR process is an acrostic which stands for a disciplined and flexible approach to urban ministry management, *Prepare, Work, and Review*.

» As a God of purpose and wisdom, the Lord desires for us to seek his wisdom in ministry as we strive to minister mercy and justice in Jesus' name.

» As we prepare our members, mobilize and release them to work, and evaluate our results, we will gain insight into what directions and deeds God the Spirit would have us take to touch the lives of our neighbors and friends in our neighborhoods.

» If we are faithful, God will be glorified and fruit will be borne.

Segue 2

Student Questions and Response

The following questions were designed to help you review the material in the second video segment. This past teaching segment addresses one of the most important concepts in urban ministry management, the idea of stewarding God's precious resources for the sake of advancing the Kingdom. As covered above, we must seek out a philosophy of ministry management that will take full advantage of the opportunities that the Holy Spirit provides us to demonstrate his love and justice in the city. We advocate a disciplined, flexible approach which we have called the *Prepare, Work, and Review* approach, or PWR. All solid ministry management is founded upon a theology of God's purpose and wisdom, a theology that can face and refute the major objections raised about planning and valid spiritual ministry. A careful review of this material will go a long way in addressing any problems you may have with the role of planning and administration in Spirit-led ministry. The following questions are designed to help you both review the facts and explore the ramifications of these principles for your life and ministry.

1. What is the meaning of the acrostic PWR, and why is it important to find a disciplined, simple, and flexible approach to manage our efforts as we seek to evangelize and do good works of justice and love mercy in urban neighborhoods? Explain your answer.

2. In what ways does the biblical teaching concerning God's purpose and wisdom help us understand the foundation of all organized and administrated efforts in spiritual ministry?

3. What are the kinds of barriers that cause many to think that planning approaches may easily undermine the leading of the Spirit? In what ways might it be possible to plan in such a way that is open to God, flexible to circumstances, and responsive to the moving of the Spirit?

4. What are the specific elements of the *Prepare phase* of PWR, and how do they help us to approach our ministry projects and initiatives with wisdom and insight? What principles and perspectives should influence us as we begin to prepare ourselves to accomplish God's task in ministry?

5. Describe some of the actions associated with the *Work phase* of PWR. What roles do gifted team members play in working a plan that is both flexible and effective?

6. Why is it important to *Review* our work and to evaluate the results of our efforts to advance the Kingdom of God? What kind of attitude is needed to give a truly *honest evaluation* of the results of our efforts in a particular project or ministry initiative?

7. How may we use the results of a particular project or initiative to discern what the Lord may want us to accomplish in the *next phase* of our ministry outreach? Why is it important not to merely continue to do the same things over again, especially if they do not accomplish the tasks we believer God has called us to do? Explain your answer.

8. What are some of the unique problems and challenges which make ministry in urban neighborhoods so difficult? What attitudes and actions may be necessary for us to overcome these problems and challenges?

9. Why is it important always to submit our plans to the Lord, regardless of how wise we believe we have been in our planning and strategy development in ministry? Find at least three Scriptures which say that God himself is the root of all ministry.

This lesson focuses upon the theological foundations of ministry, including the truths of God as *creator* and Christ as Lord, and how these truths influence us as we seek to do justice and mercy in the city. We have explored the various models of the Church in its relationship to the world, and have seen how certain images of the Church can greatly inform our urban congregational callings. We also explored the significance of careful, disciplined, and flexible approaches in preparing, working, and reviewing our ministry strategies. *PWR* is the name that we have given to our own such approach, one that acknowledges God's purpose and wisdom, and the leading of the Spirit in all phases of ministry. The following concepts below represent the central ideas and truths covered throughout the lesson.

Summary of Key Concepts

- The Nicene Creed provides critical insights that underlie our understanding of social justice: God is the *creator* of the heavens and the earth, and Jesus Christ is Lord of the Church.

- As representatives of the Kingdom of God, the Church responds to the lordship of Jesus Christ, serving both as the *locus* (place) of God's working as well as his *agent* (ambassador), that entity through whom he works.

- The Word of God teaches that there is a foundational and fundamental conflict and tension between the Church and the world, both having different sources of authority, power, and purposes.

- Throughout Church history, the Church has taken various positions in its relationship to the world. One model is to withdraw from the world and its affairs, another is to transform the world, still another is to live in tension with the world. Finally, the Church has also taken the position to be a prophetic witness in and yet not of the world.

- In connection to urban communities, four models of the Church in the world have special significance for urban outreach and ministry. The urban church is called to be a neighbor, serving the well being of those who live in the city, and called to be the salt of the earth, preserving and enriching all facets of urban life. Additionally, the urban church is called to be the light of the world, making plain the claims and life of the Kingdom of God to the city, and finally, to be a royal priesthood, interceding on behalf of those most vulnerable and voiceless in the city.

- *Prepare, Work, Review* (PWR) is the name given to a simple but effect approach to manage our efforts to do justice and love mercy in urban neighborhoods.

- All efforts toward ministry and work is rooted in God's character and work, in both his being a God of purpose in accomplishing his will in the world, and as a God of wisdom, who carries out that purpose with perfect understanding, timing, and approaches.

- Although leaders and churches may plan in such a way as to undermine the leading of the Spirit, it is also possible to plan in such a way that is open to God, flexible to circumstances, and responsive to the moving of the Spirit. PWR rightly organized can be such a disciplined, flexible approach.

- *Preparing* members of a team involves the discipline of concerted prayer for his wisdom and leading, clarifying your identity and mission, seeking God's face about ways in which he wants you to meet these needs and challenges, and making plans and assignments to help the team accomplish their tasks.

- *Working* involves mobilizing the members of the team in such a way that they both identify and use their gifts in an organized way. Team members work the plan, which is monitored during the phase of implementation.

- *Reviewing* our work includes our task to evaluate the results of our efforts in order to determine the next steps of God's leading. This involves a critical analysis of our effort, checking its fruits, and using the information to ask God what he might be suggesting about our current effort, ascertaining what the Lord wants us to do next.

- The urban scene presents leaders and churches with unique problems and challenges which make outreach in urban neighborhoods especially difficult. In order to address these challenges, we must saturate all we do with prayer, be led by the Holy Spirit during every phase of the work, expect opposition, and persevere in light of God's call and commission.

Student Application and Implications

Now is the time for you to discuss with your fellow students your questions about the Church and the strategic nature of its outreach to the urban community. Because of limited resources, difficult circumstances, few laborers, and ongoing challenges we need to use the wisdom and leading of the Lord to draft strategies that are flexible and open. The Holy Spirit wants to lead us, and so we must approach our work with a sense of purpose but also with a profound sense of submission to God. This kind of approach is neither easy nor automatic, but those mature to listen to God can in fact have profound impact for Christ. Much depends on our ability to understand the relationship between what God has called us to do, and our ability to be open to change as he leads us to do it. Answer the following questions with these insights in mind, and be open to your own particular questions as you explore now the implications of this material.

* Why is it important to affirm that God is *maker* and Jesus is Lord before one begins to attempt great things for God? Why is it important not to take *ultimate responsibility* for change upon oneself as we begin our ministry before the Lord?

* What is your role in the church today, and how is God using your role to help you better understand what your gifts and calling are to serve in the body of Christ?

* List out the various contexts and ministries in which you currently serve Christ. Of all the areas on your list, which do you feel most equipped to serve, and which do you feel list equipped to serve? What kind of input and training do you need to enhance your ability to serve Christ honorably in your present situation?

* Describe your own theology about the relationship of the Church to the world. How does your view square up with the classic models of the church/world relationships covered in this lesson?

* How would you currently describe your attitude toward your church and its relationship to your community? Is your church engaged in advancing the Kingdom, and what does it appear the Spirit is saying to the leaders in your church about your church's responsibility to be more involved in doing good works in your community?

* How would you say that you are being a neighbor, salt, light, or a priest in your community? What are the biggest challenges facing your church in fulfilling its ministry among the most vulnerable and voiceless in the city?

* Are you currently carrying out your ministry outreach or service according to a plan like the *Prepare, Work, Review* (PWR) covered in this lesson? What is your reaction to methods of planning and strategy, and how much do you believe these kinds of approaches enhance or interfere with our ability to operate in God's purposes and wisdom?

* What particular skills and aptitudes must you learn in order to make an approach like *PWR* useful and effective in your ministry context? What

pitfalls would you have to avoid so that your planning process does not undermine the leading of the Spirit in your work for the Lord?

* Of the three phases of ministry management covered in this lesson, which of the phases is your strength, and which do you need most help? How much time do you spend preparing for the ministry projects you are involved in? Do you spend time monitoring your projects in the midst of implementing them? How much time do your spend checking the fruits of your work against your goals for it?

* Of all the challenges that the urban community offers those who minister within it, which is your greatest challenge? How have you sought to overcome this challenge?

Our Plans and God's Sovereign Overrulings!

In this discussion about the nature of planning and setting goals, it is important to review for a moment some of the key Scriptures which underwrite the notion that we can and should plan, but always remain open to the leading and direction of God. He and he alone is sovereign, and as such, can alter or transcend any plan we have to coincide with his own greater plan for us, and for his glory.

- Gen. 45.4-8 - So Joseph said to his brothers, "Come near to me, please." And they came near. And he said, "I am your brother, Joseph, whom you sold into Egypt. [5] And now do not be distressed or angry with yourselves because you sold me here, for God sent me before you to preserve life. [6] For the famine has been in the land these two years, and there are yet five years in which there will be neither plowing nor harvest. [7] And God sent me before you to preserve for you a remnant on earth, and to keep alive for you many survivors. [8] So it was not you who sent me here, but God. He has made me a father to Pharaoh, and lord of all his house and ruler over all the land of Egypt."

- Gen. 50.20 - As for you, you meant evil against me, but God meant it for good, to bring it about that many people should be kept alive, as they are today.

- Job 23.13 - But he is unchangeable, and who can turn him back? What he desires, that he does.

- Prov. 16.1 - The plans of the heart belong to man, but the answer of the tongue is from the Lord.

- Prov. 16.9 - The heart of man plans his way, but the Lord establishes his steps.

- Prov. 21.1 - The king's heart is a stream of water in the hand of the Lord; he turns it wherever he will.

- Prov. 21.30 - No wisdom, no understanding, no counsel can avail against the Lord.

- Isa. 14.24-27 - The Lord of hosts has sworn: "As I have planned, so shall it be, and as I have purposed, so shall it stand, [25] that I will break the Assyrian in my land, and on my mountains trample him underfoot; and his yoke shall depart from them, and his burden from their shoulder. [26] This is the purpose that is purposed concerning the whole earth, and this is the hand that is stretched out over all the nations. [27] For the Lord of hosts has purposed, and who will annul it? His hand is stretched out, and who will turn it back?"

- Isa. 46.10 - . . . declaring the end from the beginning and from ancient times things not yet done, saying, "My counsel shall stand, and I will accomplish all my purpose."

- Dan. 4.34-35 - At the end of the days I, Nebuchadnezzar, lifted my eyes to heaven, and my reason returned to me, and I blessed the Most High, and praised and honored him who lives forever, for his dominion is an everlasting dominion, and his kingdom endures from generation to generation; [35] all the inhabitants of the earth are accounted as nothing, and he does according to his will among the host of heaven and among the inhabitants of the earth; and none can stay his hand or say to him, "What have you done?"

- Acts 5.38-39 - "So in the present case I tell you, keep away from these men and let them alone, for if this plan or this undertaking is of man, it will fail; [39] but if it is of God, you will not be able to overthrow them. You might even be found opposing God!" So they took his advice.

- Eph. 1.11 - In him we have obtained an inheritance, having been predestined according to the purpose of him who works all things according to the counsel of his will.

- Heb. 6.17-18 - So when God desired to show more convincingly to the heirs of the promise the unchangeable character of his purpose, he guaranteed it with an oath, [18] so that by two unchangeable things, in which it is impossible for God to lie, we who have fled for refuge might have strong encouragement to hold fast to the hope set before us.

CASE STUDIES

How Can the Church Compete with the Government?

Although there has been much discussion in the last years about the role of the Church to make up the shortage of government aid to the needy, many believe that the Church simply cannot address the needs of the poor. After all, the government sustained by public taxes and administration, can more effectively reach more of the nation's most vulnerable populations, and address their needs more comprehensively. Others have argued that in light of the Church's call to be salt and light in the midst of an unjust and cruel world, it is the Church's primary responsibility to display the love of God in its own efforts, projects, and programs. What is your thinking about this debate regarding the role of the government versus the Church in regards to meeting the needs of the poor? In what ways ought these two institutions cooperate to meet the needs of the poor? Does it detract from the ministry of the Church to turn it primarily into a *social organization* rather than understanding the Church primarily as a *worshiping community*?

In the World, But Not of It

For many centuries certain members of the Church (perhaps most notably those of the Anabaptist tradition) have understood the Church's relationship to the world as one of *opposition*, so much so that they have interpreted the Church's primary responsibility as one of *withdrawing from its evil influences and corrupt practices*. Often times, traditions that hold this view have literally abandoned the ways of the world, including its use of certain technologies, medias and literatures, products of culture, and even the physical presence, moving to isolated places and starting their own cloistered communities. While many find the sentiment of these groups admirable, they reject their rationale because of Jesus' affirmation that the Church would be "in the world but not of the world." What do you think about the reasoning that would advocate that Christians separate themselves emotionally, physically, and technologically from the world? Are they extreme, overdone, or on the mark?

Following the Leader versus Following the Spirit

Often times, much of what is allowed in terms of ministry outreach in many churches is determined by the core of leadership whose responsibility it is to manage the affairs of the body. Elders, pastors, boards, priests, business committees, or congregational votes are among the many ways in which the task of ministry management occurs in many thousands of congregations. While this may be highly efficient and streamlined, it tends to limit the outreach of the congregation to the imagination and initiative of its leadership. What are members of a congregation to do if they feel a deep leading of the Holy Spirit to initiate or begin a new ministry outreach, and they are not able to get any members of the leadership team to either be interested in it, or willing to provide oversight to it? Should churches encourage new initiatives of ministry which are neither recognized nor sanctioned by the leadership team of the church? Explain your answer.

A Strategy for Living Out the Gospel

In one urban church, the elders sought the Lord's face once a year to determine as best as they could what God wanted them to do for the upcoming year. Although they did not want to limit the Lord on what he might suggest to them throughout the year, they believed that in order to be good stewards they ought to set the broad direction for the church on an annual basis. The members would then be informed of this general direction, and the church would set goals and strategies based on this annual vision. Members at any time could come and suggest ways of outreach or ministry based on their observation and burden, and the elders would do their best to accommodate these new directions as the Lord led. What do you think of this particular approach to ministry management? What are its strengths, and its weaknesses? How might they have improved this strategy to do what they wanted most–to have a general plan to give direction for ministry while at the same time being open to the Lord's movement in the body as the Spirit led?

The Nicene Creed provides two critical insights that underlie our understanding of serving in the world: God as *creator* and Jesus Christ as Lord of all. The Church of Jesus Christ responds to his lordship serving both as the *locus* (place) of God's working as well as his *agent* (ambassador) through whom he works. Throughout Church history, the Church has responded in four classic ways to its relationship to the world: to withdraw from the world and its affairs, to transform the world

Restatement of the Lesson's Thesis

through direct oversight, to live in tension with the world, being in it but not of it, and finally to live as prophetic witness to the world in our model and proclamations. In responding to the world, the Church fulfills its biblical call to be neighbors, the salt of the earth, the light of the world, and a royal priesthood of God in the city.

Prepare, Work, Review (PWR) is the name given to a simple but effective approach to manage our efforts to do justice and love mercy in urban neighborhoods. All efforts toward ministry and work is rooted in God's character and work, in his being a God of purpose in accomplishing his will in the world, and as a God of wisdom, who carries out that purpose with perfect understanding, timing, and approaches. In the *Prepare phase* we enable our team to prayerfully clarify our identity and mission, brainstorm ways in which to meet these needs and challenges, and make plans and assignments to accomplish their tasks. In the *Work phase* we mobilize our gifts in an organized way to accomplish the plan. In the final *Review phase* we evaluate the results of our efforts in order to determine the next steps of God's leading. As we follow the Holy Spirit, we can address the unique challenges of urban neighborhoods, and learn to persevere in our call to advance the Kingdom in the city.

Resources and Bibliographies

If you are interested in pursuing some of the ideas of *Doing Justice and Loving Mercy: Urban Community and Neighborhood*, you might want to give these books a try:

Costas, Orlando E. *Christ Outside the Gate: Mission Beyond Christendom*. Maryknoll, NY: Orbis Press, 1982.

Sider, Ron. *Good News and Good Works: A Theology for the Whole Gospel*. Grand Rapids: Baker, 1999.

------. *Living Like Jesus: Eleven Essentials for Growing a Genuine Faith*. Grand Rapids: Baker Books, 1999.

Snyder, Howard A. *A Kingdom Manifesto*. Eugene, OR: Wipf and Stock Publishers, 1997.

Ministry Connections

This lesson began with an affirmation of two of the critical insights of the Nicene Creed about our service in the world: our God is the true God, the creator of all things, and his Son Jesus Christ is exalted as Lord of all. As an emerging leader in the Church of Jesus Christ you are called to build up the body, which by God's own design is now the *locus* (place) of God's working as well as his *agent* (ambassador) through whom he works. According to Scripture, God has equipped you with the grace and gifting to fulfill your own unique contribution to the Church as she seeks to demonstrate his love and justice through the proclamation of the Good News and doing good works. As a God of purpose and wisdom, God desires that we use our opportunities and resources to make a real difference in the lives of others, as we serve him in the Church.

Your ability to think creatively about the ways in which you might relate these truths to your own life and ministry will deeply affect your fruitfulness. You must strive to find the ways in which the Spirit might want you change, apply, or enhance your own ministry approaches to be more in sync with his truth, his purpose, and his own deep wisdom. What are the particular truths in this lesson which seem to have direct implication for your own ministry? Explore these in meditation, and ask the Holy Spirit to speak to you specifically about the way in which you may need to change your own planning, execution, and review to become a more effective servant of the Gospel in your church. Is there something that God has made known to you specifically about how he might want you to apply this material? Prayerfully seek the Lord on these and related questions, and set aside good time this week to consider how you might become more effective as you apply *PWR* kinds of planning to your ministry projects and responsibilities.

Counseling and Prayer

Prayer is a great mystery; our God allows us to participate in his work of transformation and renewal as we lay out before him the needs and opportunities that have come into our lives. God specifically suggests that those who lack wisdom–those needing his insight and direction in a particular matter or direction–need only ask him in faith, and he will liberally give his own wisdom to us (James 1.5). As you have discussed, studied, and pondered these truths, perhaps the Holy Spirit has surfaced some key issues or situations that you need God's blessing and leading in. Share these areas with your mentor, instructors, and fellow students, and receive his grace through their intercessions and encouragement. Remember, the role of your instructor is to provide you not merely clarification and help as you seek the insight of the Word of God, but also to edify you as spiritual guide and mentor. Never hesitate to set an appointment with the spiritual leaders in your church, especially your pastor, and seek the aid they can provide you as you wrestle with the difficult questions arising from your reflection on this study. God will reward your openness and humility.

ASSIGNMENTS

Scripture Memory

James 1.5-8

Reading Assignment

To prepare for class, please visit *www.tumi.org/books* to find next week's reading assignment, or ask your mentor.

Other Assignments

page 327 📖 6

It is important to not get behind in your reading assignments, Scripture memorization, and review of the previous lesson's notes. So much of a good learning experience is dependent on your ability to set a pace of study that allows you to have plenty of time to meditate, ponder, and pray over the things the Lord, the Spirit, is teaching you. As you have done in previous lessons, make certain that you come to the next class session having completed your reading assignments with a copy of your summary of the reading material for the week. Also, you must have selected the text for your exegetical project, and turned in your proposal for your ministry project.

Looking Forward to the Next Lesson

This lesson we focused on the kinds of perspectives and practices that make for effective urban ministry in and through the local church to the urban neighborhood. We reaffirmed God's role as *creator* and Jesus' lordship as the ground of all urban ministry, and affirmed the unique place and responsibility the Church has in using its resources and gifts to advance the Kingdom in the city. As we prepare, work, and review our ministry initiatives in the city, the Holy Spirit may lead us to bear much fruit for God, fruit that remains and displays the glory of the Kingdom of God.

In our next and final lesson of this module, we will begin to expand our thinking of doing justice and loving mercy to the very ends of the earth. We will explore the concept of being *world Christians*, striving to think globally but act locally. In light of the global need for justice and mercy, we will look at the issues of poverty and oppression and the issue of protecting the environment. As representatives of Christ and his Kingdom, we must be aware of and engage with clarity the great issues of our time, and lead our congregations to act consistent with our calling to be salt and light in our day and time. We will close our discussion by concentrating on what may be the central issue of the 20th century: managing difference and diversity in a world that is more and more fueled by bigotry and hatred among people. We will investigate the power of malice in the modern world, and its tragic end in violence and war that results in loss of life and destruction of property. We will explore three Christian approaches to mass violence and war, and end this module with our own passionate plea for a dynamic ministry of Christian peacemaking.

As representatives of the Kingdom, we must strive to do justice and love mercy in the midst of a world torn by malice, vengeance, and disunity. Only in Christ can we pursue a peace that is authentic and that will last.

This curriculum is the result of thousands of hours of work by The Urban Ministry Institute (TUMI) and should not be reproduced without their express permission. TUMI supports all who wish to use these materials for the advance of God's Kingdom, and affordable licensing to reproduce them is available. Please confirm with your instructor that this book is properly licensed. For more information on TUMI and our licensing program, visit *www.tumi.org* and *www.tumi.org/license*.

Capstone Curriculum

Module 16: Doing Justice and Loving Mercy
Reading Completion Sheet

Name _____

Date _____

For each assigned reading, write a brief summary (one or two paragraphs) of the author's main point. (For additional readings, use the back of this sheet.)

Reading 1

Title and Author: _____ Pages _____

Reading 2

Title and Author: _____ Pages _____

LESSON 4

Doing Justice and Loving Mercy (3)
Society and World

page 329

Lesson Objectives

Welcome in the strong name of Jesus Christ! After your reading, study, discussion, and application of the materials in this lesson, you will be able to:

- Discuss the ramifications of applying a kingdom ethic of doing justice and loving mercy to the very ends of the earth.

- Explain our responsibility as disciples of Christ in today's society to live as world Christians, striving to think globally but act locally.

- Lay out the ways in which the Church is both an outpost and beachhead of the Kingdom, called to demonstrate freedom, wholeness, and justice in its engagement with the world, responding in love, obeying the leading of its head, the Lord Jesus Christ.

- Provide a basic knowledge of four of the critical issues pertaining to world justice today: poverty and oppression, the human environment, ethnocentrism and difference, and war and violence.

- Rediscover our roles as representatives of Christ and his Kingdom, and our duty to be aware of and engage with clarity the great issues of our time, and lead our congregations to act consistent with our calling to be salt and light in them.

- Outline the biblical understanding of the concept of difference from a kingdom perspective, and detail how wrong uses of the categories of difference can fuel bigotry and hatred among people.

- Explore the three historic models of Christian approaches to mass violence and war, and the rationale behind each model.

- Give evidence of the need for Christian disciples to embrace a dynamic ministry of Christian peacemaking that will bring forgiveness, reconciliation, and grace to communities and societies torn by malice, vengeance, and disunity.

Becoming a Cheerful Giver

Devotion

2 Cor. 9.6-15 - The point is this: whoever sows sparingly will also reap sparingly, and whoever sows bountifully will also reap bountifully. [7] Each one must give as he has made up his mind, not reluctantly or under compulsion, for God loves a cheerful giver. [8] And God is able to make all grace abound to you, so that having all sufficiency in all things at all times, you may abound in every good work. [9] As it is written, "He has distributed freely, he has given to the poor; his righteousness endures forever." [10] He who supplies seed to the sower and bread for food will supply and multiply your seed for sowing and increase the harvest of your righteousness. [11] You will be enriched in every way for all your generosity, which through us will produce thanksgiving to God. [12] For the ministry of this service is not only supplying the needs of the saints, but is also overflowing in many thanksgivings to God. [13] By their approval of this service, they will glorify God because of your submission flowing from your confession of the gospel of Christ, and the generosity of your contribution for them and for all others, [14] while they long for you and pray for you, because of the surpassing grace of God upon you. [15] Thanks be to God for his inexpressible gift!

page 330

What is the secret to the blessing and abundance of God on our lives? Many Christian essays and articles are being written and Christian broadcasts being delivered over radio and television all claiming to have the answer to this question. In many cases, these messages provide a kind of technical, wooden, even mechanistic view of God. "If you do such-and-such, God *must* do so-and-so." Appeals and explanations such as this give the impression that Christianity is essentially a form of white magic: all we need for the blessing of God to penetrate every area of our lives is for us to confess the right words, over and over, never doubting, and we can affirm ourselves into prosperity, wealth, health, and abundance. Such an appeal has been the subject matter for many so-called teachers of the Word, and have garnered huge followings of people who desire to have the best of both worlds, all through the name of the Lord.

In 2 Corinthians 8-9 Paul brilliantly lays out his own argument to the Corinthians about their need to be liberal and selfless in their contribution for the provision of the needy saints in Jerusalem. Rather than lay out a kind of magical claim or word about confession or affirmation, Paul roots the promise of God's abundant provision and supply in the Corinthian's generosity and hospitality. To the extent that they learn how to be generous, hilarious, and prodigal in their giving, to that extent they would experience the supply of God. Generosity and giving, care and service, compassion and hospitality are the ways of blessing, according to the apostle. God loves the hilariously cheerful giver, the one who is looking for opportunities to make his or her goods and services available to others who cannot return the favor. In a real sense, this is the definition of godliness, it is the way in which our God responds and works on behalf of those in the world. God is neither partial nor stingy; he lavishes his goodness on others, it is his very nature to be generous and good. Let the plain teaching of the Scriptures elaborate this point:

> Matt. 5.44-48 - But I say to you, love your enemies and pray for those who persecute you, [45] so that you may be sons of your Father who is in heaven. For he makes his sun rise on the evil and on the good, and sends rain on the just and on the unjust. [46] For if you love those who love you, what reward do you have? Do not even the tax collectors do the same? [47] And if you greet only your brothers, what more are you doing than others? Do not even the Gentiles do the same? [48] You therefore must be perfect, as your heavenly Father is perfect.

> Ps. 145.9 - The Lord is good to all, and his mercy is over all that he has made.

> Ps. 36.6-7 - Your righteousness is like the mountains of God; your judgments are like the great deep; man and beast you save, O Lord. [7] How precious is your steadfast love, O God! The children of mankind take refuge in the shadow of your wings.

> Ps. 65.9-11 - You visit the earth and water it; you greatly enrich it; the river of God is full of water; you provide their grain, for so you have prepared it. [10] You water its furrows abundantly, settling its ridges, softening it with showers, and blessing its growth. [11] You crown the year with your bounty; your wagon tracks overflow with abundance.

> Ps. 104.27 - These all look to you, to give them their food in due season.

> Ps. 136.25 - . . . he who gives food to all flesh, for his steadfast love endures forever.

> Ps. 145.15-16 - The eyes of all look to you, and you give them their food in due season. [16] You open your hand; you satisfy the desire of every living thing.

> Luke 12.24-28 - Consider the ravens: they neither sow nor reap, they have neither storehouse nor barn, and yet God feeds them. Of how much more value are you than the birds! [25] And which of you by being anxious can add a single hour to his span of life? [26] If then you are not able to do as

small a thing as that, why are you anxious about the rest? [27] Consider the lilies, how they grow: they neither toil nor spin, yet I tell you, even Solomon in all his glory was not arrayed like one of these. [28] But if God so clothes the grass, which is alive in the field today, and tomorrow is thrown into the oven, how much more will he clothe you, O you of little faith!

Yes, the Scriptures are plain. Our God is generous, loving, impartial, a cheerful giver, and the root and impulse of all authentic Christian care is rooted in this recognition of God's character. This is why the person who claims to know God and shuts his bowels of compassion up to the needy, or harbors hatred and cruelty for others neither knows him nor belongs to him (cf. 1 John 3.14ff.; 4.7-21). To have been touched by the hand of God is to become a hilarious giver, one who pours out their lives for others even as God poured out his life for us in the person of his Son, Jesus Christ (2 Cor. 8.9).

So, what is the key to blessing and abundance from God? The answer is plain: *become a cheerful giver*. Cultivate each day the spirit of hospitality and generosity, living happily with an open hand and an open heart. This is the spirit of the Father in heaven, and the life of the Son as he poured out his life for us on the Cross. All we who claim intimacy with him ought to walk as he walked (cf. 1 John 2.6 whoever says he abides in him ought to walk in the same way in which he walked).

Cheerful givers are the delight of the Father. Generosity is the warmest ray from the sun of God's compassion. Are you shining today?

Nicene Creed and Prayer

After reciting and/or singing the Nicene Creed (located in the Appendix), pray the following prayer:

O God, the refuge of the poor, the strength of those who toil, and the comforter of all who sorrow, we commend to your mercy the unfortunate and needy in whatever land they may be. You alone know the number and extent of their sufferings and trials. Look down, Father of mercies, at those unhappy families suffering from war and slaughter, from hunger and disease, and other severe trials. Spare them, O Lord, for it is truly a time for mercy.

~ Peter Canisius
Ruth Connell, comp. **A Book of Prayers**.
Oxford, England: Lion Publishing, 1988. p. 111

Quiz	Put away your notes, gather up your thoughts and reflections, and take the quiz for Lesson 3, *Doing Justice and Loving Mercy: The Urban Community and Neighborhood*.
Scripture Memorization Review	Review with a partner, write out and/or recite the text for last class session's assigned memory verse: James 1.5-8.
Assignments Due	Turn in your summary of the reading assignment for last week, that is, your brief response and explanation of the main points that the authors were seeking to make in the assigned reading (Reading Completion Sheet).

Focus on the Family - Yes or No?

Many evangelicals assume without critical thought that our first and primary obligation is to focus on the family. As noble and clear as the primacy of the family is within Scripture, it seems that this doctrine can also be dangerous. After all, our first and primary allegiance must always and forever be to the Lord God himself, whom we are commanded to love with all our heart, soul, mind, and strength (cf. Deut. 6.4 with Matt. 22.34-40). The second commandment places love of neighbor next to this overwhelming love for God (cf. Lev. 19.18 with Matt. 22.34-40). Surely, the family has a significant and determinative place in our "order of loves," but are we to focus upon it? How do we care for the members of our family in such a way that does not lead us to an "us and us only" kind of mentality so indicative of so many claiming to know Christ today, but showing little or no interest in the injustice, violence, and oppression in the world?

Liberal, Conservative, or Pro-Poor?

In a world that loves to divide and separate into factions, interest groups, and political parties, what is the responsibility of believers today in their search to represent with integrity the claims and vision of Jesus in their societies? While many issues related to social justice are hammered into categories defined as either "liberal" or "progressive" or as "conservative" or "responsible," such labels do not often make it any easier for Christians to know how to vote or participate in the larger societal decision making. Can any Christian today suggest that a political party "stands for" the authentic position of the Kingdom? How are Christians to understand their duty to represent the Kingdom of God in societies where often no party in particular stands for the kind of hilarious generosity and hospitality called for by the Lord and his apostles? What stance are we to take in regard to party affiliations or social causes claiming to speak for the Lord and his people?

Personal Character or Societal Oppression?

Much controversy brews all over the world among Christians as to how we ought to best understand the nature of social injustice. Many Bible believing Christians sincerely believe that the root of all social concern is *individual responsibility*: people create their own messes, and must live in the ones that they manufactured for themselves. Such a vision tends to see all social issues as merely the outworking of personal decisions. Other Christians, equally sincere and literate in their understanding of Scripture, believe that the root of social concern is *structural evil and systemic oppression*: people are victims of messes perpetrated upon them by systems and structures of evil. This vision tends to see all social issues as the outworking of institutional injustice and structures designed to oppress the little people while making life easier for the privileged and the wealthy. These conflicting visions of social concern play themselves out in a number of ways in many different societies. What is your view on this question–should we seek to resolve the difficult social issues of our time by focusing on individual responsibility or structural and institutional injustice–or both? Explain your answer.

Doing Justice and Loving Mercy: Society and World

Segment 1: Poverty, Oppression, and the Human Environment

Rev. Dr. Don L. Davis

As disciples of Jesus Christ and members of his body, the Church, we are charged with the duty to apply his kingdom ethic of doing justice and loving mercy to the very ends of the earth. As world Christians, we are called to think globally but act locally. As members of the Church, each local congregation is both an outpost and beachhead of the Kingdom, called to demonstrate freedom, wholeness, and justice in its engagement with the world, responding in love, obeying the leading of its head, the Lord Jesus Christ. As Christ's representatives, we are called to

Summary of Segment 1

demonstrate the justice and mercy of God in the issues related to the poor and the oppressed, those most vulnerable to abuse and exploitation, in our neighborhood, as well as across the globe.

Our objective for this segment, *Poverty, Oppression, and the Human Environment*, is to enable you to see that:

- As disciples of Jesus Christ and members of his body, the Church, we are charged with the duty to apply his kingdom ethic of doing justice and loving mercy to the very ends of the earth.

- Believers are not called to live unconcerned to the issues and populations of the world. Rather, we are called by God to be "world Christians" (not *worldly* ones), thinking *globally* but acting *locally*.

- As members of the Church, each local congregation is both an outpost and beachhead of the Kingdom, called to demonstrate freedom, wholeness, and justice in its engagement with the world, responding in love, obeying the leading of its head, the Lord Jesus Christ.

- We are called to engage in open and honest dialogue with others, to seek the truth and speak it to power, and demonstrate the Kingdom's ethic as we engage the great issues of our communities and our time. We are called to engage them, even in those cases when the likelihood of change seems small.

- A sampling of some of the critical issues of our time which Christ's representatives are called to address are poverty and oppression, protection of the environment, dealing with ethnocentrism and difference, and responding to war and violence. In regards to these issues we are to act personally, congregationally, and as associations of churches together.

- We must respond aggressively to poverty and oppression and the protection of the environment in our own locales, grounding our responses in a biblical worldview that highlights God's sovereignty as *creator* and Lord of the earth. Doing so will allow us to freely and practically model in specific projects what it means to demonstrate the justice and mercy of God at home and abroad.

I. Living as World Christians: *Think Globally, Act Locally*

Video Segment 1 Outline

A. Necessity for urban churches to engage in dialogue with *global* issues

1. *The world has grown smaller*: we have live access to things taking place thousands of miles away through technology.

2. *Decisions and happenings occurring in foreign lands* affect our lives in our communities.

3. *Informed intercession* demands a critical eye toward what is taking place around us.

4. God might lead us to *respond to some global issue in a local way*.

B. Engaging the larger society: assumptions and principles

The Church of Jesus Christ, as an outpost and beachhead of the Kingdom, is called to demonstrate freedom, wholeness, and justice in its engagement with the world, responding in love, obeying the leading of its head, the Lord Jesus Christ.

1. The Church of Jesus Christ is *an outpost and beachhead of the Kingdom of God*.

   a. We are ambassadors of Jesus Christ, 2 Cor. 5.20.

   b. Our citizenship is in heaven, Phil. 3.20.

   c. Messiah Jesus is sending us into the world, Acts 26.17-18.

2. We are called to demonstrate freedom, wholeness, and justice, 2 Cor. 5.17.

3. In our engagement with the world, John 17.14-16

4. Responding in love, John 13.34-35

5. Obeying the leading of its head, the Lord Jesus Christ, Eph. 1.20-23

C. Implications of this engagement

1. According to open and honest dialogue with others

2. Seeking the truth, 1 Thess. 5.21; John 8.31-32; John 7.24

3. With a mind to demonstrate the Kingdom's ethic

    a. Witness to the reality of the Kingdom (*maturia*), Acts 1.8

    b. Servants in the world on behalf of the vulnerable and voiceless (*diakonia*), Matt. 20.28

4. The Church is called to *engagement*; only the Spirit can bring our engagement to *change* and *transformation*.

    a. We engage regardless of likelihood of final victory.

b. We engage leaving the ultimate responsibility for change with the Lord.

c. We engage to provide service (*diakonia*) and witness (*marturia*) in the name of Jesus Christ and his Kingdom.

D. Illustrations for doing justice and loving mercy in the world through four contemporary issues.

1. Critical issues on the global scene (a sampling): *thinking globally*

    a. Poverty and oppression

    b. Human environment

    c. Ethnocentrism and difference

    d. War and violence

2. Levels of response: *acting locally*

    a. Your personal response (*as individuals, couples, and families*)

    b. The local assembly corporate response (*as leaders and members of a believing congregation*)

c. The locale church (*a number of the leaders and/or congregations which unite to give witness and service in response to a pressing issue or need*)

II. Poverty and Oppression

A. Biblical analysis for the causes of poverty

1. Personal laziness and character flaws

    a. Prov. 6.6-11

    b. Prov. 12.24

    c. Prov. 19.15

    d. Prov. 19.24

    e. Prov. 20.13

    f. Eccles. 10.18

2. Oppression by the wealthy and the unjust

    a. Exod. 22.21-27

  b. Deut. 24.15

  c. Ps. 82.1-4

  d. Prov. 14.31

 3. Natural disaster or personal calamity

  a. Lev. 25.25

  b. Lev. 25.35

  c. Lev. 25.36-39

  d. Famine, Acts 11.27-29

B. Solutions correspond to the various causes

 1. Poverty due to personal sin: *exhortation, education, counseling*

 2. Poverty due to oppression: *protest, change of legislation, advocacy, aid*

 3. Poverty due to disaster or calamity: *immediate support, counseling, care*

C. Poverty (an issue of *justice*) and oppression (an issue of *freedom*)

1. All three causes of poverty may be interwoven and simultaneous.

2. Oppression may occur as a result of *systems* and *structures* which ensure that certain populations will remain unemployed or underemployed.

3. A significant issue: *liberal and conservative ideologies do not explain the complexity and seriousness of the causes and operations of poverty.*

    a. *Liberal ideologies* tend to suggest that all poverty is the result of oppression by the wealthy upon the poor.

    b. *Conservative ideologies* tend to suggest that all poverty is the result of personal laziness and lack of motivation.

D. Affirming individual value: standing for basic human rights: living out the implications of the *imago Dei*

1. The right to *live* (touches issues such as *abortion, euthanasia, health care, protection from violence and abuse*, etc.)

2. The right to *be safe in one's environment* (freedom from *torture, intimidation, abuse*)

3. The right to freedom from *forced labor and slavery*

4. The right for clothing and shelter (*fair housing, homelessness*)

5. The right for food and sustenance (*world hunger and relief*)

6. A number of congresses, conventions, and international consultations throughout the 20th century have sought to define the fundamental rights of human beings (economic, political, religious, civil, and human rights).

E. The Church's responsibility in regard to poverty and oppression

1. Conform your personal and family economic lifestyle to the kingdom ethic.

    a. Contentment, 1 Tim. 6.6-10

    b. Generosity, 2 Cor. 9.6-8

    c. Hospitality, Heb. 13.1-2

2. How the local body can seek to address particular needs of poverty and oppression in their community

    a. Function in the body of Christ according to the principles of unity and equality.

        (1) *Unity*: the earth is the Lord's, and therefore all the things we hold belong to him, Ps. 24.1-2.

(2) *Equality*: enlightened by Jesus' example, let us adjust our intake to make for generosity and hospitality in the Church, 2 Cor. 8.8-15.

b. Create programs within the church to ensure members have basic needs addressed and cared for.

c. Start servant pools within the community (where members of the body all "pool" their time and talent to address the needs of the members according to need).

3. Find practical ways, as local churches, in your area to give witness to the kingdom ethic of justice in a dramatically unjust world: the North-South inequality.

a. Organize co-ops and other shared-resource programs to reduce the cost of goods to the needy.

b. Collaborate on housing and homeless initiatives.

c. Create new locally based grass-root organizations designed to address basic human needs that are being overlooked in the community.

III. Protecting the Environment

1 Chron. 29.11 - Yours, O Lord, is the greatness and the power and the glory and the victory and the majesty, for all that is in the heavens and in the earth is yours. Yours is the kingdom, O Lord, and you are exalted as head above all.

Isa. 42.5 - Thus says God, the Lord, who created the heavens and stretched them out, who spread out the earth and what comes from it, who gives breath to the people on it and spirit to those who walk in it.

A. Causes for alarm and concern

1. Runaway population growth and urbanization

2. Shortage of and depletion of natural resources: *fossil fuels* and mineral capital

3. Pollution and erosion of the earth's natural defense mechanisms: *from ozone depletion to global warming*

4. Out-of-control technology (*fuel hungry, resource depleting, dangerous by products: e.g., nuclear technology*)

B. Biblical affirmations and insights

1. The earth belongs to God, Ps. 24.1-2.

2. The earth was given to humankind for stewardship: we were given dominion over the earth.

a. A unique dominion (based on our relationship with God and his mandate to us, Gen. 1.28)

b. A wise dominion (in sync with the earth's own ecological processes, limits, and laws, Ps. 65.9)

   c. An answerable dominion (we are stewards and tenants of God's property: the earth and all its fullness belongs to him and him alone)

      (1) Deut. 10.14

      (2) 1 Chron. 29.11

      (3) Job 41.11

   3. Trusteeship involves care as well as dominion.

C. Conservation: tending God's garden, even under the curse

   1. Dominion = trusteeship: we are trustees of God, for all the earth and its wealth belong to the Lord, Ps. 50.12.

   2. As trustees, we are responsible to God for our dominion over his creation, and answerable to him for its abuse.

      a. Exod. 19.5

      b. Deut. 10.14

   3. We are responsible to *conserve the resources of the earth* (since all life is dependent on the *biosphere*, the water, soil, and air on which we depend).

4. We are responsible to *care for the earth* (as disciples of the Kingdom, we must be concerned about an abuse of the earth's natural resources).

5. We are responsible to *share the resources of the earth* (the disparity between the haves and have-nots has direct impact on the use and/or abuse of the earth's resources).

D. The Church's responsibility in regards to the environment: *acting locally*

1. Your personal response (*as individuals, couples, and families*)

    a. Conservation: use responsible care in your personal consumption of precious resources: e.g., water.

    b. Recycling: voluntarily recycle paper, glass, and metal goods.

    c. Stay alert to local environmental issues, and increase the awareness of those in the body to such issues.

2. The local assembly corporate response (*as leaders and members of a believing congregation*)

    a. Organized efforts at conservation, recycling

    b. Neighborhood clean-ups, awareness of chemical sites, protests regarding unsafe pollutants in the neighborhood

3. The locale church response (*a number of the leaders and/or congregations which unite to give witness to and service in response to a pressing issue or need*)

   a. Dialogue and petition local civic officials about opportunities and threats that exist in your community.

   b. Advocate for congressional representation.

   c. Partner with community organizations for action.

Conclusion

» As urban Christian leaders, we are called to think globally but act locally.

» Since the Church of Jesus Christ is a beachhead and outpost of the Kingdom of God, we are called to demonstrate freedom, wholeness, and justice as we engage the world, doing justice and loving mercy under the headship of Jesus.

» Grappling with issues like poverty, oppression, and the environment will require our deepest sensitivity to the Lord and to the truth.

Segue 1

Student Questions and Response

page 334 📖 *3*

Please take as much time as you have available to answer these and other questions that the video brought out. In this first segment we discovered how as disciples of Jesus Christ and members of his body, the Church, we are charged with the duty to apply his kingdom ethic of doing justice and loving mercy, i.e., to think *globally* but act *locally*. Each congregation is an outpost and beachhead of the Kingdom, called to demonstrate freedom, wholeness, and justice in its engagement with the world, responding in love, obeying the leading of its head, the Lord Jesus Christ. You must master the underlying theology that provides warrant for our living as salt and light in the world, so rehearse the concepts covered in the segment through the questions below. Support your answers with solid Scripture and sound argument.

1. In what ways are we as believers commanded to flesh out the ethic of Jesus Christ and his Kingdom in the world? Are we responsible only for our own families and neighborhoods, or does our responsibility extend to the "ends of the earth?" Explain your answer with an appeal to Scripture.

2. Define the term "world Christians." In what way does this phrase express our responsibility to be aware of and address the various issues touching the lives of people around the world?

3. What does it means to think *globally* but act *locally*? How does one go about gaining this particular skill, and what role does the local congregation play in helping members of the body to learn this way of approaching ministry and service?

4. Explain the meaning of the phrase "each local congregation is both an outpost and beachhead of the Kingdom, called to demonstrate freedom, wholeness, and justice in its engagement with the world." Why is it so necessary that *each* congregation take on this responsibility to respond as a representative of the Kingdom where they live and work?

5. What is the relationship between engaging in open and honest dialogue with others as well as providing them with a clear witness to the Gospel of Christ? How ought we to address the practical, felt needs of the community as we seek to bear witness to Jesus and his Kingdom to others? Does one take precedence over the other? Explain.

6. If the likelihood for change or victory are small or slim on a particular issue, ought we to pursue it at all? How are we called to engage the world with the claims of Jesus and his Kingdom–ought we to share only where the likelihood for change is great?

7. Why are the issues of poverty and oppression, protection of the environment, dealing with ethnocentrism and difference, and responding to war and violence so important in today's world? As disciples of Jesus, what are the various levels at which we are called to engage these great issues, and which level is most important for our purposes as kingdom representatives?

8. What is the role of theology and doctrine as we seek to respond aggressively to poverty and oppression and the protection of the environment? What doctrines are especially important in regard to the issues of poverty and the environment?

9. How free are we to experiment in specific projects and initiatives as we seek to demonstrate the justice and mercy of God at home and abroad? Why is this freedom important to those seeking to make a difference in the world today?

Doing Justice and Loving Mercy: Society and World

Segment 2: Ethnocentrism and Difference, and War and Violence

Rev. Dr. Don L. Davis

Summary of Segment 2

page 334 📖 *4*

As representatives of the Kingdom of God, we are called to maintain a biblical vision of the concept of difference. In a world of mind-numbing diversity and cultural difference, we must grasp the various dimensions of culture and how these dimensions wrongly perceived may easily lead to bigotry and hatred. The concept of difference may erect barriers among people, causing paternalism, suspicion, and malice. When difference becomes toxic, it may easily lead to violence, terror, and even war. Christians have taken three positions in regard to war through the centuries: total pacifism, the concept of "just war," and relative pacifism (in light of the nuclear threat today). The answer to the concept of difference is the need for believers to embrace a dynamic ministry of Christian peacemaking, a strategy that celebrates difference, encourages forgiveness and reconciliation, and strives to demonstrate to all people the love and mercy of Christ.

Our objective for this segment, *Ethnocentrism and Difference, and War and Violence*, is to enable you to see that:

- Believers in Jesus Christ are called to represent the life and ethic of the Kingdom of God, and as such, we are called to affirm and express a biblical vision of the concept of difference.

- Understanding culture is critical to understanding difference in the world. Culture can be defined as "that integrated, well-established, and communally defined pattern of behavior and worldview which influences the cognitive, affective, and evaluative dimensions of its expression."

- The concept of difference has many implications for doing justice and loving mercy: differences are spiritually important, real, socially significant, and not necessarily bad or wrong. Differences tend to alienate and divide groups, and may erect barriers between and among people, leading to paternalism, suspicion, and malice.

- When differences are distorted or misunderstood they can become toxic, and lead to violence, abuse, genocide, and war.

- Historically, Christians have responded to issues of war in three ways: total pacifism, the theory of the "just war," and relative pacifism, a view which has emerged in light of the threat of nuclear destruction.

- The response of Christian disciples in a world of alienation is to adopt a strategy of Christian peacemaking which acknowledges, celebrates, and welcomes differences among people in light of Christ's incarnation. Such a strategy will cultivate practices which celebrate difference, encourage forgiveness and reconciliation, and which strive to demonstrate to all people the love and mercy of Christ, all in light of God's clear standard of righteousness in the Word of God.

I. **Dealing with the Concept of Difference in Today's World: Culture**

"Culture is that integrated, well-established, and communally defined pattern of behavior and worldview which influences the cognitive, affective, and evaluative dimensions of its expression."

Video Segment 2 Outline

A. The present reality of difference in a multi-cultural and unchurched world

1. Mind-boggling diversity: thousands of cultures and sub-cultures

2. Formidable interpersonal barriers: the present

3. Dramatic gaps in wealth and socio-economic reality

4. Technological sophistication and richness

5. Shifting, volatile ethical visions of the human good

6. Alternative religious visions and attempts at spirituality without God

B. "The Dimensions of Culture"

1. The *Cognitive* Dimension — "The knowledge shared by members of a group or society" (Paul Hiebert, *Anthropological Insights for Missionaries*, p. 30)

    a. Worldview and conceptual frameworks: cultures as systems of relationships which compose and dictate what we consider to be possible and real

    b. Different "*-ologies*"

        (1) Ontology – the study of being

        (2) Cosmology – the study of creation

        (3) Epistemology – the study of knowing

2. The *Affective* Dimension — "feelings people have, with their attitudes, notions of beauty, tastes in food and dress, likes and dislikes, and ways of enjoying themselves or experiencing sorrow" (Hiebert, p. 32)

3. The *Evaluative* Dimension — "values by which [a culture] judges human relationships to be moral or immoral"

a. Truth-falsehood claims

b. Beauty-ugliness claims

c. Right-wrong claims

d. Moral codes: the power of ultimate concern and sacredness in human society

C. Manifestations of culture

1. *Behavior*: customs, products, and languages learned as symbol systems of forms and learned meaning

2. *Products*: material objects, lived environments

3. *Explicit beliefs and value systems*: all of those forms whereby we through practice, ritual, tradition, and structure embody, articulate, and celebrate our worldview (*politics, religion, kinship relationships, economics, technology, etc.*).

II. The Implications of Difference in Doing Justice and Loving Mercy

A. The differences between people are *important*.

1. God created difference, Acts 17.26-28.

2. The Kingdom will reflect difference, Rev. 5.9-10.

B. The differences between peoples are *real*.

1. What we share in common (e.g., the *imago Dei*) is more significant than the superficial differences which separate us.

2. Our differences, nonetheless, are viewed as critical and significant, not to be ignored or eclipsed by some generic culture (cf. John 1.14-18).

C. The differences between people are *significant*.

1. These differences are more than cosmetic.

2. We divide along a number of lines, all dealing with some element where we are distinct from another.

   a. *Race*: the distinction of *color*

   b. *Gender*: the distinction of *sex*

   c. *Religion*: the distinction of *belief*

   d. *Politics*: the distinction of *ideology*

   e. *Ethnicity*: the distinction of *culture*

f. *Nationality*: the distinction of *homeland*

g. *Age*: the distinction of *generation*

3. They have profound implications for how people think, act, feel, and what they value and strive for (example- white and black differences in perception during the O.J. Simpson trial).

D. The differences between people are *not necessarily bad or wrong*.

1. Every culture has elements that are *moral*, i.e. consistent with the way that God desires us to think and act (examples- punishment for murder, care for children, etc.).

2. Every culture has elements that are *immoral*, i.e. inconsistent with or opposed to the way that God desires us to think and act (examples- infanticide of female offspring, pursuit of material wealth as an ultimate value).

3. Every culture has elements that are *amoral*, i.e. differences arising from taste, custom, tradition, and habit (examples- Eating tacos, wearing hats, speaking English, dancing at weddings).

E. The differences between people tend *to alienate and divide groups*.

1. Our differences tend to divide us because we are *ethnocentric*: we prefer our own culture and tend to judge others in light of it.

2. Anthropological roots of division: the enormous power of *enculturation*.

3. Theological roots of the division: the power of *pride*.

F. Our differences *may erect barriers* and cause us to treat people differently.

When differences are allowed to divide, we typically respond to others in three inappropriate ways.

1. We become *paternalistic*: "help the poor native syndrome"

    Our *benevolent* expression of assumed superiority often results in an attempt to modify the actions and values of a differing group (example- missionaries issuing Western clothing to South Pacific islanders).

2. In *suspicion*, we isolate and separate ourselves from people who are different.

    The *passive* expression of my group's prejudice through the deliberate limiting of contact between my group and the people, actions, and values of the group that is different (example- segregated neighborhoods).

3. In *hatred and malice*, we reject the other culture as bad or evil or undeserving, and seek to undermine and persecute it.

    The *active* expression of my group's hatred for the people, actions, and values of the group that is different (example- ethnic cleansing in Bosnia or Rwanda, the Holocaust in Germany, etc.).

III. When Difference Becomes Toxic: War and Violence

A. The peculiar modern problem: violent reaction to difference

1. The 20th century is the bloodiest century in human civilization.

   a. A *mad race* to arms and weapons

   b. *Unmatched monies* being spent on arms

   c. *More nations arming themselves* with nuclear weapons (some suggest that nearly 20-25 nations either have them, or are on the "threshold" of joining the "nuclear club" of nations).

2. Millions of dead, maimed, and tortured human beings, with countless others left orphaned, neglected, and as refugees

3. Humankind shows a nearly inexhaustible ability to malign, harm, and even kill those who differ from them.

4. With the rise of nuclear weapons, this violence and hatred can reach levels where the very existence of humankind is threatened.

   a. We are one madman away from significant nuclear destruction.

   b. There is no way to deter this except the fear of *greater annihilation*.

5. The "unleashed power of the atom has changed everything save our modes of thinking; and thus we are drifting towards unparalleled catastrophe." ~ Albert Einstein

6. The root of this malice is spiritual, Titus 3.3.

B. Finding common ground: what all Christians tend to agree upon regarding difference, violence, and war

1. Jesus Christ as Lord represents God's Kingdom of righteousness and peace.

2. Jesus' ethic involves an "upside-down" way of living: hungering for righteousness, loving enemies, pursuing peace, forgiving wrongs done, loving one another.

3. The end of righteousness will come at the completion of God's kingdom program, when war will be destroyed forever, Isa. 2.4.

C. Three historical positions of Christians to the issue of mass violence and war (see John Stott, *Involvement: Being a Responsible Christian in a Non-Christian Society*)

1. Total pacifism: *modern day obedience to the Sermon on the Mount* (Matt. 5.38-48; Luke 6.27-36)

a. Commitment to nonviolence and non-resistance based on Christ's teaching in the Sermon, and his way of the cross

b. Our responsibility is to receive Jesus' call to take up our cross and follow him.

2. Just war: *war can be justified, but its cause and process must be righteous.*

   a. Argues for a series of justifications that lay down a criteria for prosecuting a just war

      (1) A *righteous cause* (defending the vulnerable, to secure justice or remedy injustice, to protect the innocent as a last resort)

      (2) A *controlled means* (no unnecessary violence is permissible, the force should match the problem)

      (3) A *predictable outcome* (the prospect of finishing the job must be taken into account)

   b. Anchors its arguments on the legitimacy of the state to use power and authority as an agent of God's wrath on the evil doer, Rom. 12.17-13.7

3. Relative pacifism: *a new brand of nuclear pacifism*

   a. Based on the OT biblical prohibition of *"shedding of innocent blood"*

      (1) Gen. 9.6

      (2) Prov. 6.16-19

   b. This view condemns the use of indiscriminate weaponry (and claims to refute the possibility of just war theory applied to *nuclear conflicts*).

      (1) *Conventional weapons* (e.g., saturation bombing)

(2) *Indiscriminate weapons* (e.g., chemical weapons, poison gases, etc.)

(3) *Atomic weapons* (ABC's of indiscriminate weapons, *atomic, biological, and chemical*)

IV. Living as a Christian Peacemaker

A. Recognize that the differences between peoples have now been acknowledged and reconciled in the ministry of Christ.

1. Our differences are now *reconciled through the work of Christ* on the cross, between Jew and Gentile, slave and free, male and female, barbarian and Sycthian, Eph. 2; Col. 3.11; Gal. 3.28.

2. God is reconciled with all people now in his Son, 2 Cor. 5.18-21.

3. We all together share in both the guilt and the glory, Rom. 3; 1.16-17.

B. We must affirm that in a world of diversity the goal of redemption is *Christlikeness, not cultural sameness* (i.e., the goal is to enable people to be more like Jesus, not like us).

1. Colossians 3.11 and Galatians 3.28 do not advocate the obliteration of cultural identity, only the end of ungodly partiality.

2. Culture has been redeemed in the incarnation of Jesus, 1 John 1.1-3.

C. We must affirm that our *differences are displayed and celebrated* in the one, holy, apostolic, and universal Church of Jesus Christ.

1. Through faith in Christ we who were alienated by our differences have become a *new humanity* in the Church, Eph. 2.12ff..

2. Diverse, yet one: although we are many members made up of every kindred, tribe, people, and nation, from every language and clan, from every class and culture, we nevertheless are one body in Christ. We are to strive to make this unity visible in our daily lives and relationships.

3. In redemption God does not erase, shield, or obliterate our differences, but rather he acknowledges and rejoices in them (Acts 15).

4. We retain many differences, but we share a common faith and hope, Eph. 4.4-6.

    a. We share a common *parentage*, 1 John 3.1-2.

    b. We share a common *calling*, 2 Tim. 1.9.

    c. We share a common *destiny*, Rom. 8.16-17.

5. In the body, we are to love one another as Jesus loves us, John 13.34-35.

D. As representatives of the Kingdom of God, we are to demonstrate this kingdom perspective regarding difference in our works of mercy and justice.

1. We as Christian peacemakers are to pray for peace between and among people.

    a. 1 Tim. 2.1-2

    b. Ps. 122.6-8

2. We are to strive in all things to be peacemakers, aggressively following the plain teachings of our Lord on the issues of difference, reconciliation, and grace, Heb. 12.14.

    a. Matt. 5.9

    b. 2 Cor. 13.11

    c. Eph. 4.1

3. We must demonstrate in our own families and local churches the reconciliation won for us by Christ, Rom. 14.17-19.

    a. No fences, barricades, or walls can be acceptable where the Spirit fills the members, Gal. 5.22.

b. Issues of class, race, gender, background, and ethnicity must become non-issues in our midst, Col. 3.13.

c. "If charity begins at home, so does reconciliation" – John Stott, Eph. 4.1-3.

d. Learn to celebrate the differences among peoples as a gift of God in Christ.

   (1) Col. 3.11

   (2) 1 Cor. 3.21-23

   (3) Gal. 3.28

4. We must fight the tendency toward pessimism and the inevitably of war, violence, and cruelty, James 1.19-20.

   a. We must avoid being *too naive*, on the one hand, expecting the end of hatred between peoples before the Consummation of the Kingdom.

   b. We must likewise avoid becoming *too negative* about the possibility of peoples to reach a level of respect that holds aggression at arm's length.

5. We must be willing to address these issues in open discussion within our homes and our churches, Phil. 2.1-3.

   a. We are advocates of the righteousness of the Kingdom, Matt. 6.33.

b. We are to weigh all positions, liberal, conservative, and independent, and subject them to the scrutiny of the Word of God, 1 Thess. 5.21.

c. We are to stimulate in every context informed, open, and loving discussion among those who differ in opinions on the great issues of diversity today.

6. Expect to experience the rich and powerful benefits and fruits of peacemaking, James 3.16-18.

Conclusion

» Ethnocentrism and difference has caused unprecedented levels of violence, hate, and cruelty in our day.

» As Christian peacemakers, representing the Kingdom of Jesus Christ, we can be aware of the malice and division that animates our time, and transcend it by actively praying for, demonstrating, and advocating for peace between people of difference, starting right in our own neighborhoods.

» May God the Holy Spirit give us the grace and the heart to pursue the peace of Christ with all we meet, as we seek to do justice and love mercy in his name, in the city.

Segue 2

Student Questions and Response

The following questions were designed to help you review the material in the second video segment. In that section we learned how through faith in Christ we have been called to represent the Kingdom of God. As such, we have a view of culture and difference that is informed by the Word of God, especially interpreted in light of the person and work of Jesus Christ. In a world of mind-numbing diversity and cultural difference, we saw how cultural difference easily leads to bigotry and hatred, erecting the kinds of barriers that produce paternalism, suspicion, and malice. The toxic result of this is violence, ever escalating terror, and even war. As believers, we are called to embrace peacemaking, celebrate difference, encourage forgiveness and reconciliation, and strive for unity and understanding among people in the name of Christ. It is significant for your Christian leadership development to grasp these principles, so carefully review them as you answer the following questions.

1. How is it that believers in Jesus Christ have been given the high privilege and calling to represent the life and ethic of the Kingdom of God? What makes them competent to fulfill such a remarkable and high calling?

2. Define culture. What is the significance of the various elements involved in culture, i.e., the cognitive, affective, and evaluative elements involved in understanding the differences between peoples?

3. List out some of the major implications of difference in doing justice and loving mercy. In your estimation, which are the three key implications of difference, that is, the ones which determine all the others? Explain your answer.

4. What does it mean to say that a culture's actions or behaviors are either "moral," "immoral," or "amoral?"

5. When differences are allowed to divide us, we typically respond to others in three inappropriate ways. What are they, and give an example of each.

6. What are the three historical positions that Christians have held to regarding the issue of mass violence and war? Which of these seem to resonate most with the biblical teaching about war and violence? Which of these historical positions make the most sense to you?

7. In what sense are we as disciples of Jesus called to live as peacemakers in this world? In order to be such, how are we to recognize, affirm, and understand the nature of differences in light of the work of Jesus Christ?

8. What roles do concepts like forgiveness, reconciliation, and restitution play in terms of serving as Christian peacemakers? How are we as Christians to fight the tendency toward pessimism and the inevitability of war, violence, and cruelty among peoples?

9. How is the life of the Church to be a living visual aid and demonstration of the reality of the unity and love of the Kingdom in the midst of the world? How does our ability to demonstrate this love *among ourselves* condition our ability to *share it with others*? Explain with Scripture.

Summary of Key Concepts

This lesson focuses upon how we as disciples of Jesus are to apply ourselves to demonstrating Christ's kingdom ethic of doing justice and loving mercy to the very ends of the earth. We are world Christians, striving to think globally but act locally. As members of the Church we are called to demonstrate freedom, wholeness, and justice in its engagement with the world, responding in love, obeying the leading of its head, the Lord Jesus Christ. In obedience to him, we give witness of the Kingdom's ethic on the major issues pertaining to the world today, and in this lesson we have concentrated upon poverty and oppression, the human environment, ethnocentrism and difference, and war and violence. Listed below are the central concepts covered in this lesson on these issues. Review them carefully.

- As disciples of Jesus Christ and members of his body, the Church, we are charged with the duty to apply his kingdom ethic of doing justice and loving mercy to the very ends of the earth.

- Believers are not called to live unconcerned to the issues and populations of the world. Rather, we are called by God to be "world Christians" (not worldly ones), thinking *globally* but acting *locally*.

- As members of the Church, each local congregation is both an outpost and beachhead of the Kingdom, called to demonstrate freedom, wholeness, and justice in its engagement with the world, responding in love, obeying the leading of its head, the Lord Jesus Christ.

- We are called to engage in open and honest dialogue with others, to seek the truth and speak it to power, and demonstrate the Kingdom's ethic as we engage the great issues of our communities and our time. We are called to engage them, even in those cases when the likelihood of changes seems small.

- A sampling of some of the critical issues of our time which Christ's representatives are called to address are poverty and oppression, protection of the environment, dealing with ethnocentrism and difference, and responding to war and violence. In regards to these issues we are to act personally, congregationally, and as associations of churches together.

- We must respond aggressively to poverty and oppression and the protection of the environment in our own locales, grounding our responses in a biblical worldview that highlights God's sovereignty as Creator and Lord of the earth. Doing so will allow us to freely and practically model in specific projects what it means to demonstrate the justice and mercy of God at home and abroad.

- Believers in Jesus Christ are called to represent the life and ethic of the Kingdom of God, and as such, we are called to affirm and express a biblical vision of the concept of difference.

- Understanding culture is critical to understanding difference in the world, and culture can be defined as "that integrated, well-established, and communally defined pattern of behavior and worldview which influences the cognitive, affective, and evaluative dimensions of its expression."

- The concept of difference has many implications for doing justice and loving mercy: differences are spiritually important, real, socially significant, and not necessarily bad or wrong. Differences tend to alienate and divide groups, and may erect barriers between and among people, leading to paternalism, suspicion, and malice.

- When differences are distorted or misunderstood they can become toxic, and lead to violence, abuse, genocide, and war.

- Historically, Christians have responded to issues of war in three ways: total pacifism, the theory of the "just war," and relative pacifism, a view which has emerged in light of the threat of nuclear destruction.

- The response of Christian disciples in a world of alienation is to adopt a strategy of Christian peacemaking which acknowledges, celebrates, and welcomes differences among people in light of Christ's incarnation. Such a strategy will cultivate practices which celebrates difference, encourages forgiveness and reconciliation, and strives to demonstrate to all people the love and mercy of Christ, all in light of God's clear standard of righteousness in the Word of God.

Student Application and Implications

Now is the time for you to discuss with your fellow students your questions about doing justice and loving mercy as a world Christian. The following questions are designed to help you explore in what ways the particular concepts you have discovered relate to your own life and ministry.

* In what ways do you identify yourself as a person who is "charged with the duty to apply his kingdom ethic of doing justice and loving mercy to the very ends of the earth?" Would you consider yourself to live, work, play, and pray as a "world Christian," one who thinks *globally* but acts *locally*?

* How does your church view itself relative to the world around it–is it seeking to engage it, withdraw from it, confront it, or what? How has your church shown itself to be an outpost and beachhead of the Kingdom, demonstrating freedom, wholeness, and justice in its engagement with the world?

* Are you encouraged by the kinds of ministries, services, and good works your church has done as it has sought to demonstrate the Kingdom's ethic in your own neighborhood and community? How have you contributed to this demonstration–what ministry of service do you participate in your church that shows justice and mercy to others?

* Of the four critical issues of our time covered in this lesson, which moves you most to act on and to think Christianly about–poverty and oppression, protection of the environment, dealing with ethnocentrism and difference, and responding to war and violence? Which is your church most actively engaged in to address?

* What projects or initiatives are you currently involved with which allow you to express your convictions about God's justice and mercy of God, either locally or globally? What holds you back from being more involved in these kinds of projects?

* Do you grasp what the Bible teaches about the concept of difference? Can you explain the importance of difference, and what is at stake if we fail to properly understand its role in building relationships with others?

* Would you say you are understanding and tolerant of differences between and among people? Were you raised in an environment that loved people in spite of differences? Were you ever a victim of a situation where differences were distorted or misunderstood, where they became toxic, and led to hatred or even violence? How did you deal with that (those) situation(s)?

* Which of the three historical positions about war seem most convincing to you–total pacifism, the theory of the "just war," or relative pacifism? Have you served in the armed services, or could you do so, if asked? Why or why not?

* To what extent have you embraced, in your own life, a strategy of Christian peacemaking which acknowledges, celebrates, and welcomes differences among people? When does tolerating differences become an issue of moral

compromise? How can you better learn to celebrate difference, encourage forgiveness and reconciliation, and strive to demonstrate to others Christ's love for all people, regardless of background or race?

CASE STUDIES

Too Much Help?

(Based on a true story). A member of an urban church, a single mother with two children, ran into hard financial times and was evicted out of her apartment. The church leaders and its members responded in typical Christian fashion: her family was placed in a local motel, platoons of members brought potluck meals to them while in the hotel, and offerings were taken to supply them with down payment on a new home, which was secured by one of the members of the church. Workers came by and redid the cabinets, painted, got the plumbing done, and even helped move her and her family into the new (different!) home. On seeing this remarkable outpouring of love, one of the elders, a brother who grew up in a depressed urban neighborhood, expressed concern about what all of this help might ultimately do to the *motivation* and *engagement* of the young woman and her family. Although he was grateful for such a show of generous support, he shared with the other elders of the church the need for caution in giving so much support to an urban Christian family without also asking for her responsibility and involvement. What do you make of the elder's advice?

The Need to Learn the Hard Way

A young brother who was "caught between jobs" asked his church for help with his utilities and rent for his apartment. A responsible, excellent Christian, this young brother was truly in need, due to no fault of his own, and required, at least on the surface, just some financial aid to get him pass this immediate financial crisis. While much of the Church Council (those given responsibility for leading the church of which he was a part) had no problem in giving him the money, some of the leadership wondered if such a practice would be helpful. Frankly, the young brother had been in these straits before; he was not as aggressive as he could have been, too, to find a job until the last moment. Some suggested that it is important to not become too paternalistic in the lives of the members. They are adult, and responsible for their own lives. If in fact he was in this situation because he was lazy or not as aggressive in looking for a job, why should the church bail him out?

Others, disagreeing with that view, feel strongly that we ought to care for our own, no matter what? Which of these views seems to resonate most with your understanding of Scripture? Are there other alternatives that might offer a better solution?

Appropriately Patriotic or Confused Loyalty?

Some in an urban church are concerned about the pastor's constant mention of supporting the troops of the nation in every service. While some of the members have served in the armed forces, most of the members hold a view that the Church is within a country but truly is not a part of it. For them patriotism is a confused loyalty, giving to the state what only God and the Kingdom demand and deserve. Others are convinced that giving the king and country their due is distinctly Christian, and appropriate from all the NT texts which suggest that we honor the king, give to the government our due obedience, and we give to Caesar the things that are Caesar's. In a world so torn by nationalistic strife and violence, what ought to be our stand in regards to explicit showing of patriotism and "love of country" in the life and worship of the Church?

Cultural Freedom or Worldly Compromise?

Dealing with the change of the community that has taken place around it, an urban church is seeking to become more culturally relevant. Recently, the pastor decided that one of the two weekly services they host each week at the church would be handled by the young people, who have dubbed the new service "Hip Hop Hurray!" The idea is to design a service which in every way is tailored to speak to the lives and customs of the young, poor, and aggressive hip-hop teen culture which makes up the vast majority of the people on the street in the community where the church is located. The youth pastor, one who is utterly familiar with and at home with the hip-hop culture, intends on "contextualizing" every phase of the H^3 service, as it is called. From the music, to the dress, to the "rap" to the dance, all of the service will be in the language, style, and custom of hip hop culture. While many in the church are deeply excited about it and the cultural freedom it will display, others are deeply concerned that this is compromising our deepest values to vainly imitate the world's cultures. If you were asked to give a sermon on this to clarify the issues involved, what would you suggest about the service and the issues surrounding it?

Restatement of the Lesson's Thesis

As disciples of Jesus Christ and members of his body, the Church, we are charged with the duty to apply his kingdom ethic of doing justice and loving mercy to the very ends of the earth. Believers are not called to live unconcerned to the issues and populations of the world. Rather, we are called by God to be "world Christians" (not *worldly* ones), thinking *globally* but acting *locally*. As members of the Church, each local congregation is both an outpost and beachhead of the Kingdom, called to demonstrate freedom, wholeness, and justice in its engagement with the world, responding in love, obeying the leading of its head, the Lord Jesus Christ. We must respond aggressively to poverty and oppression and the protection of the environment in our own locales, grounding our responses in a biblical worldview that highlights God's sovereignty as Creator and Lord of the earth. Doing so will allow us to freely and practically model in specific projects what it means to demonstrate the justice and mercy of God at home and abroad.

Believers in Jesus Christ are called to represent the life and ethic of the Kingdom of God, and as such, we are called to affirm and express a biblical vision of the concept of difference. The concept of difference has many implications for doing justice and loving mercy: differences are spiritually important, real, socially significant, and not necessarily bad or wrong. Differences tend to alienate and divide groups, and may erect barriers between and among people, leading to paternalism, suspicion, and malice, and even to violence, abuse, genocide, and war. Historically, Christians have responded to issues of war in three ways: total pacifism, the theory of the "just war," and relative pacifism, a view which has emerged in light of the threat of nuclear destruction. We ought to adopt a strategy of Christian peacemaking which acknowledges, celebrates, and welcomes differences among people in light of Christ's incarnation.

Resources and Bibliographies

If you are interested in pursuing some of the ideas of *Doing Justice and Loving Mercy: Society and World*, you might want to give these books a try:

Carle, Robert D., and Louis A Decaro, Jr., eds. *Signs of Hope in the City: Ministries of Community Renewal*. Valley Forge, PA: Judson Press, 1997.

Linthicum, Robert C. *Empowering the Poor*. Monrovia, CA: MARC, 1991.

Perkins, John, ed. *Restoring At-Risk Communities*. Grand Rapids: Baker, 1995.

Schlossberg, Herbert, Vinay Samuel, and Ronald J. Sider, eds. *Christianity and Economics in the Post-Cold War Era: The Oxford Declaration and Beyond*. Grand Rapids: Eerdmans, 1994.

Ministry Connections	Now is the time for you to focus on your ministry assignments. You are responsible to now apply the insights of your module in a practicum that you and your mentor agree to. The goal is plain and simple: you are asked to share some of the insights you have learned in this module of doing justice and loving mercy. Your intent with your audience should be both information and edification; think of all the ways that this teaching can influence your devotional life, your prayers, your response to your church, your attitude at work, and on and on and on. What is significant is that you seek to correlate this teach with your life, work, and ministry. The ministry project is designed for this, and in the next days you will have the opportunity to share these insights in real-life, actual ministry environments. Pray that God will give you insight into his ways as you share your insights in your projects.
Counseling and Prayer	Are there any issues, persons, situations, or opportunities that need to be prayed for as a result of your studies in this lesson or module? What particular issues or people has God laid upon your heart that require focused supplication and prayer for in this lesson? Take the time to ponder this, and receive the necessary support in counsel and prayer for what the Spirit has shown you. No amount of study, information, or effort can begin to match the power of prayer in your life, for the sake of your own life and those whom you live and teach. Never underestimate the power of faith-filled, godly prayer: James 5.16 - "The prayer of a righteous person has great power as it is working."

ASSIGNMENTS

Scripture Memory	No assignment due.
Reading Assignment	No assignment due.
Other Assignments page 336 📖 5	By this time in your study of this module, you should have determined, outlined, and submitted all information pertaining to you ministry and exegetical project. Your instructor should now be outlined, determined, and accepted by your instructor. Make sure that you plan ahead, so you will not be late in turning in your assignments.

Final Exam Notice

The final will be a take home exam, and will include questions taken from the first three quizzes, new questions on material drawn from this lesson, and essay questions which will ask for your short answer responses to key integrating questions. Also, you should plan on reciting or writing out the verses memorized for the course on the exam. When you have completed your exam, please notify your mentor and make certain that they get your copy.

Please note: Your module grade cannot be determined if you do not take the final exam and turn in all outstanding assignments to your mentor (ministry project, exegetical project, and final exam).

The Last Word about this Module

In this lesson we have explored the concept of a global Christian vision, one which would allow for us as urban Christian leaders to think globally but act locally. We are members of the Church of Jesus Christ, God's very own beachhead and outpost of the Kingdom of God. As ambassadors of that Kingdom we are called to demonstrate freedom, wholeness, and justice as we engage the world. We are called to bear witness of the Rule of God in our lives, our words, and our deeds, in the midst of a crooked and perverse generation. As such, we are equally called to grapple with issues like poverty, oppression, the environment, ethnocentrism, and the issues of war and violence.

Truly, to be a Christian is to be in the world, but not of it, to bear witness to the Age to come in the midst of this present age. Only through Christ and his Spirit can we become the kind of Christian peacemakers that our tortured world so desperately needs. Our sincere prayer for you is that as you represent the Kingdom of Jesus Christ you will give living demonstration of its power and beauty, and flesh out in practical, tangible ways the life-giving power of God through Christ and his people.

May God, the Holy Spirit, give you the desire and the ability to pursue God's justice and mercy in the midst of the urban communities where you live, work, and witness. Amen!

Appendices

193	Appendix 1: **The Nicene Creed** *(with Scripture memory passages)*
194	Appendix 2: **We Believe: Confession of the Nicene Creed (Common Meter)**
195	Appendix 3: **The Story of God: Our Sacred Roots**
196	Appendix 4: **The Theology of Christus Victor**
197	Appendix 5: **Christus Victor: An Integrated Vision for the Christian Life**
198	Appendix 6: **Old Testament Witness to Christ and His Kingdom**
199	Appendix 7: **Summary Outline of the Scriptures**
201	Appendix 8: **From Before to Beyond Time**
203	Appendix 9: **There Is a River**
204	Appendix 10: **A Schematic for a Theology of the Kingdom and the Church**
205	Appendix 11: **Living in the Already and the Not Yet Kingdom**
206	Appendix 12: **Jesus of Nazareth: The Presence of the Future**
207	Appendix 13: **Traditions**
215	Appendix 14: **A Theology of the Church in Kingdom Perspective**
216	Appendix 15: **Kingdom of God Timeline**
217	Appendix 16: **Models of the Kingdom**
219	Appendix 17: **A Theology of the Church**
238	Appendix 18: **Our Declaration of Dependence: Freedom in Christ**
240	Appendix 19: **Dealing with Old Ways**
241	Appendix 20: **Discipling the Faithful: Establishing Leaders for the Urban Church**
242	Appendix 21: **Readings on the Church**
245	Appendix 22: **Five Views of the Relationship between Christ and Culture**

246	Appendix 23: **That We May Be One**
256	Appendix 24: **The Oikos Factor: Spheres of Relationship and Influence**
257	Appendix 25: **Culture, Not Color: Interaction of Class, Culture, and Race**
258	Appendix 26: **Authentic Freedom in Jesus Christ**
259	Appendix 27: **World Impact's Vision: Toward a Biblical Strategy to Impact the Inner City**
260	Appendix 28: **Empowering People for Freedom, Wholeness, and Justice**
290	Appendix 29: **Documenting Your Work**

APPENDIX 1
The Nicene Creed

Memory Verses ⇩

Rev. 4.11 (ESV) Worthy are you, our Lord and God, to receive glory and honor and power, for you created all things, and by your will they existed and were created.

John 1.1 (ESV) In the beginning was the Word, and the Word was with God, and the Word was God.

1 Cor.15.3-5 (ESV) For what I received I passed on to you as of first importance: that Christ died for our sins according to the Scriptures, that he was buried, that he was raised on the third day according to the Scriptures, and that he appeared to Peter, and then to the Twelve.

Rom. 8.11 (ESV) If the Spirit of him who raised Jesus from the dead dwells in you, he who raised Christ Jesus from the dead will also give life to your mortal bodies through his Spirit who dwells in you.

1 Pet. 2.9 (ESV) But you are a chosen race, a royal priesthood, a holy nation, a people for his own possession, that you may proclaim the excellencies of him who called you out of darkness into his marvelous light.

1 Thess. 4.16-17 (ESV) For the Lord himself will descend from heaven with a cry of command, with the voice of an archangel, and with the sound of the trumpet of God. And the dead in Christ will rise first. Then we who are alive, who are left, will be caught up together with them in the clouds to meet the Lord in the air, and so we will always be with the Lord.

We believe in one God,   *(Deut. 6.4-5; Mark 12.29; 1 Cor. 8.6)*
    the Father Almighty,   *(Gen. 17.1; Dan. 4.35; Matt. 6.9; Eph. 4.6; Rev. 1.8)*
    Maker of heaven and earth   *(Gen 1.1; Isa. 40.28; Rev. 10.6)*
    and of all things visible and invisible.   *(Ps. 148; Rom. 11.36; Rev. 4.11)*

We believe in one Lord Jesus Christ, the only Begotten Son of God,
    begotten of the Father before all ages,
    God from God, Light from Light, True God from True God,
    begotten not created,
    of the same essence as the Father,   *(John 1.1-2; 3.18; 8.58; 14.9-10; 20.28; Col. 1.15, 17; Heb. 1.3-6)*
    through whom all things were made.   *(John 1.3; Col. 1.16)*

Who for us men and for our salvation came down from heaven
    and was incarnate by the Holy Spirit and the virgin Mary
    and became human.   *(Matt. 1.20-23; John 1.14; 6.38; Luke 19.10)*
    Who for us too, was crucified under Pontius Pilate,
    suffered, and was buried.   *(Matt. 27.1-2; Mark 15.24-39, 43-47; Acts 13.29; Rom. 5.8; Heb. 2.10; 13.12)*
    The third day he rose again
    according to the Scriptures,   *(Mark 16.5-7; Luke 24.6-8; Acts 1.3; Rom. 6.9; 10.9; 2 Tim. 2.8)*
    ascended into heaven,
    and is seated at the right hand of the Father.   *(Mark 16.19; Eph. 1.19-20)*
    He will come again in glory
    to judge the living and the dead,
    and his Kingdom will have no end.
      (Isa. 9.7; Matt. 24.30; John 5.22; Acts 1.11; 17.31; Rom. 14.9; 2 Cor. 5.10; 2 Tim. 4.1)

We believe in the Holy Spirit, the Lord and life-giver,
    (Gen. 1.1-2; Job 33.4; Ps. 104.30; 139.7-8; Luke 4.18-19; John 3.5-6; Acts 1.1-2; 1 Cor. 2.11; Rev. 3.22)
    who proceeds from the Father and the Son,   *(John 14.16-18, 26; 15.26; 20.22)*
    who together with the Father and Son
    is worshiped and glorified,   *(Isa. 6.3; Matt. 28.19; 2 Cor. 13.14; Rev. 4.8)*
    who spoke by the prophets.   *(Num. 11.29; Mic. 3.8; Acts 2.17-18; 2 Pet. 1.21)*

We believe in one holy, catholic, and apostolic Church.
    (Matt. 16.18; Eph. 5.25-28; 1 Cor. 1.2; 10.17; 1 Tim. 3.15; Rev. 7.9)

We acknowledge one baptism for the forgiveness of sin,   *(Acts 22.16; 1 Pet. 3.21; Eph. 4.4-5)*
    And we look for the resurrection of the dead
    And the life of the age to come.   *(Isa. 11.6-10; Mic. 4.1-7; Luke 18.29-30; Rev. 21.1-5; 21.22-22.5)*

Amen.

APPENDIX 2

We Believe: Confession of the Nicene Creed (Common Meter*)

Rev. Dr. Don L. Davis, 2007. All Rights Reserved.

* This song is adapted from the Nicene Creed, and set to Common Meter (8.6.8.6.), meaning it can be sung to tunes of the same meter, such as: *O, for a Thousand Tongues to Sing; Alas, and Did My Savior Bleed?; Amazing Grace; All Hail the Power of Jesus' Name; There Is a Fountain; Joy to the World*

The Father God Almighty rules, Maker of earth and heav'n.
Yes, all things seen and those unseen, by him were made, and given!

We hold to one Lord Jesus Christ, God's one and only Son,
Begotten, not created, too, he and our Lord are one!

Begotten from the Father, same, in essence, God and Light;
Through him all things were made by God, in him were given life.

Who for us all, for salvation, came down from heav'n to earth,
Was incarnate by the Spirit's pow'r, and the Virgin Mary's birth.

Who for us too, was crucified, by Pontius Pilate's hand,
Suffered, was buried in the tomb, on third day rose again.

According to the Sacred text all this was meant to be.
Ascended to heav'n, to God's right hand, now seated high in glory.

He'll come again in glory to judge all those alive and dead.
His Kingdom rule shall never end, for he will reign as Head.

We worship God, the Holy Spirit, our Lord, Life-giver known,
With Fath'r and Son is glorified, Who by the prophets spoke.

And we believe in one true Church, God's people for all time,
Cath'lic in scope, and built upon the apostolic line.

Acknowledging one baptism, for forgiv'ness of our sin,
We look for Resurrection day–the dead shall live again.

We look for those unending days, life of the Age to come,
When Christ's great Reign shall come to earth, and God's will shall be done!

APPENDIX 3
The Story of God: Our Sacred Roots
Rev. Dr. Don L. Davis

The Alpha and the Omega	Christus Victor	Come, Holy Spirit	Your Word Is Truth	The Great Confession	His Life in Us	Living in the Way	Reborn to Serve
The LORD God is the source, sustainer, and end of all things in the heavens and earth. All things were formed and exist by his will and for his eternal glory, the triune God, Father, Son, and Holy Spirit, Rom. 11.36.							
THE TRIUNE GOD'S UNFOLDING DRAMA *God's Self-Revelation in Creation, Israel, and Christ*				**THE CHURCH'S PARTICIPATION IN GOD'S UNFOLDING DRAMA** *Fidelity to the Apostolic Witness to Christ and His Kingdom*			
The Objective Foundation: The Sovereign Love of God *God's Narration of His Saving Work in Christ*				**The Subjective Practice: Salvation by Grace through Faith** *The Redeemed's Joyous Response to God's Saving Work in Christ*			
The Author of the Story	*The Champion of the Story*	*The Interpreter of the Story*	*The Testimony of the Story*	*The People of the Story*	*Re-enactment of the Story*	*Embodiment of the Story*	*Continuation of the Story*
The Father as Director	Jesus as Lead Actor	The Spirit as Narrator	Scripture as Script	As Saints, Confessors	As Worshipers, Ministers	As Followers, Sojourners	As Servants, Ambassadors
Christian Worldview	Communal Identity	Spiritual Experience	Biblical Authority	Orthodox Theology	Priestly Worship	Congregational Discipleship	Kingdom Witness
Theistic and Trinitarian Vision	Christ-centered Foundation	Spirit-Indwelt and -Filled Community	Canonical and Apostolic Witness	Ancient Creedal Affirmation of Faith	Weekly Gathering in Christian Assembly	Corporate, Ongoing Spiritual Formation	Active Agents of the Reign of God
Sovereign Willing	Messianic Representing	Divine Comforting	Inspired Testifying	Truthful Retelling	Joyful Excelling	Faithful Indwelling	Hopeful Compelling
Creator True Maker of the Cosmos	Recapitulation Typos and Fulfillment of the Covenant	Life-Giver Regeneration and Adoption	Divine Inspiration God-breathed Word	The Confession of Faith Union with Christ	Song and Celebration Historical Recitation	Pastoral Oversight Shepherding the Flock	Explicit Unity Love for the Saints
Owner Sovereign Disposer of Creation	Revealer Incarnation of the Word	Teacher Illuminator of the Truth	Sacred History Historical Record	Baptism into Christ Communion of Saints	Homilies and Teachings Prophetic Proclamation	Shared Spirituality Common Journey through the Spiritual Disciplines	Radical Hospitality Evidence of God's Kingdom Reign
Ruler Blessed Controller of All Things	Redeemer Reconciler of All Things	Helper Endowment and the Power	Biblical Theology Divine Commentary	The Rule of Faith Apostles' Creed and Nicene Creed	The Lord's Supper Dramatic Re-enactment	Embodiment Anamnesis and Prolepsis through the Church Year	Extravagant Generosity Good Works
Covenant Keeper Faithful Promisor	Restorer Christ, the Victor over the powers of evil	Guide Divine Presence and Shekinah	Spiritual Food Sustenance for the Journey	The Vincentian Canon Ubiquity, antiquity, universality	Eschatological Foreshadowing The Already/Not Yet	Effective Discipling Spiritual Formation in the Believing Assembly	Evangelical Witness Making Disciples of All People Groups

APPENDIX 4

The Theology of Christus Victor
A Christ-Centered Biblical Motif for Integrating and Renewing the Urban Church

Rev. Dr. Don L. Davis

	The Promised Messiah	The Word Made Flesh	The Son of Man	The Suffering Servant	The Lamb of God	The Victorious Conqueror	The Reigning Lord in Heaven	The Bridegroom and Coming King
Biblical Framework	Israel's hope of Yahweh's anointed who would redeem his people	In the person of Jesus of Nazareth, the Lord has come to the world	As the promised king and divine Son of Man, Jesus reveals the Father's glory and salvation to the world	As Inaugurator of the Kingdom of God, Jesus demonstrates God's reign present through his words, wonders, and works	As both High Priest and Paschal Lamb, Jesus offers himself to God on our behalf as a sacrifice for sin	In his resurrection from the dead and ascension to God's right hand, Jesus is proclaimed as Victor over the power of sin and death	Now reigning at God's right hand till his enemies are made his footstool, Jesus pours out his benefits on his body	Soon the risen and ascended Lord will return to gather his Bride, the Church, and consummate his work
Scripture References	Isa. 9.6-7 Jer. 23.5-6 Isa. 11.1-10	John 1.14-18 Matt. 1.20-23 Phil. 2.6-8	Matt. 2.1-11 Num. 24.17 Luke 1.78-79	Mark 1.14-15 Matt. 12.25-30 Luke 17.20-21	2 Cor. 5.18-21 Isa. 52-53 John 1.29	Eph. 1.16-23 Phil. 2.5-11 Col. 1.15-20	1 Cor. 15.25 Eph. 4.15-16 Acts. 2.32-36	Rom. 14.7-9 Rev. 5.9-13 1 Thess. 4.13-18
Jesus' History	The pre-incarnate, only begotten Son of God in glory	His conception by the Spirit, and birth to Mary	His manifestation to the Magi and to the world	His teaching, exorcisms, miracles, and mighty works among the people	His suffering, crucifixion, death, and burial	His resurrection, with appearances to his witnesses, and his ascension to the Father	The sending of the Holy Spirit and his gifts, and Christ's session in heaven at the Father's right hand	His soon return from heaven to earth as Lord and Christ: the Second Coming
Description	The biblical promise for the seed of Abraham, the prophet like Moses, the son of David	In the Incarnation, God has come to us; Jesus reveals to humankind the Father's glory in fullness	In Jesus, God has shown his salvation to the entire world, including the Gentiles	In Jesus, the promised Kingdom of God has come visibly to earth, demonstrating his binding of Satan and rescinding the Curse	As God's perfect Lamb, Jesus offers himself up to God as a sin offering on behalf of the entire world	In his resurrection and ascension, Jesus destroyed death, disarmed Satan, and rescinded the Curse	Jesus is installed at the Father's right hand as Head of the Church, Firstborn from the dead, and supreme Lord in heaven	As we labor in his harvest field in the world, so we await Christ's return, the fulfillment of his promise
Church Year	Advent	Christmas	Season after Epiphany Baptism and Transfiguration	Lent	Holy Week Passion	Eastertide Easter, Ascension Day, Pentecost	Season after Pentecost Trinity Sunday	Season after Pentecost All Saints Day, Reign of Christ the King
	The Coming of Christ	*The Birth of Christ*	*The Manifestation of Christ*	*The Ministry of Christ*	*The Suffering and Death of Christ*	*The Resurrection and Ascension of Christ*	*The Heavenly Session of Christ*	*The Reign of Christ*
Spiritual Formation	As we await his Coming, let us proclaim and affirm the hope of Christ	O Word made flesh, let us every heart prepare him room to dwell	Divine Son of Man, show the nations your salvation and glory	In the person of Christ, the power of the reign of God has come to earth and to the Church	May those who share the Lord's death be resurrected with him	Let us participate by faith in the victory of Christ over the power of sin, Satan, and death	Come, indwell us, Holy Spirit, and empower us to advance Christ's Kingdom in the world	We live and work in expectation of his soon return, seeking to please him in all things

APPENDIX 5
Christus Victor
An Integrated Vision for the Christian Life
Rev. Dr. Don L. Davis

For the Church
- The Church is the primary extension of Jesus in the world
- Ransomed treasure of the victorious, risen Christ
- *Laos:* The people of God
- God's new creation: presence of the future
- Locus and agent of the Already/Not Yet Kingdom

For Gifts
- God's gracious endowments and benefits from *Christus Victor*
- Pastoral offices to the Church
- The Holy Spirit's sovereign dispensing of the gifts
- Stewardship: divine, diverse gifts for the common good

For Theology and Doctrine
- The authoritative Word of Christ's victory: the Apostolic Tradition: the Holy Scriptures
- Theology as commentary on the grand narrative of God
- *Christus Victor* as core theological framework for meaning in the world
- The Nicene Creed: the Story of God's triumphant grace

Christus Victor
Destroyer of Evil and Death
Restorer of Creation
Victor o'er Hades and Sin
Crusher of Satan

For Evangelism and Mission
- Evangelism as unashamed declaration and demonstration of *Christus Victor* to the world
- The Gospel as Good News of kingdom pledge
- We proclaim God's Kingdom come in the person of Jesus of Nazareth
- The Great Commission: go to all people groups making disciples of Christ and his Kingdom
- Proclaiming Christ as Lord and Messiah

For Spirituality
- The Holy Spirit's presence and power in the midst of God's people
- Sharing in the disciplines of the Spirit
- Gatherings, lectionary, liturgy, and our observances in the Church Year
- Living the life of the risen Christ in the rhythm of our ordinary lives

For Worship
- People of the Resurrection: unending celebration of the people of God
- Remembering, participating in the Christ event in our worship
- Listen and respond to the Word
- Transformed at the Table, the Lord's Supper
- The presence of the Father through the Son in the Spirit

For Justice and Compassion
- The gracious and generous expressions of Jesus through the Church
- The Church displays the very life of the Kingdom
- The Church demonstrates the very life of the Kingdom of heaven right here and now
- Having freely received, we freely give (no sense of merit or pride)
- Justice as tangible evidence of the Kingdom come

APPENDIX 6
Old Testament Witness to Christ and His Kingdom
Rev. Dr. Don L. Davis

Christ Is Seen in the OT's:	Covenant Promise and Fulfillment	Moral Law	Christophanies	Typology	Tabernacle, Festival, and Levitical Priesthood	Messianic Prophecy	Salvation Promises
Passage	Gen. 12.1-3	Matt. 5.17-18	John 1.18	1 Cor. 15.45	Heb. 8.1-6	Mic. 5.2	Isa. 9.6-7
Example	The Promised Seed of the Abrahamic covenant	The Law given on Mount Sinai	Commander of the Lord's army	Jonah and the great fish	Melchizedek, as both High Priest and King	The Lord's Suffering Servant	Righteous Branch of David
Christ As	Seed of the woman	The Prophet of God	God's present Revelation	Antitype of God's drama	Our eternal High Priest	The coming Son of Man	Israel's Redeemer and King
Where Illustrated	Galatians	Matthew	John	Matthew	Hebrews	Luke and Acts	John and Revelation
Exegetical Goal	To see Christ as heart of God's sacred drama	To see Christ as fulfillment of the Law	To see Christ as God's revealer	To see Christ as antitype of divine typos	To see Christ in the Temple *cultus*	To see Christ as true Messiah	To see Christ as coming King
How Seen in the NT	As fulfillment of God's sacred oath	As *telos* of the Law	As full, final, and superior revelation	As substance behind the historical shadows	As reality behind the rules and roles	As the Kingdom made present	As the One who will rule on David's throne
Our Response in Worship	God's veracity and faithfulness	God's perfect righteousness	God's presence among us	God's inspired Scripture	God's ontology: his realm as primary and determinative	God's anointed servant and mediator	God's resolve to restore his kingdom authority
How God Is Vindicated	God does not lie: he's true to his word	Jesus fulfills all righteousness	God's fulness is revealed to us in Jesus of Nazareth	The Spirit spoke by the prophets	The Lord has provided a mediator for humankind	Every jot and tittle written of him will occur	Evil will be put down, creation restored, under his reign

APPENDIX 7
Summary Outline of the Scriptures
Rev. Dr. Don L. Davis

1. GENESIS - Beginnings
   a. Adam
   b. Noah
   c. Abraham
   d. Isaac
   e. Jacob
   f. Joseph

2. EXODUS - Redemption, (out of)
   a. Slavery
   b. Deliverance
   c. Law
   d. Tabernacle

3. LEVITICUS - Worship and Fellowship
   a. Offerings, sacrifices
   b. Priests
   c. Feasts, festivals

4. NUMBERS - Service and Walk
   a. Organized
   b. Wanderings

5. DEUTERONOMY - Obedience
   a. Moses reviews history and law
   b. Civil and social laws
   c. Palestinian Covenant
   d. Moses' blessing and death

6. JOSHUA - Redemption (into)
   a. Conquer the land
   b. Divide up the land
   c. Joshua's farewell

7. JUDGES - God's Deliverance
   a. Disobedience and judgment
   b. Israel's twelve judges
   c. Lawless conditions

8. RUTH - Love
   a. Ruth chooses
   b. Ruth works
   c. Ruth waits
   d. Ruth rewarded

9. 1 SAMUEL - Kings, Priestly Perspective
   a. Eli
   b. Samuel
   c. Saul
   d. David

10. 2 SAMUEL - David
    a. King of Judah
       (9 years - Hebron)
    b. King of all Israel
       (33 years - Jerusalem)

11. 1 KINGS - Solomon's Glory, Kingdom's Decline
    a. Solomon's glory
    b. Kingdom's decline
    c. Elijah the prophet

12. 2 KINGS - Divided Kingdom
    a. Elisha
    b. Israel (N. Kingdom falls)
    c. Judah (S. Kingdom falls)

13. 1 CHRONICLES - David's Temple Arrangements
    a. Genealogies
    b. End of Saul's reign
    c. Reign of David
    d. Temple preparations

14. 2 CHRONICLES - Temple and Worship Abandoned
    a. Solomon
    b. Kings of Judah

15. EZRA - The Minority (Remnant)
    a. First return from exile - Zerubbabel
    b. Second return from exile - Ezra (priest)

16. NEHEMIAH - Rebuilding by Faith
    a. Rebuild walls
    b. Revival
    c. Religious reform

17. ESTHER - Female Savior
    a. Esther
    b. Haman
    c. Mordecai
    d. Deliverance: Feast of Purim

18. JOB - Why the Righteous Suffer
    a. Godly Job
    b. Satan's attack
    c. Four philosophical friends
    d. God lives

19. PSALMS - Prayer and Praise
    a. Prayers of David
    b. Godly suffer; deliverance
    c. God deals with Israel
    d. Suffering of God's people - end with the Lord's reign
    e. The Word of God (Messiah's suffering and glorious return)

20. PROVERBS - Wisdom
    a. Wisdom versus folly
    b. Solomon
    c. Solomon - Hezekiah
    d. Agur
    e. Lemuel

21. ECCLESIASTES - Vanity
    a. Experimentation
    b. Observation
    c. Consideration

22. SONG OF SOLOMON - Love Story

23. ISAIAH - The Justice (Judgment) and Grace (Comfort) of God
    a. Prophecies of punishment
    b. History
    c. Prophecies of blessing

24. JEREMIAH - Judah's Sin Leads to Babylonian Captivity
    a. Jeremiah's call; empowered
    b. Judah condemned; predicted Babylonian captivity
    c. Restoration promised
    d. Prophesied judgment inflicted
    e. Prophesies against Gentiles
    f. Summary of Judah's captivity

25. LAMENTATIONS - Lament over Jerusalem
    a. Affliction of Jerusalem
    b. Destroyed because of sin
    c. The prophet's suffering
    d. Present desolation versus past splendor
    e. Appeal to God for mercy

26. EZEKIEL - Israel's Captivity and Restoration
    a. Judgment on Judah and Jerusalem
    b. Judgment on Gentile nations
    c. Israel restored; Jerusalem's future glory

27. DANIEL - The Time of the Gentiles
    a. History; Nebuchadnezzar, Belshazzar, Daniel
    b. Prophecy

28. HOSEA - Unfaithfulness
    a. Unfaithfulness
    b. Punishment
    c. Restoration

29. JOEL - The Day of the Lord
    a. Locust plague
    b. Events of the future day of the Lord
    c. Order of the future day of the Lord

30. AMOS - God Judges Sin
    a. Neighbors judged
    b. Israel judged
    c. Visions of future judgment
    d. Israel's past judgment blessings

31. OBADIAH - Edom's Destruction
    a. Destruction prophesied
    b. Reasons for destruction
    c. Israel's future blessing

32. JONAH - Gentile Salvation
    a. Jonah disobeys
    b. Other suffer
    c. Jonah punished
    d. Jonah obeys; thousands saved
    e. Jonah displeased, no love for souls

33. MICAH - Israel's Sins, Judgment, and Restoration
    a. Sin and judgment
    b. Grace and future restoration
    c. Appeal and petition

34. NAHUM - Nineveh Condemned
    a. God hates sin
    b. Nineveh's doom prophesied
    c. Reasons for doom

35. HABAKKUK - The Just Shall Live by Faith
    a. Complaint of Judah's unjudged sin
    b. Chaldeans will punish
    c. Complaint of Chaldeans' wickedness
    d. Punishment promised
    e. Prayer for revival; faith in God

36. ZEPHANIAH - Babylonian Invasion Prefigures the Day of the Lord
    a. Judgment on Judah foreshadows the Great Day of the Lord
    b. Judgment on Jerusalem and neighbors foreshadows final judgment of all nations
    c. Israel restored after judgments

37. HAGGAI - Rebuild the Temple
    a. Negligence
    b. Courage
    c. Separation
    d. Judgment

38. ZECHARIAH - Two Comings of Christ
    a. Zechariah's vision
    b. Bethel's question; Jehovah's answer
    c. Nation's downfall and salvation

39. MALACHI - Neglect
    a. The priest's sins
    b. The people's sins
    c. The faithful few

Summary Outline of the Scriptures (continued)

1. MATTHEW - Jesus the King
  a. The Person of the King
  b. The Preparation of the King
  c. The Propaganda of the King
  d. The Program of the King
  e. The Passion of the King
  f. The Power of the King
 	
2. MARK - Jesus the Servant
  a. John introduces the Servant
  b. God the Father identifies the Servant
  c. The temptation initiates the Servant
  d. Work and word of the Servant
  e. Death, burial, resurrection
 	
3. LUKE - Jesus Christ the Perfect Man
  a. Birth and family of the Perfect Man
  b. Testing of the Perfect Man; hometown
  c. Ministry of the Perfect Man
  d. Betrayal, trial, and death of the Perfect Man
  e. Resurrection of the Perfect Man
 	
4. JOHN - Jesus Christ is God
  a. Prologue - the Incarnation
  b. Introduction
  c. Witness of Jesus to his Apostles
  d. Passion - witness to the world
  e. Epilogue
 	
5. ACTS - The Holy Spirit Working in the Church
  a. The Lord Jesus at work by the Holy Spirit through the Apostles at Jerusalem
  b. In Judea and Samaria
  c. To the uttermost parts of the Earth
 	
6. ROMANS - The Righteousness of God
  a. Salutation
  b. Sin and salvation
  c. Sanctification
  d. Struggle
  e. Spirit-filled living
  f. Security of salvation
  g. Segregation
  h. Sacrifice and service
  i. Separation and salutation
	7. 1 CORINTHIANS - The Lordship of Christ
	  a. Salutation and thanksgiving
	  b. Conditions in the Corinthian body
	  c. Concerning the Gospel
	  d. Concerning collections
	
	8. 2 CORINTHIANS - The Ministry in the Church
	  a. The comfort of God
	  b. Collection for the poor
	  c. Calling of the Apostle Paul
	
	9. GALATIANS - Justification by Faith
	  a. Introduction
	  b. Personal - Authority of the Apostle and glory of the Gospel
	  c. Doctrinal - Justification by faith
	  d. Practical - Sanctification by the Holy Spirit
	  e. Autographed conclusion and exhortation
	
	10. EPHESIANS - The Church of Jesus Christ
	  a. Doctrinal - the heavenly calling of the Church
	    A Body
	    A Temple
	    A Mystery
	  b. Practical - The earthly conduct of the Church
	    A New Man
	    A Bride
	    An Army
	
	11. PHILIPPIANS - Joy in the Christian Life
	  a. Philosophy for Christian living
	  b. Pattern for Christian living
	  c. Prize for Christian living
	  d. Power for Christian living
	
	12. COLOSSIANS - Christ the Fullness of God
	  a. Doctrinal - In Christ believers are made full
	  b. Practical - Christ's life poured out in believers, and through them
	
	13. 1 THESSALONIANS - The Second Coming of Christ:
	  a. Is an inspiring hope
	  b. Is a working hope
	  c. Is a purifying hope
	  d. Is a comforting hope
	  e. Is a rousing, stimulating hope
		14. 2 THESSALONIANS - The Second Coming of Christ
		  a. Persecution of believers now; judgment of unbelievers hereafter (at coming of Christ)
		  b. Program of the world in connection with the coming of Christ
		  c. Practical issues associated with the coming of Christ
		
		15. 1 TIMOTHY - Government and Order in the Local Church
		  a. The faith of the Church
		  b. Public prayer and women's place in the Church
		  c. Officers in the Church
		  d. Apostasy in the Church
		  e. Duties of the officer of the Church
		
		16. 2 TIMOTHY - Loyalty in the Days of Apostasy
		  a. Afflictions of the Gospel
		  b. Active in service
		  c. Apostasy coming; authority of the Scriptures
		  d. Allegiance to the Lord
		
		17. TITUS - The Ideal New Testament Church
		  a. The Church is an organization
		  b. The Church is to teach and preach the Word of God
		  c. The Church is to perform good works
		
		18. PHILEMON - Reveal Christ's Love and Teach Brotherly Love
		  a. Genial greeting to Philemon and family
		  b. Good reputation of Philemon
		  c. Gracious plea for Onesimus
		  d. Guiltless illustration of Imputation
		  e. General and personal requests
		
		19. HEBREWS - The Superiority of Christ
		  a. Doctrinal - Christ is better than the Old Testament economy
		  b. Practical - Christ brings better benefits and duties
		
		20. JAMES - Ethics of Christianity
		  a. Faith tested
		  b. Difficulty of controlling the tongue
		  c. Warning against worldliness
		  d. Admonitions in view of the Lord's coming
			21. 1 PETER - Christian Hope in the Time of Persecution and Trial
			  a. Suffering and security of believers
			  b. Suffering and the Scriptures
			  c. Suffering and the sufferings of Christ
			  d. Suffering and the Second Coming of Christ
			
			22. 2 PETER - Warning Against False Teachers
			  a. Addition of Christian graces gives assurance
			  b. Authority of the Scriptures
			  c. Apostasy brought in by false testimony
			  d. Attitude toward Return of Christ: test for apostasy
			  e. Agenda of God in the world
			  f. Admonition to believers
			
			23. 1 JOHN - The Family of God
			  a. God is Light
			  b. God is Love
			  c. God is Life
			
			24. 2 JOHN - Warning against Receiving Deceivers
			  a. Walk in truth
			  b. Love one another
			  c. Receive not deceivers
			  d. Find joy in fellowship
			
			25. 3 JOHN - Admonition to Receive True Believers
			  a. Gaius, brother in the Church
			  b. Diotrephes
			  c. Demetrius
			
			26. JUDE - Contending for the Faith
			  a. Occasion of the epistle
			  b. Occurrences of apostasy
			  c. Occupation of believers in the days of apostasy
			
			27. REVELATION - The Unveiling of Christ Glorified
			  a. The person of Christ in glory
			  b. The possession of Jesus Christ - the Church in the World
			  c. The program of Jesus Christ - the scene in Heaven
			  d. The seven seals
			  e. The seven trumpets
			  f. Important persons in the last days
			  g. The seven vials
			  h. The fall of Babylon
			  i. The eternal state

APPENDIX 8

From Before to Beyond Time:

The Plan of God and Human History

Adapted from: Suzanne de Dietrich. ***God's Unfolding Purpose.*** *Philadelphia: Westminster Press, 1976.*

I. Before Time (Eternity Past) 1 Cor. 2.7
A. The Eternal Triune God
B. God's Eternal Purpose
C. The Mystery of Iniquity
D. The Principalities and Powers

II. Beginning of Time (Creation and Fall) Gen. 1.1
A. Creative Word
B. Humanity
C. Fall
D. Reign of Death and First Signs of Grace

III. Unfolding of Time (God's Plan Revealed Through Israel) Gal. 3.8
A. Promise (Patriarchs)
B. Exodus and Covenant at Sinai
C. Promised Land
D. The City, the Temple, and the Throne (Prophet, Priest, and King)
E. Exile
F. Remnant

IV. Fullness of Time (Incarnation of the Messiah) Gal. 4.4-5
A. The King Comes to His Kingdom
B. The Present Reality of His Reign
C. The Secret of the Kingdom: the Already and the Not Yet
D. The Crucified King
E. The Risen Lord

V. The Last Times (The Descent of the Holy Spirit) Acts 2.16-18
A. Between the Times: the Church as Foretaste of the Kingdom
B. The Church as Agent of the Kingdom
C. The Conflict Between the Kingdoms of Darkness and Light

VI. The Fulfillment of Time (The Second Coming) Matt. 13.40-43
A. The Return of Christ
B. Judgment
C. The Consummation of His Kingdom

VII. Beyond Time (Eternity Future) 1 Cor. 15.24-28
A. Kingdom Handed Over to God the Father
B. God as All in All

From Before to Beyond Time
Scriptures for Major Outline Points

I. Before Time (Eternity Past)

1 Cor. 2.7 (ESV) - But we impart a secret and hidden wisdom of God, *which God decreed before the ages* for our glory (cf. Titus 1.2).

II. Beginning of Time (Creation and Fall)

Gen. 1.1 (ESV) - *In the beginning*, God created the heavens and the earth.

III. Unfolding of Time (God's Plan Revealed Through Israel)

Gal. 3.8 (ESV) - And the Scripture, foreseeing that God would justify the Gentiles by faith, *preached the Gospel beforehand to Abraham*, saying, "In you shall all the nations be blessed" (cf. Rom. 9.4-5).

IV. Fullness of Time (The Incarnation of the Messiah)

Gal. 4.4-5 (ESV) - *But when the fullness of time had come*, God sent forth his Son, born of woman, born under the law, to redeem those who were under the law, so that we might receive adoption as sons.

V. The Last Times (The Descent of the Holy Spirit)

Acts 2.16-18 (ESV) - But this is what was uttered through the prophet Joel: "'*And in the last days it shall be*,' God declares, 'that I will pour out my Spirit on all flesh, and your sons and your daughters shall prophesy, and your young men shall see visions, and your old men shall dream dreams; even on my male servants and female servants in those days I will pour out my Spirit, and they shall prophesy.'"

VI. The Fulfillment of Time (The Second Coming)

Matt. 13.40-43 (ESV) - Just as the weeds are gathered and burned with fire, *so will it be at the close of the age*. The Son of Man will send his angels, and they will gather out of his kingdom all causes of sin and all lawbreakers, and throw them into the fiery furnace. In that place there will be weeping and gnashing of teeth. Then the righteous will shine like the sun in the Kingdom of their Father. He who has ears, let him hear.

VII. Beyond Time (Eternity Future)

1 Cor. 15.24-28 (ESV) - Then comes the end, when he delivers the Kingdom to God the Father after destroying every rule and every authority and power. For he must reign until he has put all his enemies under his feet. The last enemy to be destroyed is death. For "God has put all things in subjection under his feet." But when it says, "all things are put in subjection," it is plain that he is excepted who put all things in subjection under him. When all things are subjected to him, then the Son himself will also be subjected to him who put all things in subjection under him, that God may be all in all.

APPENDIX 9
"There Is a River"
Identifying the Streams of a Revitalized Authentic Christian Community in the City[1]
Rev. Dr. Don L. Davis • Psalm 46.4 (ESV) - There is a river whose streams make glad the city of God, the holy habitation of the Most High.

Tributaries of Authentic Historic Biblical Faith			
Recognized Biblical Identity	**Revived Urban Spirituality**	**Reaffirmed Historical Connectivity**	**Refocused Kingdom Authority**
The Church Is **One**	The Church Is **Holy**	The Church Is **Catholic**	The Church Is **Apostolic**
A Call to Biblical Fidelity *Recognizing the Scriptures as the anchor and foundation of the Christian faith and practice*	A Call to the Freedom, Power, and Fullness of the Holy Spirit *Walking in the holiness, power, gifting, and liberty of the Holy Spirit in the body of Christ*	A Call to Historic Roots and Continuity *Confessing the common historical identity and continuity of authentic Christian faith*	A Call to the Apostolic Faith *Affirming the apostolic tradition as the authoritative ground of the Christian hope*
A Call to Messianic Kingdom Identity *Rediscovering the story of the promised Messiah and his Kingdom in Jesus of Nazareth*	A Call to Live as Sojourners and Aliens as the People of God *Defining authentic Christian discipleship as faithful membership among God's people*	A Call to Affirm and Express the Global Communion of Saints *Expressing cooperation and collaboration with all other believers, both local and global*	A Call to Representative Authority *Submitting joyfully to God's gifted servants in the Church as undershepherds of true faith*
A Call to Creedal Affinity *Embracing the Nicene Creed as the shared rule of faith of historic orthodoxy*	A Call to Liturgical, Sacramental, and Catechetical Vitality *Experiencing God's presence in the context of the Word, sacrament, and instruction*	A Call to Radical Hospitality and Good Works *Expressing kingdom love to all, and especially to those of the household of faith*	A Call to Prophetic and Holistic Witness *Proclaiming Christ and his Kingdom in word and deed to our neighbors and all peoples*

[1] *This schema is an adaptation and is based on the insights of the **Chicago Call** statement of May 1977, where various leading evangelical scholars and practitioners met to discuss the relationship of modern evangelicalism to the historic Christian faith.*

APPENDIX 10
A Schematic for a Theology of the Kingdom and the Church
The Urban Ministry Institute

The Reign of the One, True, Sovereign, and Triune God, the LORD God, Yahweh, God the Father, Son, and Holy Spirit			
The Father Love - 1 John 4.8 Maker of heaven and earth and of all things visible and invisible	**The Son** Faith - Heb. 12.2 Prophet, Priest, and King	**The Spirit** Hope - Rom. 15.13 Lord of the Church	
Creation All that exists through the creative action of God.	**Kingdom** The Reign of God expressed in the rule of his Son Jesus the Messiah.	**Church** The one, holy, apostolic community which functions as a witness to (Acts 28.31) and a foretaste of (Col. 1.12; James 1.18; 1 Pet. 2.9; Rev. 1.6) the Kingdom of God.	
The eternal God, sovereign in power, infinite in wisdom, perfect in holiness, and steadfast in love, is the source and goal of all things.	**Rom. 8.18-21 →** **Freedom** (Slavery) Jesus answered them, "Truly, truly, I say to you, everyone who commits sin is a slave to sin. The slave does not remain in the house forever; the son remains forever. So if the Son sets you free, you will be free indeed." - John 8.34-36 (ESV)	*The Church is an Apostolic Community Where the Word is Rightly Preached, Therefore it is a Community of:* **Calling** - For freedom Christ has set us free; stand firm therefore, and do not submit again to a yoke of slavery. - Gal. 5.1 (ESV) (cf. Rom. 8.28-30; 1 Cor. 1.26-31; Eph. 1.18; 2 Thess. 2.13-14; Jude 1.1) **Faith** - ". . . for unless you believe that I am he you will die in your sins". . . . So Jesus said to the Jews who had believed in him, "If you abide in my word, you are truly my disciples, and you will know the truth, and the truth will set you free." - John 8.24b, 31-32 (ESV) (cf. Ps. 119.45; Rom. 1.17; 5.1-2; Eph. 2.8-9; 2 Tim. 1.13-14; Heb. 2.14-15; James 1.25) **Witness** - The Spirit of the Lord is upon me, because he has anointed me to proclaim good news to the poor. He has sent me to proclaim liberty to the captives and recovering of sight to the blind, to set at liberty those who are oppressed, to proclaim the year of the Lord's favor. - Luke 4.18-19 (ESV) (cf. Lev. 25.10; Prov. 31.8; Matt. 4.17; 28.18-20; Mark 13.10; Acts 1.8; 8.4, 12; 13.1-3; 25.20; 28.30-31)	
O, the depth of the riches and wisdom and knowledge of God! How unsearchable are his judgments, and how inscrutable his ways! For who has known the mind of the Lord, or who has been his counselor? Or who has ever given a gift to him, that he might be repaid?" For from him and through him and to him are all things. To him be glory forever! Amen! - Rom. 11.33-36 (ESV) (cf. 1 Cor. 15.23-28, Rev.)	**Rev. 21.1-5 →** **Wholeness** (Sickness) But he was wounded for our transgressions; he was crushed for our iniquities; upon him was the chastisement that brought us peace, and with his stripes we are healed. - Isa. 53.5 (ESV)	*The Church is One Community Where the Sacraments are Rightly Administered, Therefore it is a Community of:* **Worship** - You shall serve the Lord your God, and he will bless your bread and your water, and I will take sickness away from among you. - Exod. 23.25 (ESV) (cf. Ps. 147.1-3; Heb. 12.28; Col. 3.16; Rev. 15.3-4; 19.5) **Covenant** - And the Holy Spirit also bears witness to us; for after the saying, "This is the covenant that I will make with them after those days, declares the Lord: I will put my laws on their hearts, and write them on their minds," then he adds, "I will remember their sins and their lawless deeds no more." - Heb. 10.15-17 (ESV) (cf. Isa. 54.10-17; Ezek. 34.25-31; 37.26-27; Mal. 2.4-5; Luke 22.20; 2 Cor. 3.6; Col. 3.15; Heb. 8.7-13; 12.22-24; 13.20-21) **Presence** - In him you also are being built together into a dwelling place for God by his Spirit. - Eph. 2.22 (ESV) (cf. Exod. 40.34-38; Ezek. 48.35; Matt. 18.18-20)	
	Isa. 11.6-9 → **Justice** (Selfishness) Behold, my servant whom I have chosen, my beloved with whom my soul is well pleased. I will put my Spirit upon him, and he will proclaim justice to the Gentiles. He will not quarrel or cry aloud, nor will anyone hear his voice in the streets; a bruised reed he will not break, and a smoldering wick he will not quench, until he brings justice to victory. - Matt. 12.18-20 (ESV)	*The Church is a Holy Community Where Discipline is Rightly Ordered, Therefore it is a Community of:* **Reconciliation** - For he himself is our peace, who has made us both one and has broken down in his flesh the dividing wall of hostility by abolishing the law of commandments and ordinances, that he might create in himself one new man in place of the two, so making peace, and might reconcile us both to God in one body through the cross, thereby killing the hostility. And he came and preached peace to you who were far off and peace to those who were near. For through him we both have access in one Spirit to the Father. - Eph. 2.14-18 (ESV) (cf. Exod. 23.4-9; Lev. 19.34; Deut. 10.18-19; Ezek. 22.29; Mic. 6.8; 2 Cor. 5.16-21) **Suffering** - Since therefore Christ suffered in the flesh, arm yourselves with the same way of thinking, for whoever has suffered in the flesh has ceased from sin, so as to live for the rest of the time in the flesh no longer for human passions but for the will of God. - 1 Pet. 4.1-2 (ESV) (cf. Luke 6.22; 10.3; Rom. 8.17; 2 Tim. 2.3; 3.12; 1 Pet. 2.20-24; Heb. 5.8; 13.11-14) **Service** - But Jesus called them to him and said, "You know that the rulers of the Gentiles lord it over them, and their great ones exercise authority over them. It shall not be so among you. But whoever would be great among you must be your servant, and whoever would be first among you must be your slave even as the Son of Man came not to be served but to serve, and to give his life as a ransom for many." - Matt. 20.25-28 (ESV) (cf. 1 John 4.16-18; Gal. 2.10)	

APPENDIX 11
Living in the Already and the Not Yet Kingdom
Rev. Dr. Don L. Davis

The Spirit: The pledge of the inheritance (***arrabon***)
The Church: The foretaste (***aparche***) of the Kingdom
"In Christ": The rich life (***en Christos***) we share as citizens of the Kingdom

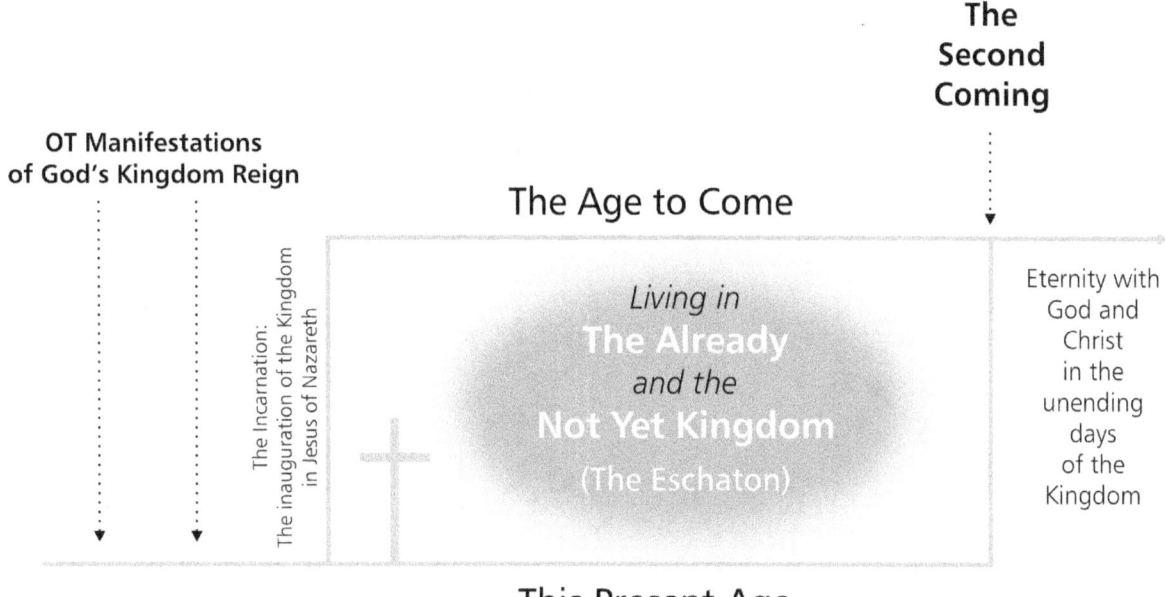

Internal enemy: The flesh (*sarx*) and the sin nature
External enemy: The world (*kosmos*) the systems of greed, lust, and pride
Infernal enemy: The devil (*kakos*) the animating spirit of falsehood and fear

Jewish View of Time

This Present Age   The Age to Come

The Coming of Messiah
The restoration of Israel
The end of Gentile oppression
The return of the earth to Edenic glory
Universal knowledge of the Lord

APPENDIX 12

Jesus of Nazareth: The Presence of the Future

Rev. Dr. Don L. Davis

Creation: The Reign of Almighty God

Glorification: New Heavens and New Earth

The Cross: The Center of Revelation and Redemption

Creation

Covenant

Church

Consummation

The Fall
- Curse (Death)
- Slavery
- Selfishness
- Sickness

The Divine Promise
- Abraham
- Isaac
- Jacob
- Judah
- David

The Incarnation
"The Kingdom is at hand!"
Invasion of Satan's Dominion
Rescinding of the Curse
Emblems of the Age to Come
Promise of the Holy Spirit
Defeat of the Powers and Principalities

The Church

The Spirit of God — "The Age of the Spirit"

Sign and Foretaste
Prophetic Witness
The Promise Fulfilled

Between the Times

APPENDIX 13

Traditions

(Paradosis)

Dr. Don L. Davis and Rev. Terry G. Cornett

Strong's Definition

Paradosis. Transmission, i.e. (concretely) a precept; specifically, the Jewish traditionary law

Vine's Explanation

denotes "a tradition," and hence, by metonymy, (a) "the teachings of the rabbis," . . . (b) "apostolic teaching," . . . of instructions concerning the gatherings of believers, of Christian doctrine in general . . . of instructions concerning everyday conduct.

1. **The concept of tradition in Scripture is essentially positive.**

    Jer. 6.16 (ESV) - Thus says the Lord: "Stand by the roads, and look, and ask for the ancient paths, where the good way is; and walk in it, and find rest for your souls. But they said, 'We will not walk in it'" (cf. Exod. 3.15; Judg. 2.17; 1 Kings 8.57-58; Ps. 78.1-6).

    2 Chron. 35.25 (ESV) - Jeremiah also uttered a lament for Josiah; and all the singing men and singing women have spoken of Josiah in their laments to this day. They made these a rule in Israel; behold, they are written in the Laments (cf. Gen. 32.32; Judg. 11.38-40).

    Jer. 35.14-19 (ESV) - The command that Jonadab the son of Rechab gave to his sons, to drink no wine, has been kept, and they drink none to this day, for they have obeyed their father's command. I have spoken to you persistently, but you have not listened to me. I have sent to you all my servants the prophets, sending them persistently, saying, 'Turn now every one of you from his evil way, and amend your deeds, and do not go after other gods to serve them, and then you shall dwell in the land that I gave to you and your fathers.' But you did not incline your ear or listen to me. The sons of Jonadab the son of Rechab have kept the command that their father gave them, but this people has not obeyed me. Therefore, thus says the

Traditions (continued)

Lord, the God of hosts, the God of Israel: Behold, I am bringing upon Judah and all the inhabitants of Jerusalem all the disaster that I have pronounced against them, because I have spoken to them and they have not listened, I have called to them and they have not answered." But to the house of the Rechabites Jeremiah said, "Thus says the Lord of hosts, the God of Israel: Because you have obeyed the command of Jonadab your father and kept all his precepts and done all that he commanded you, therefore thus says the Lord of hosts, the God of Israel: Jonadab the son of Rechab shall never lack a man to stand before me."

2. **Godly tradition is a wonderful thing, but not all tradition is godly.**

   Any individual tradition must be judged by its faithfulness to the Word of God and its usefulness in helping people maintain obedience to Christ's example and teaching.[1] In the Gospels, Jesus frequently rebukes the Pharisees for establishing traditions that nullify rather than uphold God's commands.

   Mark 7.8 (ESV) - You leave the commandment of God and hold to the tradition of men" (cf. Matt. 15.2-6; Mark 7.13).

   Col. 2.8 (ESV) - See to it that no one takes you captive by philosophy and empty deceit, according to human tradition, according to the elemental spirits of the world, and not according to Christ.

3. **Without the fullness of the Holy Spirit, and the constant edification provided to us by the Word of God, tradition will inevitably lead to dead formalism.**

   Those who are spiritual are filled with the Holy Spirit, whose power and leading alone provides individuals and congregations a sense of freedom and vitality in all they practice and believe. However, when the practices and teachings of any given tradition are no longer infused by the power of the Holy Spirit and the Word of God, tradition loses its effectiveness, and may actually become counterproductive to our discipleship in Jesus Christ.

   Eph. 5.18 (ESV) - And do not get drunk with wine, for that is debauchery, but be filled with the Spirit.

---

[1] *"All Protestants insist that these traditions must ever be tested against Scripture and can never possess an independent apostolic authority over or alongside of Scripture." (J. Van Engen, "Tradition,"* **Evangelical Dictionary of Theology***, Walter Elwell, Gen. ed.) We would add that Scripture is itself the "authoritative tradition" by which all other traditions are judged. See "Appendix A, The Founders of Tradition: Three Levels of Christian Authority," p. 4.*

Traditions (continued)

Gal. 5.22-25 (ESV) - But the fruit of the Spirit is love, joy, peace, patience, kindness, goodness, faithfulness, gentleness, self-control; against such things there is no law. And those who belong to Christ Jesus have crucified the flesh with its passions and desires. If we live by the Spirit, let us also walk by the Spirit.

2 Cor. 3.5-6 (ESV) - Not that we are sufficient in ourselves to claim anything as coming from us, but our sufficiency is from God, who has made us competent to be ministers of a new covenant, not of the letter but of the Spirit. For the letter kills, but the Spirit gives life.

4. **Fidelity to the Apostolic Tradition (teaching and modeling) is the essence of Christian maturity.**

    2 Tim. 2.2 (ESV) - and what you have heard from me in the presence of many witnesses entrust to faithful men who will be able to teach others also.

    1 Cor. 11.1-2 (ESV) - Be imitators of me, as I am of Christ. Now I commend you because you remember me in everything and maintain the traditions even as I delivered them to you (cf.1 Cor. 4.16-17, 2 Tim. 1.13-14, 2 Thess. 3.7-9, Phil. 4.9).

    1 Cor. 15.3-8 (ESV) - For I delivered to you as of first importance what I also received: that Christ died for our sins in accordance with the Scriptures, that he was buried, that he was raised on the third day in accordance with the Scriptures, and that he appeared to Cephas, then to the twelve. Then he appeared to more than five hundred brothers at one time, most of whom are still alive, though some have fallen asleep. Then he appeared to James, then to all the apostles. Last of all, as to one untimely born, he appeared also to me.

5. **The Apostle Paul often includes an appeal to the tradition for support in doctrinal practices.**

    1 Cor. 11.16 (ESV) - If anyone is inclined to be contentious, we have no such practice, nor do the churches of God (cf. 1 Cor. 1.2, 7.17, 15.3).

Traditions (continued)

> 1 Cor. 14.33-34 (ESV) - For God is not a God of confusion but of peace. As in all the churches of the saints, the women should keep silent in the churches. For they are not permitted to speak, but should be in submission, as the Law also says.

6. **When a congregation uses received tradition to remain faithful to the "Word of God," they are commended by the apostles.**

   > 1 Cor. 11.2 (ESV) - Now I commend you because you remember me in everything and maintain the traditions even as I delivered them to you.

   > 2 Thess. 2.15 (ESV) - So then, brothers, stand firm and hold to the traditions that you were taught by us, either by our spoken word or by our letter.

   > 2 Thess. 3.6 (ESV) - Now we command you, brothers, in the name of our Lord Jesus Christ, that you keep away from any brother who is walking in idleness and not in accord with the tradition that you received from us.

Appendix A

The Founders of Tradition: Three Levels of Christian Authority

Exod. 3.15 (ESV) - God also said to Moses, "Say this to the people of Israel, 'The Lord, the God of your fathers, the God of Abraham, the God of Isaac, and the God of Jacob, has sent me to you.' This is my name forever, and thus I am to be remembered throughout all generations."

1. **The Authoritative Tradition: the Apostles and the Prophets (The Holy Scriptures)**

   Eph. 2.19-21 (ESV) - So then you are no longer strangers and aliens, but you are fellow citizens with the saints and members of the household of God, built on the foundation of the apostles and prophets, Christ Jesus himself being the cornerstone, in whom the whole structure, being joined together, grows into a holy temple in the Lord.

   ~ The Apostle Paul

Traditions (continued)

Those who gave eyewitness testimony to the revelation and saving acts of Yahweh, first in Israel, and ultimately in Jesus Christ the Messiah. This testimony is binding for all people, at all times, and in all places. It is the authoritative tradition by which all subsequent tradition is judged.

2. The Great Tradition: the Ecumenical Councils and their Creeds[2]

[2] See Appendix B, "Defining the Great Tradition."

What has been believed everywhere, always, and by all.

~ Vincent of Lerins

The Great Tradition is the core dogma (doctrine) of the Church. It represents the teaching of the Church as it has understood the Authoritative Tradition (the Holy Scriptures), and summarizes those essential truths that Christians of all ages have confessed and believed. To these doctrinal statements the whole Church, (Catholic, Orthodox, and Protestant)[3] gives its assent. The worship and theology of the Church reflects this core dogma, which finds its summation and fulfillment in the person and work of Jesus Christ. From earliest times, Christians have expressed their devotion to God in its Church calendar, a yearly pattern of worship which summarizes and reenacts the events of Christ's life.

[3] Even the more radical wing of the Protestant reformation (Anabaptists) who were the most reluctant to embrace the creeds as dogmatic instruments of faith, did not disagree with the essential content found in them. "They assumed the Apostolic Creed–they called it 'The Faith,' Der Glaube, as did most people." See John Howard Yoder, Preface to Theology: Christology and Theological Method. Grand Rapids: Brazos Press, 2002. pp. 222-223.

3. Specific Church Traditions: the Founders of Denominations and Orders

The Presbyterian Church (U.S.A.) has approximately 2.5 million members, 11,200 congregations and 21,000 ordained ministers. Presbyterians trace their history to the 16th century and the Protestant Reformation. Our heritage, and much of what we believe, began with the French lawyer John Calvin (1509-1564), whose writings crystallized much of the Reformed thinking that came before him.

~ The Presbyterian Church, U.S.A.

Christians have expressed their faith in Jesus Christ in various ways through specific movements and traditions which embrace and express the Authoritative Tradition and the Great Tradition in unique ways. For instance,

Traditions (continued)

Catholic movements have arisen around people like Benedict, Francis, or Dominic, and among Protestants people like Martin Luther, John Calvin, Ulrich Zwingli, and John Wesley. Women have founded vital movements of Christian faith (e.g., Aimee Semple McPherson of the Foursquare Church), as well as minorities (e.g., Richard Allen of the African Methodist Episcopal Church or Charles H. Mason of the Church of God in Christ, who also helped to spawn the Assemblies of God), all which attempted to express the Authoritative Tradition and the Great Tradition in a specific way consistent with their time and expression.

The emergence of vital, dynamic movements of the faith at different times and among different peoples reveal the fresh working of the Holy Spirit throughout history. Thus, inside Catholicism, new communities have arisen such as the Benedictines, Franciscans, and Dominicans; and outside Catholicism, new denominations have emerged (Lutherans, Presbyterians, Methodists, Church of God in Christ, etc.). Each of these specific traditions have "founders," key leaders whose energy and vision helped to establish a unique expression of Christian faith and practice. Of course, to be legitimate, these movements must adhere to and faithfully express both the Authoritative Tradition and the Great Tradition. Members of these specific traditions embrace their own unique practices and patterns of spirituality, but these unique features are not necessarily binding on the Church at large. They represent the unique expressions of that community's understanding of and faithfulness to the Authoritative and Great Traditions.

Specific traditions seek to express and live out this faithfulness to the Authoritative and Great Traditions through their worship, teaching, and service. They seek to make the Gospel clear within new cultures or sub-cultures, speaking and modeling the hope of Christ into new situations shaped by their own set of questions posed in light of their own unique circumstances. These movements, therefore, seek to contextualize the Authoritative tradition in a way that faithfully and effectively leads new groups of people to faith in Jesus Christ, and incorporates those who believe into the community of faith that obeys his teachings and gives witness of him to others.

Traditions (continued)

Appendix B

Defining the "Great Tradition"

The Great Tradition (sometimes called the "classical Christian tradition") is defined by Robert E. Webber as follows:

> *[It is] the broad outline of Christian belief and practice developed from the Scriptures between the time of Christ and the middle of the fifth century*
>
> ~ Webber. **The Majestic Tapestry**.
> Nashville: Thomas Nelson Publishers, 1986. p. 10.

This tradition is widely affirmed by Protestant theologians both ancient and modern.

> *Thus those ancient Councils of Nicea, Constantinople, the first of Ephesus, Chalcedon, and the like, which were held for refuting errors, we willingly embrace, and reverence as sacred, in so far as relates to doctrines of faith, for they contain nothing but the pure and genuine interpretation of Scripture, which the holy Fathers with spiritual prudence adopted to crush the enemies of religion who had then arisen.*
>
> ~ John Calvin. **Institutes**. IV, ix. 8.

> *. . . most of what is enduringly valuable in contemporary biblical exegesis was discovered by the fifth century.*
>
> ~ Thomas C. Oden. **The Word of Life**.
> San Francisco: HarperSanFrancisco, 1989. p. xi

> *The first four Councils are by far the most important, as they settled the orthodox faith on the Trinity and the Incarnation.*
>
> ~ Philip Schaff. **The Creeds of Christendom**. Vol. 1.
> Grand Rapids: Baker Book House, 1996. p. 44.

Our reference to the Ecumenical Councils and Creeds is, therefore, focused on those Councils which retain a widespread agreement in the Church among Catholics, Orthodox, and Protestants. While Catholic and Orthodox share common agreement on the first seven councils, Protestants tend to affirm and use primarily the first four. Therefore, those councils which continue to be shared by the whole Church are completed with the Council of Chalcedon in 451.

Traditions (continued)

It is worth noting that each of these four Ecumenical Councils took place in a pre-European cultural context and that none of them were held in Europe. They were councils of the whole Church and they reflected a time in which Christianity was primarily an eastern religion in it's geographic core. By modern reckoning, their participants were African, Asian, and European. The councils reflected a church that ". . . has roots in cultures far distant from Europe and preceded the development of modern European identity, and [of which] some of its greatest minds have been African" (Oden, *The Living God*, San Francisco: HarperSanFrancisco, 1987, p. 9).

Perhaps the most important achievement of the Councils was the creation of what is now commonly called the Nicene Creed. It serves as a summary statement of the Christian faith that can be agreed on by Catholic, Orthodox, and Protestant Christians.

The first four Ecumenical Councils are summarized in the following chart:

Name/Date/Location	Purpose
First Ecumenical Council 325 A.D. Nicea, Asia Minor	Defending against: *Arianism* Question answered: *Was Jesus God?* Action: *Developed the initial form of the Nicene Creed to serve as a summary of the Christian faith*
Second Ecumenical Council 381 A.D. Constantinople, Asia Minor	Defending against: *Macedonianism* Question answered: *Is the Holy Spirit a personal and equal part of the Godhead?* Action: *Completed the Nicene Creed by expanding the article dealing with the Holy Spirit*
Third Ecumenical Council 431 A.D. Ephesus, Asia Minor	Defending against: *Nestorianism* Question answered: *Is Jesus Christ both God and man in one person?* Action: *Defined Christ as the Incarnate Word of God and affirmed his mother Mary as **theotokos** (God-bearer)*
Fourth Ecumenical Council 451 A.D. Chalcedon, Asia Minor	Defending against: *Monophysitism* Question answered: *How can Jesus be both God and man?* Action: *Explained the relationship between Jesus' two natures (human and Divine)*

APPENDIX 14
A Theology of the Church in Kingdom Perspective
Don Davis and Terry Cornett

APPENDIX 15
Kingdom of God Timeline
Rev. Dr. Don L. Davis

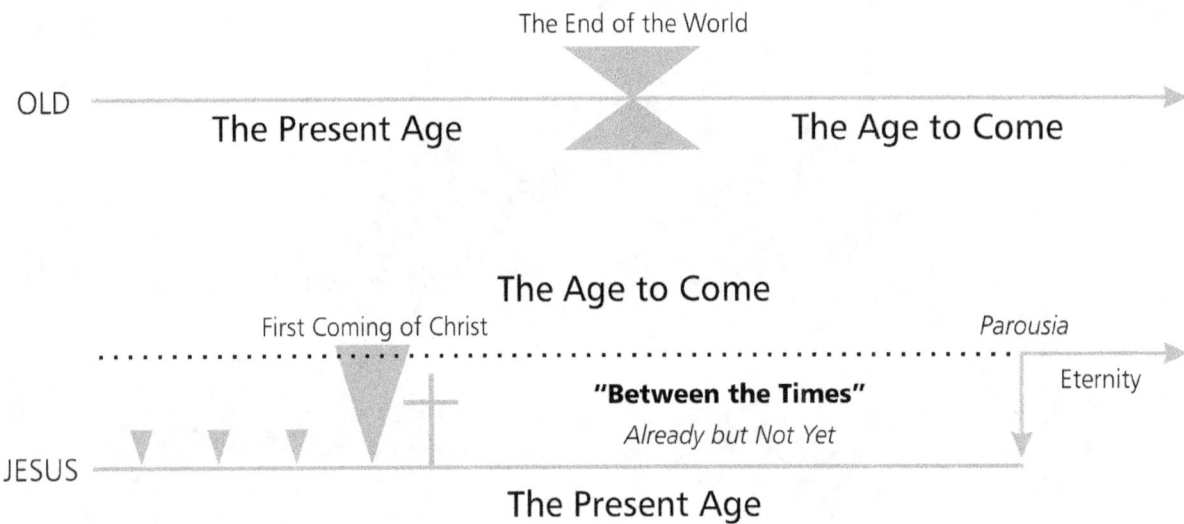

The "*malkuth*" of Yahweh, the "*basileia tou Theou.*" First century Palestinian Jews saw God as King, of his people Israel and all the earth. Yet, due to the rebellion of humankind and Satan and his angels, God's reign in the earth is **yet future**. It shall be: 1) nationalistic--the salvation and sovereignty of Israel over her enemies, 2) universal knowledge and reign of God, 3) *tsidkenu* (righteousness, justice) and *shalom* (peace), 4) obedience to the Law of God, 5) the final battle with the Gentile nations - Armageddon, 6) occur by a supernatural cataclysm realized at the end of time, 7) transformation of the heavens and earth to pre-Edenic splendor, 8) rule by the son of David-son of Man, 9) rescinding the effects of the curse, 10) the resurrection of the dead, 11) and judgment and destruction of all of God's enemies - sin, death, evil, the "world," the devil and his angels, and 12) eternal life.

Jesus' proclamation: **The Kingdom of God has now appeared in the life, person, and ministry of Messiah Jesus.** In Jesus' words (*kerygma*), his deeds of compassion (*diakinia*), his miracles, his exorcisms of demons, his passion, death, and resurrection, and the sending of the Spirit, **the promised-for Kingdom has come**. The Kingdom is **both** present and future; he announces **the presence of the future**. Present kingdom blessings include 1) the Church as sign and foretaste, 2) the pledge of the Holy Spirit, 3) the forgiveness of sin, 4) the proclamation of the Kingdom worldwide, 5) reconciliation and peace with God, 6) the binding of Satan, with authority given to Christ's disciples.

APPENDIX 16
Models of the Kingdom
Howard A Snyder, March 2002.

1. The Kingdom as Future Hope - the Future Kingdom

This has been a dominant model in the history of the Church. The emphasis is strongly on the future: a final culmination and reconciliation of all things which is more than merely the eternal existence of the soul. The model draws heavily on NT material. While some of the following models also represent future hope, here the note of futurity is determinative.

2. The Kingdom as Inner Spiritual Experience - the Interior Kingdom

A "spiritual kingdom" to be experienced in the heart or soul; "beatific vision." Highly mystical, therefore individualistic; an experience that can't really be shared with others. Examples: Julian of Norwich, other mystics; also some contemporary Protestant examples.

3. The Kingdom as Mystical Communion - the Heavenly Kingdom

The "communion of saints"; the Kingdom as essentially identified with heaven. Less individualistic. Often centers especially in worship and liturgy. Examples: John of Damascus, John Tauler; in somewhat different ways, Wesley and 19th and 20th-century revivalistic and Evangelical Protestantism. Kingdom is primarily other-worldly and future.

4. The Kingdom as Institutional Church - the Ecclesiastical Kingdom

The dominant view of medieval Christianity; dominant in Roman Catholicism until Vatican II. Pope as Vicar of Christ rules on earth in Christ's stead. The tension between the Church and the Kingdom largely dissolves. Traces to Augustine's City of God, but was developed differently from what Augustine believed. Protestant variations appear whenever the Church and Kingdom are too closely identified. Modern "Church Growth" thinking has been criticized at this point.

Models of the Kingdom (continued)

5. The Kingdom as Counter-System - the Subversive Kingdom

May be a protest to #4; sees the Kingdom as a reality which prophetically judges the sociopolitical order as well as the Church. One of the best examples: Francis of Assisi; also 16th century Radical Reformers; "Radical Christians" today; Sojourners magazine. Sees Church as counter-culture embodying the new order of the Kingdom.

6. The Kingdom as Political State - the Theocratic Kingdom

Kingdom may be seen as a political theocracy; Church and society not necessarily to be organized democratically. Tends to work from O.T. models, especially the Davidic Kingdom. Constantinian model; Byzantine Christianity a good example. Calvin's Geneva, perhaps, in a somewhat different sense. Problem of Luther's "two kingdoms" view.

7. The Kingdom as Christianized Society - the Transforming Kingdom

Here also the Kingdom provides a model for society, but more in terms of values & principles to be worked out in society. Kingdom in its fullness would be society completely leavened by Christian values. Post-millennialism; many mid-19th-century Evangelicals; early 20th-century Social Gospel. Kingdom manifested progressively in society, in contrast to premillennialism.

8. The Kingdom as Earthly Utopia - the Earthly Kingdom

May be seen as #7 taken to extreme. This view of the Kingdom is literally utopian. Tends to deny or downplay sin, or see evil as purely environmental. The view of many utopian communities (Cohn, *Pursuit of the Millennium*) including 19th-century U.S. and British examples. In a different way, the view of many of America's Founding Fathers. Most influential 20th-century example: Marxism. Liberation theology, to some degree. In a starkly different way: U.S. Fundamentalist premillennialism, combining this model with #1, #2 and/or #3 -Kingdom has no contemporary relevance, but will be literal utopia in the future. Thus similarities between Marxism and Fundamentalism.

APPENDIX 17
A Theology of the Church
Don L. Davis and Terry Cornett ©1996 World Impact Press

The Church Is an Apostolic Community
Where the Word Is Rightly Preached

I. **A Community of Calling**

   A. The essential meaning of Church is *Ekklesia*: those who have been "*called out*" in order to be "*called to*" a New Community.

      1. Like the Thessalonians, the Church is called out from idolatry to serve the living God and *called to* wait for his Son from heaven.

      2. The Church is *called out* in order that it may belong to Christ (Rom. 1.6). Jesus speaks of the Church as "my *ekklesia*" that is the "called out ones" who are his unique possession (Matt. 16.18; Gal. 5.24; James 2.7).

      3. The components of God's call:

         a. The foundation is God's desire to save (John 3.16, 1 Tim. 2.4).

         b. The message is the good news of the Kingdom (Matt. 24.14).

         c. The recipients are "whosoever will" (John 3.15).

         d. The method is through faith in the shed blood of Christ and acknowledgment of his lordship (Rom. 3.25; 10.9-10; Eph. 2.8).

         e. The result is regeneration and placement into the body of Christ (2 Cor. 5.17; Rom. 12.4-5; Eph. 3.6; 5.30).

   B. The Church is *called out*.

      1. Called out of the world:

         a. The world is under Satan's dominion and stands in opposition to God.

         b. Conversion and incorporation in Christ's Church involves repentance (*metanoia*) and a transfer of kingdom allegiances.

A Theology of the Church (continued)

    c. The Church exists as strangers and aliens who are "in" but not "of" this world system.

2. Called out from sin:

    a. Those in the Church are being sanctified, set apart for holy action, so that they may live out their calling as saints of God (1 Cor. 1.2; 2 Tim. 1.9, 1 Pet. 1.15).

    b. The Church must be available for God's purpose and use (Rom. 8.28-29; Eph. 1.11; Rom. 6.13).

    c. The Church must bring glory to God alone (Isa. 42.8; John 13.31-32; 17.1; Rom. 15.6; 1 Pet. 2.12).

    d. The Church must now be characterized by obedience to God (2 Thess. 1.8; Heb. 5.8-9; 1 John 2.3).

C. The Church is *called to*:

1. Salvation and new life

    a. Forgiveness and cleansing from sin (Eph. 1.7; 5.26; 1 John 1.9).

    b. Justification (Rom. 3.24; 8.30; Titus 3.7) in which God pronounces us guiltless as to the penalty of his divine law.

    c. Regeneration (John 3.5-8; Col. 3.9-10) by which a "new self" is birthed in us through the Spirit.

    d. Sanctification (John 17.19; 1 Cor. 1.2) in which we are "set apart" by God for holiness of life.

    e. Glorification and Life Eternal (Rom. 8.30, 1 Tim. 6.12; 2 Thess. 2.14) in which we are changed to be like Christ and prepared to live forever in the presence of God (Rom. 8.23; 1 Cor. 15.51-53; 1 John 3.2).

A Theology of the Church (continued)

2. Participation in a new community of God's chosen people (1 Pet. 2.9-10)

    a. Members of Christ's body (1 Cor. 10.16-17; 12.27).

    b. Sheep of God's flock under one Shepherd (John 10; Heb. 13.20; 1 Pet. 5.2-4).

    c. Members of God's family and household (Gal. 6.10; 1 Tim. 3.15).

    d. Children of Abraham and recipients of covenant promise (Rom. 4.16; Gal. 3.29; Eph. 2.12).

    e. Citizens of the New Jerusalem (Phil. 3.20; Rev. 3.12).

    f. The firstfruits of the Kingdom of God (Luke 12.32; James 1.18).

3. Freedom (Gal. 5.1, 13)

    a. Called out of the dominion of darkness which suppresses freedom (Col. 1.13-14).

    b. Called away from sin which enslaves (John 8.34-36).

    c. Called to God the Father who is the Liberator of his people (Exod. 6.6).

    d. Called to God the Son who gives the truth which sets free (John 8.31-36).

    e. Called to God the Spirit whose presence creates liberty (2 Cor. 3.17).

II. A Community of Faith

A. The Church is a community of faith, which has, by faith, confessed Jesus as Lord and Savior.

Faith refers both to ***the content of our belief*** and to ***the act of believing*** itself. Jesus is the object (content) of our faith and his life is received through faith (our belief) in him and his word. In both of these senses, the Church is a community of faith.

A Theology of the Church (continued)

1. The Church places its faith:

   a. in the Living Word (Jesus the Messiah),

   b. who is revealed in the written Word (Sacred Scripture),

   c. and who is now present, teaching and applying his Word to the Church (through the ministry of the Holy Spirit).

2. The Church guards the deposit of faith, given by Christ and the apostles, through sound teaching and the help of the Holy Spirit who indwells its members (2 Tim. 1.13-14).

B. Because it is a community of faith, the Church is also a community of grace.

   1. The Church exists by grace-through faith rather than through human merit or works (Gal. 2.21; Eph. 2.8).

   2. The Church announces, in faith, the grace of God to all humanity (Titus 2.11-15).

   3. The Church lives by grace in all actions and relationships (Eph. 4.1-7).

C. The Church is a community where the Scriptures are preached, studied, meditated upon, memorized, believed, and obeyed (Ezek. 7.10; Jos. 1.8; Ps. 119; Col. 3.16; 1 Tim. 4.13; James 1.22-25).

   1. The Church preaches the Gospel of the Kingdom, as revealed in Scripture, and calls people to repentance and faith which leads to obedience (Matt. 4.17; 28.19-20; Acts 2.38-40).

   2. The Church studies and applies the Scriptures through teaching, rebuking, correcting, and training in righteousness so that all members of the community are equipped to live godly lives characterized by good works (2 Tim. 3.16-17; 4.2).

   3. The Church intentionally reflects on the Scriptures in light of reason, tradition, and experience, learning and doing theology as a means of more fully understanding and acting upon truth (Ps. 119.97-99; 1 Tim. 4.16; 2 Tim. 2.15).

A Theology of the Church (continued)

4. The Church functions as a listening community which is aware of the Spirit's presence and relies upon him to interpret and apply the Scriptures to the present moment (John 14.25-26).

D. The Church contends for the faith that was once for all entrusted to the saints (Jude 3).

III. A Community of Witness

A. The Church witnesses to the fact that in the incarnation, life, teaching, death and resurrection of Jesus the Christ, God's Kingdom has begun (Mark 1.15; Luke 4.43; 6.20; 11.20; Acts 1.3; 28.23; 1 Cor. 4.20; Col. 1.12-13).

1. The Church proclaims Jesus as *Christus Victor* whose reign will:

    a. Rescind the curse over creation and humankind (Rev. 22.3).

    b. Defeat Satan and the powers and destroy their work (1 John 3.8).

    c. Reverse the present order by defending and rewarding the meek, the humble, the despised, the lowly, the righteous, the hungry, and the rejected (Luke 1.46-55; 4.18-19; 6.20-22).

    d. Propitiate God's righteous anger (Gal. 3.10-14; 1 John 2.1-2).

    e. Create a new humanity (1 Cor. 15.45-49; Eph. 2.15; Rev. 5.9-10).

    f. Destroy the last enemy- death (1 Cor. 15.26).

2. Ultimately, the very Kingdom itself will be turned over to God the Father, and the freedom, wholeness, and justice of the Lord will abound throughout the universe (Isa. 10.2-7; 11.1-9; 53.5; Mic. 4.1-3; 6.8; Matt. 6.33; 23.23; Luke 4.18-19; John 8.34-36; 1 Cor. 15.28; Rev. 21).

A Theology of the Church (continued)

B. The Church witnesses by:

1. Functioning as a sign and foretaste of the Kingdom of God; the Church is a visible community where people see that:

   a. Jesus is acknowledged as Lord (Rom. 10.9-10).

   b. The truth and power of the Gospel is growing and producing fruit among every kindred, tribe, and nation (Acts 2.47; Rom. 1.16; Col. 1.6; Rev. 7.9-10).

   c. The values of God's Kingdom are accepted and acted upon (Matt. 6.33).

   d. God's commands are obeyed on earth as they are in heaven (Matt. 6.10; John 14.23-24).

   e. The presence of God is experienced (Matt. 18.20; John 14.16-21).

   f. The power of God is demonstrated (1 Cor. 4.20).

   g. The love of God is freely received and given (Eph. 5.1-2; 1 John 3.18; 4.7-8).

   h. The compassion of God is expressed in bearing each other's burdens, first within the Church, and then, in sacrificial service to the whole world (Matt. 5.44-45; Gal. 6.2, 10; Heb. 13.16).

   i. The redemptiveness of God transcends human frailty and sin so that the treasure of the Kingdom is evident in spite of being contained in earthen vessels (2 Cor. 4.7).

2. Performing signs and wonders which confirm the Gospel (Mark 16.20; Acts 4.30; 8.6,13; 14.3; 15.12; Rom. 15.18-19; Heb. 2.4)

3. Accepting the call to mission

   a. Going into all the world to preach the Gospel (Matt. 24.14; 28.18-20; Acts 1.8, Col. 1.6).

   b. Evangelizing and making disciples of Christ and his Kingdom (Matt. 28.18-20; 2 Tim. 2.2).

A Theology of the Church (continued)

    c. Establishing churches among those unreached by the Gospel (Matt. 16.18; 28.19; Acts 2.41-42; 16.5; 2 Cor. 11.28; Heb. 12.22-23).

    d. Displaying the excellencies of Christ's Kingdom by engendering freedom, wholeness, and justice in his Name (Isa. 53.5; Mic. 6.8; Matt. 5.16; 12.18-20; Luke 4.18-19; John 8.34-36; 1 Pet. 3.11).

4. Acting as a prophetic community

    a. Speaking the Word of God into situations of error, confusion, and sin (2 Cor. 4.2; Heb. 4.12; James 5.20; Titus 2.15).

    b. Speaking up for those who cannot speak up for themselves so that justice is defended (Prov. 31.8-9).

    c. Announcing judgment against sin in all its forms (Rom. 2.5; Gal. 6.7-8; 1 Pet. 4.17).

    d. Announcing hope in situations where sin has produced despair (Jer. 32.17; 2 Thess. 2.16; Heb. 10.22-23; 1 Pet. 1.3-5).

    e. Proclaiming the return of Jesus, the urgency of the hour, and the reality that soon every knee will bow and every tongue confess that Jesus is Lord to the glory of God the Father (Matt. 25.1-13; Phil. 2.10-11; 2 Tim. 4.1, Titus 2.12-13).

The Church Is One Community
Where the Sacraments Are Rightly Administered

IV. A Community of Worship

  A. The Church recognizes that worship is the primary end of all creation.

    1. The worshiper adores, praises, and gives thanks to God for his character and actions, ascribing to him the worth and glory due his Person. This worship is directed to:

      a. The Father Almighty who is the Maker of all things visible and invisible.

A Theology of the Church (continued)

      b. The Son who by his incarnation, death, and resurrection accomplished salvation and who is now glorified at the Father's right hand.

      c. The Spirit who is the Lord and Giver of Life.

  2. Worship is the primary purpose of the material heavens and earth, and all life therein (Pss. 148-150; Luke 19.37-40; Rom. 11.36; Rev. 4.11; 15.3-4).

  3. Worship is the central activity of the angelic hosts who honor God in his presence (Isa. 6; Rev. 5).

  4. Worship is the chief vocation of the "community of saints," all true Christians, living and dead, who seek to glorify God in all things (Ps. 29.2; Rom. 12.1-2; 1 Cor. 10.31; Col. 3.17).

B. The Church offers acceptable worship to God. This means:

  1. The worshipers have renounced all false gods or belief systems that lay claim to their allegiance and have covenanted to serve and worship the one true God (Exod. 34.14; 1 Thess. 1.9-10).

  2. The worshipers worship:

      a. In Spirit - as regenerated people who, through saving faith in Jesus Christ, are filled with the Holy Spirit and under his direction.

      b. In Truth - understanding God as he is revealed in Scripture and worshiping in accordance with the teaching of the Word.

      c. In Holiness - Living lives that demonstrate their genuine commitment to serve the Living God.

C. The Church worships as a royal priesthood, wholeheartedly offering up sacrifices of praise to God and employing all its creative resources to worship him with excellence.

  1. The Christian Church is a people who worship, not a place of worship.

A Theology of the Church (continued)

2. The entire congregation ministers to the Lord, each one contributing a song, a word, a testimony, a prayer, etc. according to their gifts and capacities (1 Cor. 14.26).

3. The Church worships with the full range of human emotion, intellect, and creativity:

    a. Physical expression- raising of hands, dancing, kneeling, bowing, etc.

    b. Intellectual engagement- striving to understand God's nature and works.

    c. Artistic expression- through music and the other creative arts.

    d. Celebratory expression- the Church plays in the presence of God (Prov. 8.30-31) experiencing "Sabbath rest" through festivals, celebrations, and praise.

4. The Church worships liturgically by together reenacting the story of God and his people.

    a. The Church proclaims and embodies the drama of God's redemptive action in its ritual, tradition, and order of worship.

    b. The Church, like the covenant people Israel, orders its life around the celebration of the Lord's Supper and Baptism which reenact the story of God's salvation (Deut. 16.3; Matt. 28.19; Rom. 6.4; 1 Cor. 11.23-26).

    c. The Church remembers the worship and service of saints through the ages, learning from their experiences with the Spirit of God (Deut. 32.7; Pss. 77.10-12; 143.5; Isa. 46.9; Heb. 11).

5. The Church worships in freedom:

    a. Constantly experiencing new forms and expressions of worship which honor God and allow his people to delight in him afresh (Pss. 33.3; 40.3; 96.1; 149.1; Isa. 42.9-10; Luke 5.38; Rev. 5.9).

A Theology of the Church (continued)

      b. Being led by the Spirit so that its worship is responsive to God himself (2 Cor. 3.6; Gal. 5.25; Phil. 3.3).

      c. Expressing the unchanging nature of God in forms that are conducive to the particular cultures and personalities of the worshipers (Acts 15).

  6. The Church worships in right order, making sure that each act of worship edifies the body, and stands in accordance with the Word of God (1 Cor. 14.12, 33, 40; Gal. 5.13-15, 22-25; Eph. 4.29; Phil. 4.8).

D. The Church's worship leads to wholeness:

  1. Health and blessing attend the worshiping community (Exod. 23.25; Ps. 147.1-3).

  2. The community takes on the character of the One who is worshiped (Exod. 29.37; Ps. 27.4; Jer. 2.5; 10.8; Matt. 6.21; Col. 3.1-4; 1 John 3.2).

V. A Community of Covenant

A. The Church is the gathering of those who participate in the New Covenant. This New Covenant:

  1. Is mediated by Jesus Christ, the Great High Priest, and is purchased and sealed by his blood (Matt. 26.28; 1 Tim. 2.5; Heb. 8.6; 4.14-16).

  2. Is initiated and participated in only through the electing grace of God (Rom. 8.29-30; 2 Tim. 1.9; Titus 1.1; 1 Pet. 1.1).

  3. Is a covenant of peace (*Shalom*) which gives access to God (Ezek. 34.23-31; Rom. 5.1-2; Eph. 2.17-18; Heb. 7.2-3).

  4. Is uniquely celebrated and experienced in the Lord's Supper and Baptism (Mark 14.22-25; 1 Cor. 10.16; Col. 2.12; 1 Pet. 3.21).

A Theology of the Church (continued)

5. By faith, both imputes and imparts righteousness to the participants so that God's laws are put in the hearts and written on their minds (Jer. 31.33; Rom. 1.17; 2 Cor. 5.21; Gal. 3.21-22; Phil. 1.11; 3.9; Heb. 10.15-17; 12.10-11; 1 Pet. 2.24).

B. The Covenant enables us to understand and experience Christian sanctification:

1. Righteousness: right relationships with God and others (Exod. 20.1-17; Mic. 6.8; Mark 12.29-31; James 2.8).

2. Truth: right beliefs about God and others (Ps. 86.11; Isa. 45.19; John 8.31-32, 17.17; 1 Pet. 1.22).

3. Holiness: right actions toward God and others (Lev. 11.45; 20.8; Eccles. 12.13; Matt. 7.12; 2 Cor. 7.1; Col. 3.12; 2 Pet. 3.11).

C. The purpose of the New Covenant is to enable the Church to be like Christ Jesus:

1. Jesus is the new pattern for humanity:

   a. The second Adam (Rom. 5.12-17; 1 Cor. 15.45-49).

   b. The likeness into which the Church is fashioned (Rom. 8.29; 1 John 3.2).

   c. His life, character, and teaching are the standard for faith and practice (John 13.17; 20.21; 2 John 6, 9, 1 Cor. 11.1).

2. This covenant is made possible by the sacrifice of Christ himself (Matt. 26.27-29; Heb. 8-10).

3. The apostolic ministry of the new covenant is meant to conform believers to the image of Christ (2 Cor. 3; Eph. 4.12-13).

A Theology of the Church (continued)

  D. The Covenant binds us to those who have gone before.

  1. It recognizes that the Church is one (Eph. 4.4-5).

  2. It reminds us that we are surrounded by a cloud of witnesses who have participated in the same covenant (Heb. 12.1).

  3. It reminds us that we are part of a sacred chain:

     God-Christ-Apostles-Church.

  4. It reminds us that we share the same:

     a. Spiritual parentage (John 1.13; 3.5-6; 2 Cor. 1.2; Gal. 4.6; 1 John 3.9).

     b. Family likeness (Eph. 3.15; Heb. 2.11).

     c. Lord, faith and baptism (Eph. 4.5).

     d. Indwelling Spirit (John 14.17; Rom. 8.9; 2 Cor. 1.22).

     e. Calling and mission (Eph. 4.1; Heb. 3.1; 2 Pet. 1.10).

     f. Hope and destiny (Gal. 5.5; Eph. 1.18; Eph. 4.4; Col. 1.5).

  5. Causes us to understand that since we share the same covenant, administered by the same Lord, under the leadership of the same Spirit with those Christians who have come before us, we must necessarily reflect upon the creeds, the councils, and the actions of the Church throughout history in order to understand the apostolic tradition and the ongoing work of the Holy Spirit (1 Cor. 11.16).

VI. A Community of Presence

  A. "Where Jesus Christ is, there is the Church" - Ignatius of Antioch (Matt. 18.20).

A Theology of the Church (continued)

B. The Church is the dwelling place of God (Eph. 2.19-21):

   1. His nation

   2. His household

   3. His temple

C. The Church congregates in eager anticipation of God's presence (Eph. 2.22).

   1. The Church now comes into the presence of God at every gathering:

      a. Like the covenant people in the Old Testament, the Church gathers in the presence of God (Exod. 18.12; 34.34; Deut. 14.23; 15.20; Ps. 132.7; Heb. 12.18-24).

      b. The gathered Church makes manifest the reality of the Kingdom of God by being in the presence of the King (1 Cor. 14.25).

   2. The Church anticipates the future gathering of the people of God when the fullness of God's presence will be with them all (Ezek. 48.35; 2 Cor. 4.14; 1 Thess. 3.13; Rev. 21.13).

D. The Church is absolutely dependent on the presence of the Spirit of Christ.

   1. Without the presence of the Holy Spirit there is no Church (Acts 2.38; Rom. 8.9; 1 Cor. 12.13; Gal. 3.3; Eph. 2.22; 4.4; Phil. 3.3).

   2. The Holy Spirit creates, directs, empowers, and teaches congregations of believers (John 14.16-17, 26; Acts 1.8; 2.17; 13.1; Rom. 15.13, 19; 2 Cor. 3.18).

   3. The Holy Spirit gives gifts to the Church so that it can accomplish its mission, bringing honor and glory to God (Rom. 12.4-8; 1 Cor. 12.1-31; Heb. 2.4).

   4. The Holy Spirit binds the Church together as the family of God and the body of Christ (2 Cor. 13.14; Eph. 4.3).

A Theology of the Church (continued)

E. The Church is a Kingdom of priests which stands in God's presence (1 Pet. 2.5, 9):

1. Ministering before the Lord (Ps. 43.4; Ps. 134.1-2).

2. Placing God's blessing on his people (Num. 6.22-27; 2 Cor. 13.14).

3. Bringing people before the attention of God (1 Thess. 1.3; 2 Tim. 1.3).

4. Offering themselves and the fruit of their ministry to God (Isa. 66.20, Rom. 12.1; 15.16).

F. The Church lives in God's presence through prayer.

1. Prayer as access to the Holy of holies (Rev. 5.8).

2. Prayer as communion with God (Ps. 5.3; Rom. 8.26-27).

3. Prayer as intercession.

    a. For the world (1 Tim. 2.1-2).

    b. For the saints (Eph. 6.18-20, 1 Thess. 5.25).

4. Prayer as thanksgiving (Phil. 4.6; Col. 1.3).

5. Prayer as the warfare of the Kingdom.

    a. Binding and loosing (Matt. 16.19).

    b. Engaging the principalities and powers (Eph. 6.12,18).

The Church Is a Holy Community Where Discipline Is Rightly Ordered

VII. A Community of Reconciliation

A. The Church is a community that is reconciled to God: all reconciliation is ultimately dependent on God's reconciling actions toward humanity.

A Theology of the Church (continued)

1. God's desire to reconcile is evidenced by sending his prophets and in the last days by his Son (Heb. 1.1-2).

2. The incarnation, the life, the death, and the resurrection of Jesus are the ultimate acts of reconciliation from God toward humanity (Rom. 5.8).

3. The Gospel is now a message of reconciliation, made possible by Christ's death, that God offers to humanity (2 Cor. 5.16-20).

B. The Church is a community of individuals and peoples that are reconciled to each other by their common identity as one body.

1. By his death Christ united his people who are born of the same seed (1 John 3.9), reconciled as fellow citizens and members of a new humanity (Eph. 2.11-22).

2. The Church community treats all members of God's household with love and justice in spite of differences in race, class, gender, and culture because they are organically united by their participation in the body of Christ (Gal. 3.26-29; Col. 3.11).

C. The Church is a community that is concerned for reconciliation among all peoples.

1. The Church functions an ambassador that invites all people to be reconciled to God (2 Cor. 5.19-20). This task of mission lays the foundation for all the reconciling activities of the Church.

2. The Church promotes reconciliation with and between all people.

   a. Because the Church is commanded to love its enemies (Matt. 5.44-48).

   b. Because the Church is an incarnational community which seeks, like Christ, to identify with those alienated from itself.

A Theology of the Church (continued)

    c. Because the Church embodies and works for the vision of the Kingdom of God in which peoples, nations, and nature itself will be completely reconciled and at peace (Isa. 11.1-9; Mic. 4.2-4; Matt. 4.17; Acts 28.31).

    d. Because the Church recognizes the eternal plan of God to reconcile all things in heaven and on earth under one head, the Lord Jesus Christ, in order that the Kingdom may be handed over to God the Father who will be all in all (Eph. 1.10; Rom. 11.36; 1 Cor. 15.27-28; Rev. 11.15, 21.1-17).

D. The Church is a community of friendship: friendship is a key part of reconciliation and spiritual development.

  1. Spiritual maturity results in friendship with God (Exod. 33.11; James 2.23).

  2. Spiritual discipleship results in friendship with Christ (John 15.13-15).

  3. Spiritual unity is expressed in friendship with the saints (Rom. 16.5, 9, 12; 2 Cor. 7.1; Phil. 2.12; Col. 4.14; 1 Pet. 2.11; 1 John 2.7; 3 John 1.14).

VIII. A Community of Suffering

A. The Church community suffers because it exists in the world as "sheep among wolves" (Luke 10.3).

  1. Hated by those who reject Christ (John 15.18-20).

  2. Persecuted by the world system (Matt. 5.10; 2 Cor. 4.9; 2 Tim. 3.12).

  3. It is uniquely the community of the poor, the hungry, the weeping, the hated, the excluded, the insulted, and the rejected (Matt. 5.20-22).

  4. It is founded on the example and experience of Christ and the apostles (Isa. 53.3; Luke 9.22; Luke 24.46; Acts 5.41; 2 Tim. 1.8; 1 Thess. 2.2).

A Theology of the Church (continued)

B. The Church community imitates Christ in his suffering.

1. Because it purifies from sin (1 Pet. 4.1-2).

2. Because it teaches obedience (Heb. 5.8).

3. Because it allows them to know Christ more fully (Phil. 3.10).

4. Because those who share in Christ's suffering will also share in his comfort and glory (Rom. 8.17-18; 2 Cor. 1.5; 1 Pet. 5.1).

C. The Church community suffers because it identifies with those who suffer.

1. The body of Christ suffers whenever one of its members suffers (1 Cor. 12.26).

2. The body of Christ suffers because it voluntarily identifies itself with the despised, the rejected, the oppressed, and the unlovely (Prov. 29.7; Luke 7.34; Luke 15.1-2).

D. The cross of Christ is both the instrument of salvation and the pattern for Christian life. The cross embodies the values of the Church community.

1. The cross of Christ is the most fundamental Christian symbol. It serves as a constant reminder that the Church is a community of suffering.

2. The basic requirement of discipleship is a willingness to take up the cross daily and follow Jesus (Mark 8.34; Luke 9.23; Luke 14.27).

IX. A Community of Works

A. "Works of Service" are the hallmark of Christian congregations as they do justice, love mercy, and walk humbly with God.

1. The leadership of the Church is charged with preparing God's people for "works of service" (Eph. 4.12).

2. These good works are central to the new purpose and identity which is given us during the new birth. "For we are his workmanship, created in

A Theology of the Church (continued)

> Christ Jesus for good works, which God prepared beforehand, that we should walk in them" (Eph. 2.10).
>
> 3. These works of service reveal God's character to the world and lead people to give him praise (Matt. 5.16; 2 Cor. 9.13).

B. Servanthood characterizes the Christian's approach to relationships, resources, and ministry.

1. The Church community serves based on the example of Christ who came "not to be served but to serve" (Matt. 20.25-28; Luke 22.27; Phil. 2.7).

2. The Church community serves based on the command of Christ and the apostles (Mark 10.42-45; Gal. 5.13; 1 Pet. 4.10).

3. The Church community serves, first of all, "the least of these" according to the mandates of Christ's teaching (Matt. 18.2-5; Matt. 25. 34-46; Luke 4.18-19).

C. Generosity and hospitality are the twin signs of kingdom service.

1. Generosity results in the giving of one's self and one's good for the sake of announcing and obeying Christ and his kingdom reign.

2. Hospitality results in treating the stranger, the foreigner, the prisoner, and the enemy as one of your very own people (Heb. 13.2).

3. These signs are the true fruit of repentance (Luke 3.7-14; Luke 19.8-10; James 1.27)

D. Stewardship is the foundational truth which governs the way the Church uses resources in order to do "Works of Service."

1. Our resources (time, money, authority, health, position, etc.) belong not to ourselves but to God.

A Theology of the Church (continued)

      a. We answer to God for our management of the things entrusted to us personally and corporately (Matt. 25.14-30).

      b. Money should be managed in such as way that treasures are laid up in heaven (Matt. 6.19-21; Luke 12.32-34; Luke 16.1-15; 1 Tim. 6.17-19).

      c. Seeking first the Kingdom of God is the standard by which our stewardship is measured and the basis upon which more will be entrusted (Matt. 6.33).

  2. Proper stewardship should contribute to equality and mutual sharing (2 Cor. 8.13-15).

  3. Greed is indicative of dishonest stewardship and a repudiation of God as the owner and giver of all things (Luke 12.15; Luke 16.13; Eph. 5.5; Col. 3.5; 1 Pet. 5.2).

E. Justice is a key goal of the Church as it serves God and others.

  1. Doing justice is an essential part of fulfilling our service to God (Deut. 16.20; 27.19; Pss. 33.5; 106.3; Prov. 28.5; Mic. 6.8; Matt. 23.23).

  2. Justice characterizes the righteous servant but is absent from the hypocrite and the unrighteous (Prov. 29.7; Isa. 1.17; 58.1-14; Matt. 12.18-20; Luke 11.42).

APPENDIX 18
Our Declaration of Dependence: Freedom in Christ

It is important to teach morality within the realm of freedom (i.e., Gal. 5.1, "It is for freedom Christ has set you free"), and always in the context of using your freedom in the framework of bringing God glory and advancing Christ's Kingdom. I emphasize the "6-8-10" principles of 1 Corinthians, and apply them to all moral issues.

1. 1 Cor. 6.9-11, Christianity is about transformation in Christ; no amount of excuses will get a person into the Kingdom.

2. 1 Cor. 6.12a, We are free in Christ, but not everything one does is edifying or helpful.

3. 1 Cor. 6.12b, We are free in Christ, but anything that is addictive and exercising control over you is counter to Christ and his Kingdom.

4. 1 Cor. 8.7-13, We are free in Christ, but we ought never to flaunt our freedom, especially in the face of Christians whose conscience would be marred and who would stumble if they saw us doing something they found offensive.

5. 1 Cor. 10.23, We are free in Christ; all things are lawful for us, but neither is everything helpful, nor does doing everything build oneself up.

6. 1 Cor. 10.24, We are free in Christ, and ought to use our freedom to love our brothers and sisters in Christ, and nurture them for other's well being (cf. Gal. 5.13).

7. 1 Cor. 10.31, We are free in Christ, and are given that freedom in order that we might glorify God in all that we do, whether we eat or drink, or anything else.

8. 1 Cor. 10.32-33, We are free in Christ, and ought to use our freedom in order to do what we can to give no offense to people in the world or the Church, but do what we do in order to influence them to know and love Christ, i.e., that they might be saved.

This focus on freedom, in my mind, places all things that we say to adults or teens in context. Often, the way in which many new Christians are discipled is through a

Our Declaration of Dependence - Freedom in Christ (continued)

rigorous taxonomy (listing) of different vices and moral ills, and this can at times give them the sense that Christianity is an anti-act religion (a religion of simply not doing things), and/or a faith overly concerned with not sinning. Actually, the moral focus in Christianity is on freedom, a freedom won at a high price, a freedom to love God and advance the Kingdom, a freedom to live a surrendered life before the Lord. The moral responsibility of urban Christians is to live free in Jesus Christ, to live free unto God's glory, and to not use their freedom from the law as a license for sin.

The core of the teaching, then, is to focus on the freedom won for us through Christ's death and resurrection, and our union with him. We are now set free from the law, the principle of sin and death, the condemnation and guilt of our own sin, and the conviction of the law on us. We serve God now out of gratitude and thankfulness, and the moral impulse is living free in Christ. Yet, we do not use our freedom to be wiseguys or knuckle-heads, but to glorify God and love others. This is the context in which we address the thorny issues of homosexuality, abortion, and other social ills. Those who engage in such acts feign freedom, but, lacking a knowledge of God in Christ, they are merely following their own internal predispositions, which are not informed either by God's moral will or his love.

Freedom in Christ is a banner call to live holy and joyously as urban disciples. This freedom will enable them to see how creative they can be as Christians in the midst of so-called "free" living which only leads to bondage, shame, and remorse.

APPENDIX 19
Dealing With Old Ways
Adapted from Paul Hiebert

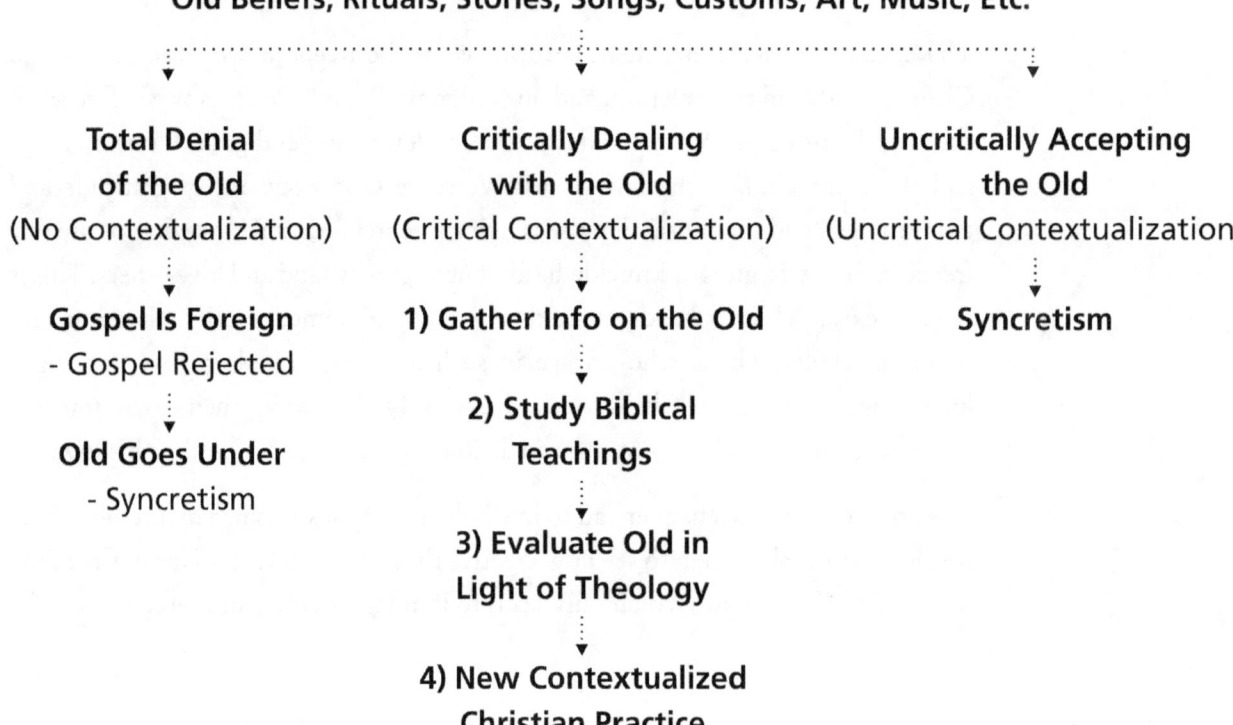

APPENDIX 20
Discipling the Faithful: Establishing Leaders for the Urban Church
Crowns of Beauty Conference. Don Davis. February 1998.

	Commission	Character	Competence	Community
Definition	Recognizes the call of God and replies with prompt obedience to his lordship and leading	Reflects the character of Christ in their personal convictions, conduct, and lifestyle	Responds in the power of the Spirit with excellence in carrying out their appointed tasks and ministry	Regards multiplying disciples in the body of Christ as the primary role of ministry
Key Scripture	2 Tim. 1.6-14; 1 Tim. 4.14; Acts 1.8; Matt. 28.18-20	John 15.4-5; 2 Tim. 2.2; 1 Cor. 4.2; Gal. 5.16-23	2 Tim. 2.15; 3.16-17; Rom. 15.14; 1 Cor. 12	Eph. 4.9-15; 1 Cor. 12.1-27
Critical Concept	The Authority of God: God's leader acts on God's recognized call and authority, acknowledged by the saints and God's leaders	The Humility of Christ: God's leader demonstrates the mind and lifestyle of Christ in his or her actions and relationships	The Power of the Spirit: God's leader operates in the gifting and anointing of the Holy Spirit	The Growth of the Church: God's leader uses all of his or her resources to equip and empower the body of Christ for his/her goal and task
Central Elements	A clear call from God Authentic testimony before God and others Deep sense of personal conviction based on Scripture Personal burden for a particular task or people Confirmation by leaders and the body	Passion for Christlikeness Radical lifestyle for the Kingdom Serious pursuit of holiness Discipline in the personal life Fulfills role-relationships as bondslave of Jesus Christ Provides an attractive model for others in their conduct, speech, and lifestyle (the fruit of the Spirit)	Endowments and gifts from the Spirit Sound discipling from an able mentor Skill in the spiritual disciplines Ability in the Word Able to evangelize, follow up, and disciple new converts Strategic in the use of resources and people to accomplish God's task	Genuine love for and desire to serve God's people Disciples faithful individuals Facilitates growth in small groups Pastors and equips believers in the congregation Nurtures associations and networks among Christians and churches Advances new movements among God's people locally
Satanic Strategy to Abort	Operates on the basis of personality or position rather than on God's appointed call and ongoing authority	Substitutes ministry activity and/or hard work and industry for godliness and Christlikeness	Functions on natural gifting and personal ingenuity rather than on the Spirit's leading and gifting	Exalts tasks and activities above equipping the saints and developing Christian community
Key Steps	Identify God's call Discover your burden Be confirmed by leaders	Abide in Christ Discipline for godliness Pursue holiness in all	Discover the Spirit's gifts Receive excellent training Hone your performance	Embrace God's Church Learn leadership's contexts Equip concentrically
Results	Deep confidence in God arising from God's call	Powerful Christlike example provided for others to follow	Dynamic working of the Holy Spirit	Multiplying disciples in the Church

APPENDIX 21
Readings on the Church

The People of God: Living the Adventure of the *Ekklesia*

1 Pet. 2.9-12 (ESV) - But you are a chosen race, a royal priesthood, a holy nation, a people for his own possession, that you may proclaim the excellencies of him who called you out of darkness into his marvelous light. [10] Once you were not a people, but now you are God's people; once you had not received mercy, but now you have received mercy. [11] Beloved, I urge you as sojourners and exiles to abstain from the passions of the flesh, which wage war against your soul. [12] Keep your conduct among the Gentiles honorable, so that when they speak against you as evildoers, they may see your good deeds and glorify God on the day of visitation.

The identification of Christians as "the people of God" appears a number of times in the New Testament (e.g. Luke 1.17; Acts 15.14; Titus 2.14; Heb. 4.9; 8.10; 1 Pet. 2.9-10; Rev. 18.4; 21.3). But it is used by Paul with special significance in Romans 9.25-26; 11.1-2; 15.10, and 2 Corinthians 6.16 to set the Christian church in the context of the long story of God's dealing with his chosen people Israel. "People of God," a covenant expression, speaks of God's choosing and calling a particular people into covenantal relationship (Exod. 19.5; Deut. 7.6; 14.2; Ps. 135.4; Heb. 8.10; 1 Pet. 2.9-10; Rev. 21.3). They are God's gracious initiative and magnanimous action in creating, calling, saving, judging, and sustaining them. And as God's people, they experience God's presence among them.

~ Richard Longenecker, ed.
Community Formation in the Early Church and in the Church Today.
Peabody, MA: Hendrickson Publishers, 2002. p. 75.

Where Biblical Study of Leadership Begins: The Church as Context for World Change

[A] biblical study on leadership must begin with the story of the church that came into existence on the Day of Pentecost. The term *ekklesia* is used more than one hundred times in the New Testament. In fact, it's virtually impossible to understand God's will for our lives as believers without comprehending this wonderful "mystery of Christ" that has "been revealed by the Spirit to God's holy apostles and prophets" (Eph. 3.4-5).

Readings on the Church (continued)

Beyond the Gospels, most of the NT is the story of "local churches" and how God intended them to function. True, Jesus Christ came to lay the foundation and to build his *ekklesia* (Matt. 16.18) and when he said to Peter, "I will build my *church*," He was certainly thinking more broadly than establishing a "local church" in Caesarea Philippi where this conversation took place (Matt. 16.13-20). . . .

On the other hand, Jesus was also anticipating the multitude of *local churches* that would be established in Judea and Samaria and throughout the Roman Empire--and eventually all over the world as we know it today. This story begins in the book of Acts and spans a significant period during the first century (approximately from A.D. 33 to A.D. 63). Furthermore, during this time frame, most of the New Testament letters were written to these local churches--or to men like Timothy and Titus who were helping to establish these churches.

~ Gene Getz. **Elders and Leaders**. Chicago: Moody, 2003. pp. 47-48.

A World to Change, a World to Win

If anyone is going to change the world for the better, it may be argued, it ought to be the Christians, not the Communists. For myself, I would say that if we started applying our Christianity to the society in which we live, then it would be we, indeed, who would change the world. Christians, too, have a world to change and a world to win. Had the early Christians gone in for slogans these might well have been theirs. They might be ours too. There is no reason at all why they should be the monopoly of the Communists *[and the Muslims, and the atheists, and the hedonists, and the secular humanists, and the . . .]*

~ Douglas Hyde, **Dedication and Leadership**, pp. 32-33

Those Who Turn the World Upside Down Have Themselves Been Turned Inside Out

The bitterest foe became the greatest friend. The Blasphemer became the preacher of Christ's love. The hand that wrote the indictment of the disciples of Christ when he brought them before magistrates and into prison now penned epistles of God's redeeming love. The heart that once beat with joy when Stephen sank beneath the bloody stones now rejoiced in scourgings and stonings for the sake of Christ.

Readings on the Church (continued)

From this erstwhile enemy, persecutor, blasphemer came the greater part of the New Testament, the noblest statements of theology, the sweetest lyrics of Christian love.

~ C. E. Macartney in **Dynamic Spiritual Leadership** by J. Oswald Sanders. pp. 33-34

APPENDIX 22
Five Views of the Relationship between Christ and Culture
Based on **Christ and Culture** by H. Richard Niebuhr. New York: Harper and Row, 1951.

Christ Against Culture	Christ and Culture in Paradox	Christ the Transformer of Culture	Christ Above Culture	The Christ of Culture
Opposition	Tension	Conversion	Cooperation	Acceptance
Therefore come out from them and be separate, says the Lord. Touch no unclean thing, and I will receive you. - 2 Cor. 6.17 (cf. 1 John 2.15)	Give to Caesar what is Caesar's, and to God what is God's. - Matt. 22.21 (cf. 1 Pet. 2.13-17)	In putting everything under him, God left nothing that is not subject to him. Yet at present we do not see everything subject to him. - Heb. 2.8 (cf. Col. 1.16-18)	Indeed, when Gentiles, who do not have the law, do by nature things required by the law, they are a law for themselves. - Rom. 2.14 (cf. Rom. 13.1, 5-6)	Every good and perfect gift is from above, coming down from the Father of the heavenly lights, who does not change like shifting shadows. - James 1.17 (cf. Phil. 4.8)
Culture is radically affected by sin and constantly opposes the will of God. Separation and opposition are the natural responses of the Christian community which is itself an alternative culture.	Culture is radically affected by sin but does have a role to play. It is necessary to delineate between spheres: Culture as law (restrains wickedness), Christianity as grace (gives righteousness). Both are an important part of life but the two cannot be confused or merged.	Culture is radically affected by sin but can be redeemed to play a positive role in restoring righteousness. Christians should work to have their culture acknowledge Christ's lordship and be changed by it.	Culture is a product of human reason and is part of a God-given way to discover truth. Although culture can discern real truth, sin limits its capacities which must be aided by revelation. Seeks to use culture as a first step toward the understanding of God and his revelation.	Culture is God's gift to help man overcome his bondage to nature and fear and advance in knowledge and goodness. Human culture is what allows us to conserve the truth humanity has learned. Jesus' moral teaching moves human culture upward to a new level.
Tertullian, Menno Simons Anabaptists	Martin Luther Lutherans	St. Augustine, John Calvin Reformed	Thomas Aquinas Roman Catholic	Peter Abelard, Immanual Kant Liberal Protestant

APPENDIX 23
That We May Be One
Elements of an Integrated Church Planting Movement Among the Urban Poor
Rev. Dr. Don L. Davis

Church Planting Movements among the Urban Poor = an integrated and aggressive advance of the Kingdom of God among the urban poor resulting in a significant increase of indigenous churches which fundamentally share in common a constellation of elements which provides them with a distinct and unique identity, purpose, and practice.

Ministry among the urban poor must be grounded in a vision and understanding of the liberty we have in Christ to conceive of coherent, integrated movements of followers of Jesus who because of shared experience, proximity, culture, and history *determine to reflect their unique faith and practice in a way consistent with the historic faith but distinct to their life and times.* This is not an arbitrary act; movements cannot ignore the nature of the one (unity), holy (sanctity), catholic (universality), and apostolic (apostolicity) Church, the one true people of God.

Nevertheless, as was affirmed by the emerging leaders of the then American Episcopal Church, the freedom that we have in Christ allows for different forms and usages of worship in the body of Christ without any offense whatsoever, as long as we are faithful to the historic orthodox beliefs of the Church as taught to us by the prophets and apostles of our Lord. Doctrine must remain anchored and complete; discipline, however, can be based on the contingencies and exigencies of the people who embrace them, as long as all that is shaped and conceived builds up the body of Christ, and glorifies God our Father through our Lord Jesus Christ.

"The congregations in an Integrated Church Planting Movement Among the Urban Poor *will exhibit together:*"

1. *A shared history and identity* (i.e., *a common name and heritage*). CPMs among the urban poor will seek to link themselves to and identify themselves by a well defined and joyfully shared history and persona that all members and congregations share.

It is a most invaluable part of that blessed "liberty wherewith Christ hath made us free," that in his worship different forms and usages may without offence be allowed, provided the substance of the Faith be kept entire; and that, in every Church, what cannot be clearly determined to belong to Doctrine must be referred to Discipline; and therefore, by common consent and authority, may be altered, abridged, enlarged, amended, or otherwise disposed of, as may seem most convenient for the edification of the people, "according to the various exigency of times and occasions."
~ 1789 Preface to the *Book of Common Prayer.* 1928 Episcopal edition.

That We May Be One (continued)

2. *A shared liturgy and celebration* (i.e., *a common worship*). CPMs among the urban poor should reflect a shared hymnody, practice of the sacraments, theological focus and imagery, aesthetic vision, vestments, liturgical order, symbology, and spiritual formation that enables us to worship and glorify God in a way that lifts up the Lord and attracts urbanites to vital worship.

3. *A shared membership, well-being, welfare, and support* (i.e., *a common order and discipline*). CPMs among the urban poor must be anchored in evangelical and historically orthodox presentations of the Gospel that result in conversions to Jesus Christ and incorporation into local churches.

4. *A shared catechism and doctrine* (i.e., *a common faith*). CPMs among the urban poor must embrace a common biblical theology and express it practically in a Christian education that reflects their commonly held faith.

5. *A shared church government and authority* (i.e., *a common polity*). CPMs among the urban poor must be organized around a common polity, ecclesial management, and submit to flexible governing policies that allow for effective and efficient management of their resources and congregations.

6. *A shared leadership development structure* (i.e., *a common pastoral strategy*). CPMs among the urban poor are committed with supplying each congregation with godly undershepherds, and seek to identify, equip, and support its pastors and missionaries in order that their members may grow to maturity in Christ.

7. *A shared financial philosophy and procedure* (i.e., *a common stewardship*). CPMs among the urban poor strive to handle all of their financial affairs and resources with wise, streamlined, and reproducible policies that allow for the good management of their monies and goods, locally, regionally, and nationally.

8. *A shared care and support ministry* (i.e., *a common service*). CPMs among the urban poor seek to practically demonstrate the love and justice of the Kingdom among its members and towards others in the city in ways that allow individuals and congregations to love their neighbors as they love themselves.

9. *A shared evangelism and outreach* (i.e., *a common mission*): CPMs among the urban poor network and collaborate among their members in order to clearly present Jesus and his Kingdom to the lost in the city in order to multiply new congregations in unreached urban areas as quickly as possible.

That We May Be One (continued)

10. *A shared vision for connection and association* (i.e., *a common partnership*). CPMs among the urban poor must seek to make fresh connections, links, and relationships with other movements for the sake of regular communication, fellowship, and mission.

These principles of belonging, camaraderie, and identity lay the foundation for a new paradigm of authentic ecumenical unity, the kind that can lead to partnerships and collaboration of grand scope and deep substance. Below is a short overview of the TUMI biblical basis for the kind of partnerships which can fuel and sustain credible church planting movements among the urban poor.

God's Partners and Fellow Workers

1 Cor. 3.1-9 (ESV) - But I, brothers, could not address you as spiritual people, but as people of the flesh, as infants in Christ. [2] I fed you with milk, not solid food, for you were not ready for it. And even now you are not yet ready, [3] for you are still of the flesh. For while there is jealousy and strife among you, are you not of the flesh and behaving only in a human way? [4] For when one says, "I follow Paul," and another, "I follow Apollos," are you not being merely human? [5] What then is Apollos? What is Paul? Servants through whom you believed, as the Lord assigned to each. [6] I planted, Apollos watered, but God gave the growth. [7] So neither he who plants nor he who waters is anything, but only God who gives the growth. [8] He who plants and he who waters are one, and each will receive his wages according to his labor. [9] For we are God's fellow workers. You are God's field, God's building.

To Facilitate Pioneer Church Planting Movements Among America's Unreached C_1 Communities

As a ministry of World Impact, TUMI is dedicated to generating and strategically facilitating dynamic, indigenous C_1 church planting movements targeted to reach the 80% Window of America's inner cities. In order to attain this purpose, we will help form strategic alliances between and among urban missionaries and pastors, theologians and missiologists, churches and denominations, and other kingdom-minded individuals and organizations in order to trigger robust pioneer

That We May Be One (continued)

church planting movements that multiply thousands of culturally conducive evangelical C₁ churches among America's urban poor. We will offer our expertise to assure that these churches in every way glorify God the Father in their Christ-centered identity, Spirit-formed worship and community life, historically orthodox doctrine, and kingdom-oriented practice and mission.

I. Partnership₁ Involves Recognizing our Fundamental Unity in Christ: We Share the Same Spiritual DNA.

A. *Our faith in Jesus has made us one together.*

1. 1 John 1.3 (ESV) - that which we have seen and heard we proclaim also to you, so that you too may have fellowship with us; and indeed our fellowship is with the Father and with his Son Jesus Christ.

2. John 17.11 (ESV) - And I am no longer in the world, but they are in the world, and I am coming to you. Holy Father, keep them in your name, which you have given me, that they may be one, even as we are one.

B. *The organic unity between the Father and Son, and the people of God,* John 17.21-22 (ESV) - that they may all be one, just as you, Father, are in me, and I in you, that they also may be in us, so that the world may believe that you have sent me. [22] The glory that you have given me I have given to them, that they may be one even as we are one.

C. *Our unity leads to a common effort in glorifying God the Father of our Lord,* Rom. 15.5-6 (ESV) - May the God of endurance and encouragement grant you to live in such harmony with one another, in accord with Christ Jesus, [6] that together you may with one voice glorify the God and Father of our Lord Jesus Christ.

D. *God's will for the body is unity in mind and judgment*, 1 Cor. 1.10 (ESV) - I appeal to you, brothers, by the name of our Lord Jesus Christ, that all of you agree and that there be no divisions among you, but that you be united in the same mind and the same judgment.

E. *The Holy Spirit's baptism has made us of one spiritual body and spirit*, 1 Cor. 12.12-13 (ESV) - For just as the body is one and has many members, and all the members of the body, though many, are one body, so it is with Christ.

That We May Be One (continued)

[13] For in one Spirit we were all baptized into one body— Jews or Greeks, slaves or free—and all were made to drink of one Spirit.

F. *The very essence of biblical faith is unity*, Eph. 4.4-6 (ESV) - There is one body and one Spirit—just as you were called to the one hope that belongs to your call [5] one Lord, one faith, one baptism, [6] one God and Father of all, who is over all and through all and in all.

G. *Our bond of partnership precludes unity with those not united to Christ*, 2 Cor. 6.14-16 (ESV) - Do not be unequally yoked with unbelievers. For what partnership has righteousness with lawlessness? Or what fellowship has light with darkness? [15] What accord has Christ with Belial? Or what portion does a believer share with an unbeliever? [16] What agreement has the temple of God with idols? For we are the temple of the living God; as God said, "I will make my dwelling among them and walk among them, and I will be their God, and they shall be my people.

II. **Partnership$_2$ Involves the Sharing of Monies, Persons, and Resources to Fund a Common Cause: We Share a Common Source, Table, and Pot.**

A. *The partnership between those who share the Word and receive it involves concrete blessing and giving.*

1. *The taught share with the teacher*, Gal. 6.6 (ESV) - One who is taught the word must share all good things with the one who teaches.

2. *Illustrated in the relationship of the Jew to the Gentile in the body*, Rom. 15.27 (ESV) - They were pleased to do it, and indeed they owe it to them. For if the Gentiles have come to share in their spiritual blessings, they ought also to be of service to them in material blessings.

B. *The power of unity extends to those who are appointed by God to serve his people*, Deut. 12.19 (ESV) - Take care that you do not neglect the Levite as long as you live in your land.

C. *Those who labor deserve the generous supply of those who benefit from that labor.*

1. *Christ's exhortation to the disciples*, Matt. 10.10 (ESV) - No bag for your journey, nor two tunics nor sandals nor a staff, for the laborer deserves his food.

That We May Be One (continued)

    2. *Illustrated from OT Scripture and analogy*, 1 Cor. 9.9-14 (ESV) - For it is written in the Law of Moses, "You shall not muzzle an ox when it treads out the grain." Is it for oxen that God is concerned? [10] Does he not speak entirely for our sake? It was written for our sake, because the plowman should plow in hope and the thresher thresh in hope of sharing in the crop. [11] If we have sown spiritual things among you, is it too much if we reap material things from you? [12] If others share this rightful claim on you, do not we even more? Nevertheless, we have not made use of this right, but we endure anything rather than put an obstacle in the way of the gospel of Christ. [13] Do you not know that those who are employed in the temple service get their food from the temple, and those who serve at the altar share in the sacrificial offerings? [14] In the same way, the Lord commanded that those who proclaim the gospel should get their living by the gospel.

    3. *Double honor: respect and sharing of resources*, 1 Tim. 5.17-18 (ESV) - Let the elders who rule well be considered worthy of double honor, especially those who labor in preaching and teaching. [18] For the Scripture says, "You shall not muzzle an ox when it treads out the grain," and, "The laborer deserves his wages."

D. *The Philippian relationship with Paul is a prototype of this kind of essential partnership.*

    1. *From the beginning they shared tangibly with Paul*, Phil. 1.3-5 (ESV) - I thank my God in all my remembrance of you, [4] always in every prayer of mine for you all making my prayer with joy, [5] because of your partnership in the gospel from the first day until now.

    2. *Epaphroditus was their messenger to transport their aid to Paul*, Phil. 2.25 (ESV) - I have thought it necessary to send to you Epaphroditus my brother and fellow worker and fellow soldier, and your messenger and minister to my need

    3. *The Philippians were completely engaged in the support of Paul's ministry from the first*, Phil. 4.15-18 (ESV) - And you Philippians yourselves know that in the beginning of the gospel, when I left Macedonia, no church entered into partnership with me in giving and receiving, except you only. [16] Even in Thessalonica you sent me help for my needs once

That We May Be One (continued)

and again. [17] Not that I seek the gift, but I seek the fruit that increases to your credit. [18] I have received full payment, and more. I am well supplied, having received from Epaphroditus the gifts you sent, a fragrant offering, a sacrifice acceptable and pleasing to God.

III. Partnership₃ Involves Collaborating Together as Co-workers and Co-laborers in the Work of Advancing the Kingdom: We Share a Common Cause and Task.

A. *Partnership assumes that each person and congregation brings their unique experience, perspective, and gifting to the table for use*, Gal. 2.6-8 (ESV) - And from those who seemed to be influential (what they were makes no difference to me; God shows no partiality)—those, I say, who seemed influential added nothing to me. [7] On the contrary, when they saw that I had been entrusted with the gospel to the uncircumcised, just as Peter had been entrusted with the gospel to the circumcised [8] (for he who worked through Peter for his apostolic ministry to the circumcised worked also through me for mine to the Gentiles).

B. *Authentic partnerships involve discerning the Lord's leading, opportunity, and blessing on those who are called to represent his interests in the places where he has led them*, Gal. 2.9-10 (ESV) - and when James and Cephas and John, who seemed to be pillars, perceived the grace that was given to me, they gave the right hand of fellowship to Barnabas and me, that we should go to the Gentiles and they to the circumcised. [10] Only, they asked us to remember the poor, the very thing I was eager to do.

C. *Partnership in terms of co-working and co-laboring involves a shared vision and commitment to a common cause*, e.g., Timothy, Phil. 2.19-24 (ESV) - I hope in the Lord Jesus to send Timothy to you soon, so that I too may be cheered by news of you. [20] For I have no one like him, who will be genuinely concerned for your welfare. [21] They all seek their own interests, not those of Jesus Christ. [22] But you know Timothy's proven worth, how as a son with a father he has served with me in the gospel. [23] I hope therefore to send him just as soon as I see how it will go with me, [24] and I trust in the Lord that shortly I myself will come also.

That We May Be One (continued)

D. *Paul's unique words for his partners in the Gospel*

1. Co-worker (*synergos*), Rom. 16.3, 7, 9, 21; 2 Cor. 8.23; Phil. 2.25; 4.3; Col. 4.7, 10, 11, 14; Philem. 1, 24.

2. Co-prisoner (*synaichmalotos*), Col. 4.10; Philem. 23

3. Co-slave (*syndoulos*), Col. 1.7, 4.7

4. Co-soldier (*systratiotes*) Phil. 2.25; Philem. 2

5. Co-laborer (*synatheleo*), Phil. 4.2-3

E. A brief listing of Paul's partners in ministry (these accompanied him at every phase and effort of the work, with diverse backgrounds, giftings, tasks, and responsibilities along the way of his ministry)

1. John Mark (Col. 4.10; Philem. 24)

2. Artistarchus (Col. 4.10; Philem. 24)

3. Andronicus and Junia (Rom. 16.7)

4. Philemon (Philem. 1)

5. Epaphroditus (same as Epaphras) (Col. 1.7; Philem. 23; Phil. 2.25)

6. Clement (Phil. 4.3)

7. Urbanus (Rom. 16.9)

8. Jesus (Justus) (Col. 4.11)

9. Demas (who later apostocized in the world), (Col. 4.14; Philem. 24; 2 Tim. 4.20)

10. Tychicus (Col. 4.7; Phil. 4.3)

11. Archippus (Philem. 2)

12. Euodia (Phil. 4.2-3)

13. Syntyche (Phil. 4.2-3)

14. Tertius (Rom. 16.22)

That We May Be One (continued)

15. Phoebe (Rom. 16.1)
16. Erastus (Rom. 16.23)
17. Quartus (Rom. 16.23)
18. Tryphaena (Rom. 16.12)
19. Tryphosa (Rom. 16.12)
20. Persis (Rom. 16.12)
21. Mary (Rom. 16.6)
22. Onesiphorus (2 Tim. 1.16-18)

IV. Implications of Partnership Principles in Light of TUMI's Visions

To Facilitate Pioneer Church Planting Movements Among America's Unreached C_1 Communities

As a ministry of World Impact, TUMI is dedicated to generating and strategically facilitating dynamic, indigenous C_1 church planting movements targeted to reach the 80% Window of America's inner cities. In order to attain this purpose, we will help form strategic alliances between and among urban missionaries and pastors, theologians and missiologists, churches and denominations, and other kingdom-minded individuals and organizations in order to trigger robust pioneer church planting movements that multiply thousands of culturally conducive evangelical C_1 churches among America's urban poor. We will offer our expertise to assure that these churches in every way glorify God the Father in their Christ-centered identity, Spirit-formed worship and community life, historically orthodox doctrine, and kingdom-oriented practice and mission.

A. *TUMI will help form strategic alliances to trigger urban church plant movements.*

B. *TUMI seeks to support dynamic movements which produce and sustain healthy C_1 churches.*

That We May Be One (continued)

C. Clear implications of this for us

1. We don't recruit people to ourselves, but to participate in Christ's kingdom advance.

2. We don't own the vision, it is God's desire to impact the world, and we contribute alongside others.

3. Our contribution is no better or worse than others: we are co-laborers with others.

4. The work that others do will probably be more critical and fruitful than our own.

Bottom Line

There is virtually no limit to what we can accomplish if we as a team are willing to give our all for the sake of our common cause, if we do not care what role we have to play in order to win, nor care who gets the credit after the victory.

APPENDIX 24
The *Oikos* Factor
Spheres of Relationship and Influence
Rev. Dr. Don L. Davis

Survey: 42,000 asked: Who or what was responsible for your coming to Christ and your church:

Special need	1-2%
Walk-in	2-3%
Pastor	5-6%
Visitation	1-2%
Sunday School	4-5%
Evangelistic crusade/TV	1/2%
Church program	2-3%
Friend or relative	75-90%!!

--Church Growth, Inc. Monrovia, CA

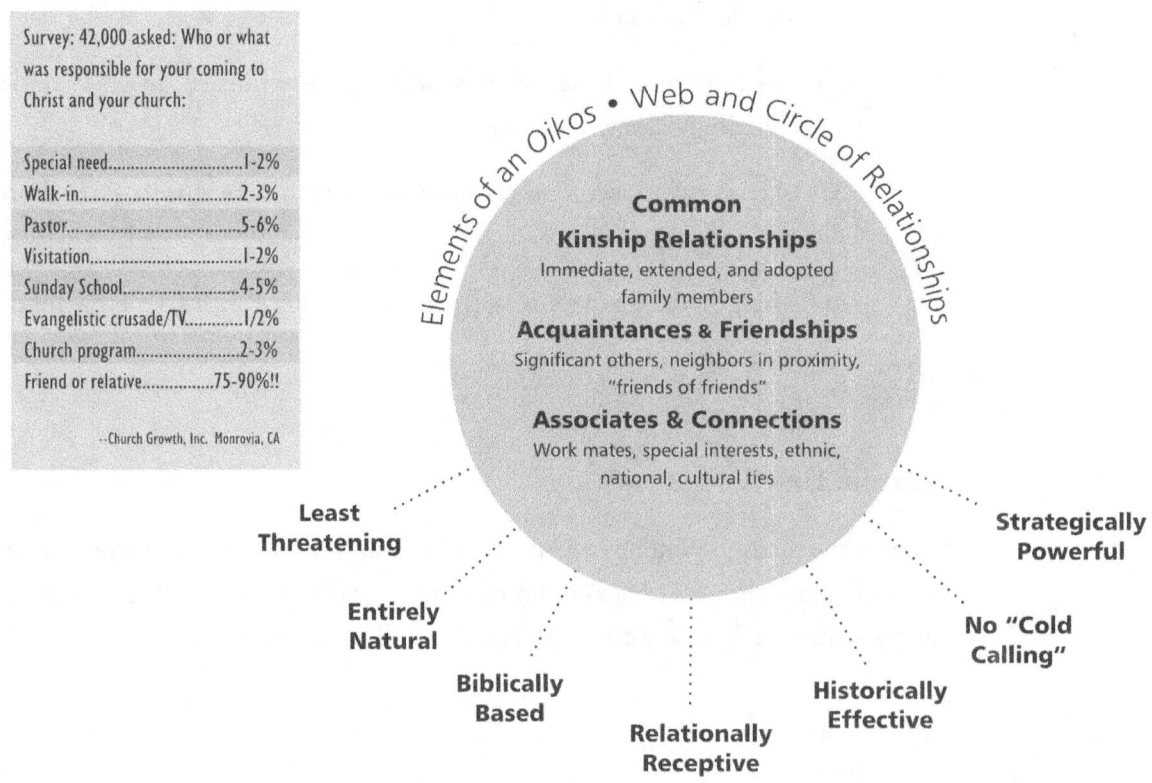

Elements of an Oikos • Web and Circle of Relationships

Common Kinship Relationships
Immediate, extended, and adopted family members

Acquaintances & Friendships
Significant others, neighbors in proximity, "friends of friends"

Associates & Connections
Work mates, special interests, ethnic, national, cultural ties

- Least Threatening
- Entirely Natural
- Biblically Based
- Relationally Receptive
- Historically Effective
- No "Cold Calling"
- Strategically Powerful

Oikos (household) in the OT
"A household usually contained four generations, including men, married women, unmarried daughters, slaves of both sexes, persons without citizenship, and "sojourners," or resident foreign workers." – Hans Walter Wolff, *Anthology of the Old Testament*

Oikos (household) in the NT
Evangelism and disciple making in our NT narratives are often described as following the flow of the relational networks of various people within their *oikoi* (households), that is, those natural lines of connection in which they resided and lived (c.f., Mark 5.19; Luke 19.9; John 4.53; 1.41-45, etc.). Andrew to Simon (John 1.41-45), and both Cornelius (Acts 10-11) and the Philippian jailer (Acts 16) are notable cases of evangelism and discipling through *oikoi*.

Oikos (household) among the urban poor
While great differences exist between cultures, kinship relationships, special interest groups, and family structures among urban populations, it is clear that urbanites connect with others far more on the basis of connections through relationships, friendships, and family than through proximity and neighborhood alone. Often times the closest friends of urban poor dwellers are not immediately close-by in terms of neighborhood; family and friends may dwell blocks, even miles away. Taking the time to study the precise linkages of relationships among the dwellers in a certain area can prove extremely helpful in determining the most effective strategies for evangelism and disciple making in inner city contexts.

APPENDIX 25
Culture, Not Color: Interaction of Class, Culture, and Race
World Impact, Inc.

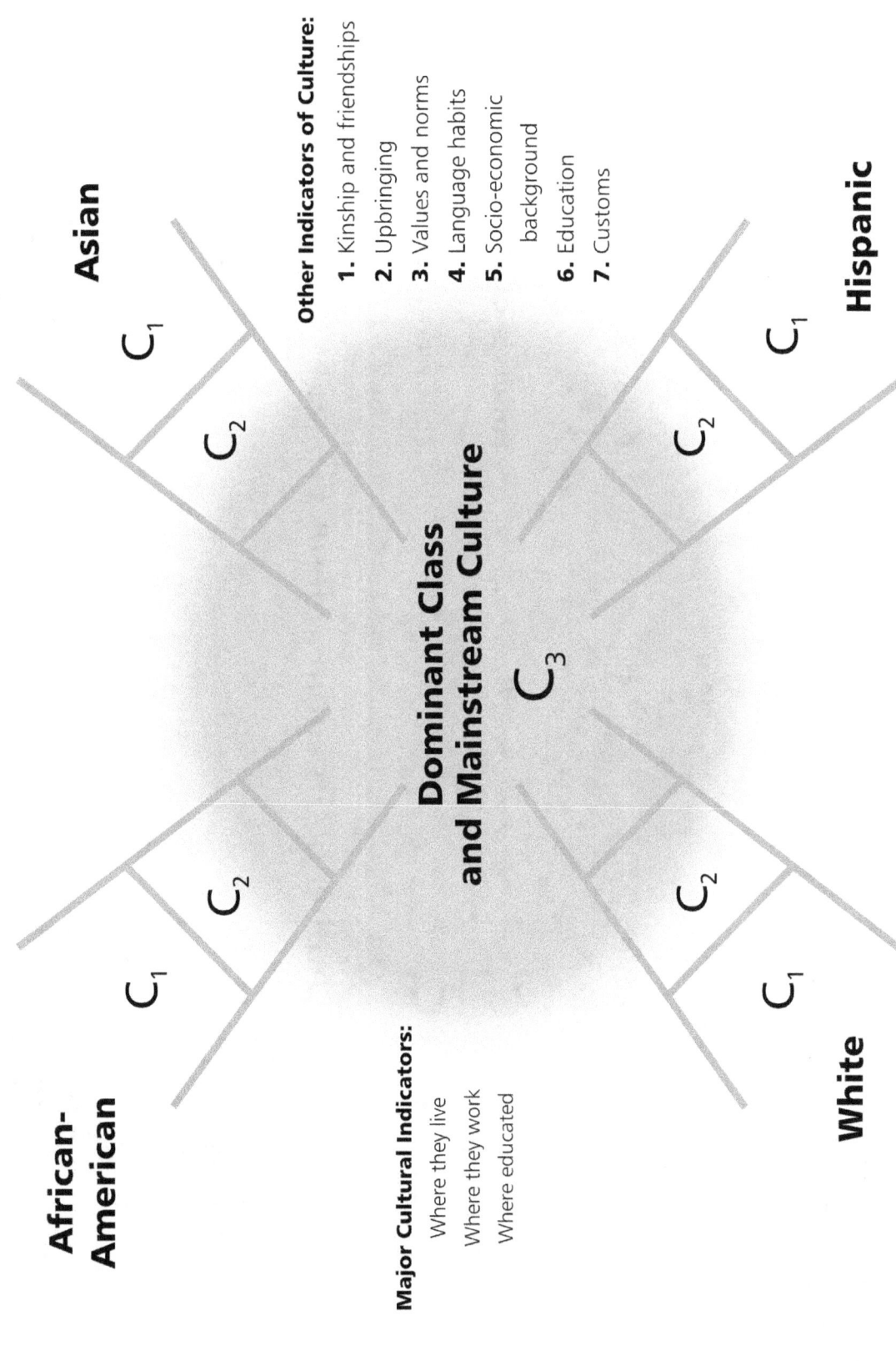

APPENDIX 26
Authentic Freedom in Jesus Christ
Rev. Dr. Don L. Davis

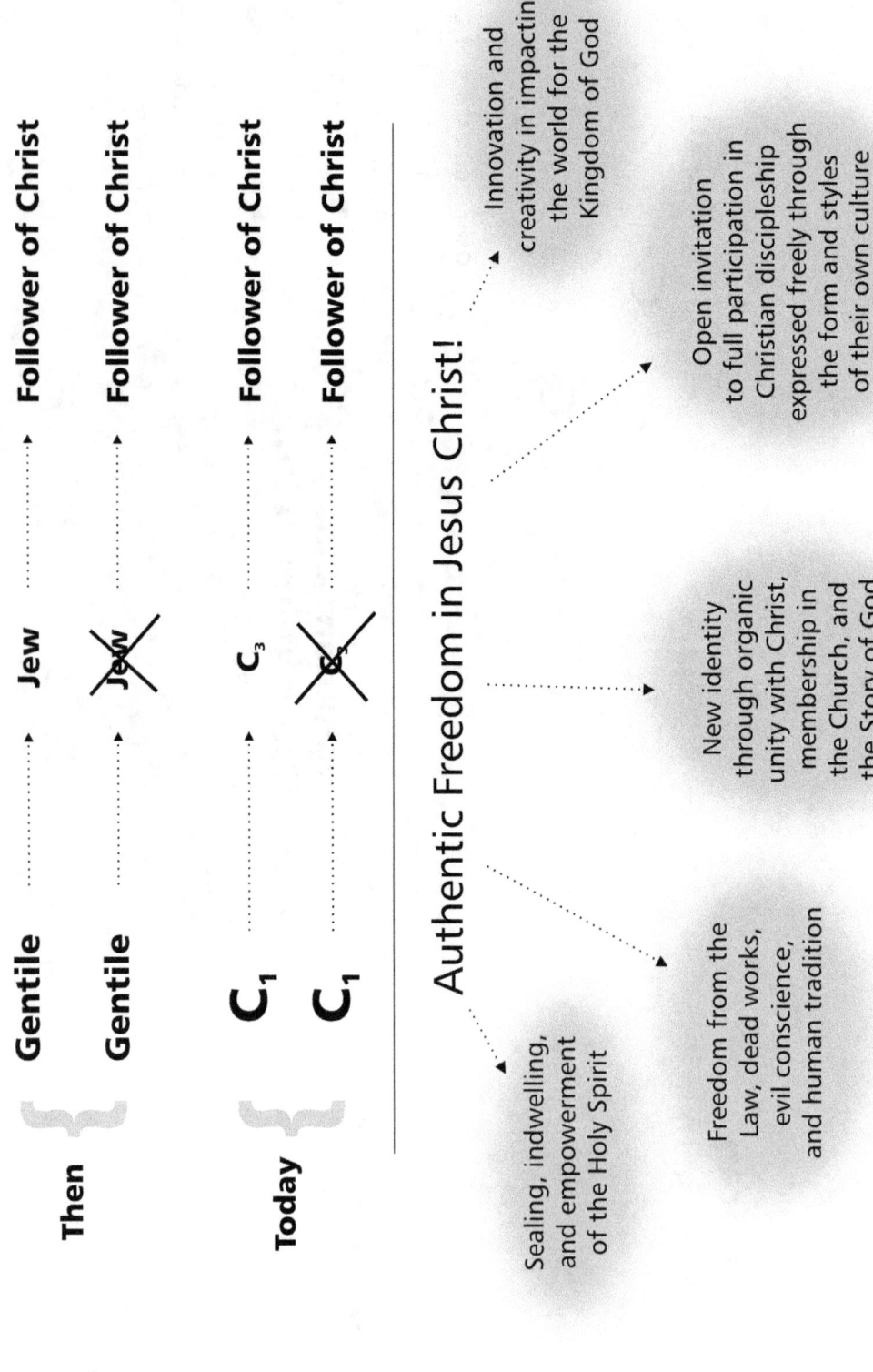

APPENDIX 27
World Impact's Vision: Toward a Biblical Strategy to Impact the Inner City
World Impact, Inc.

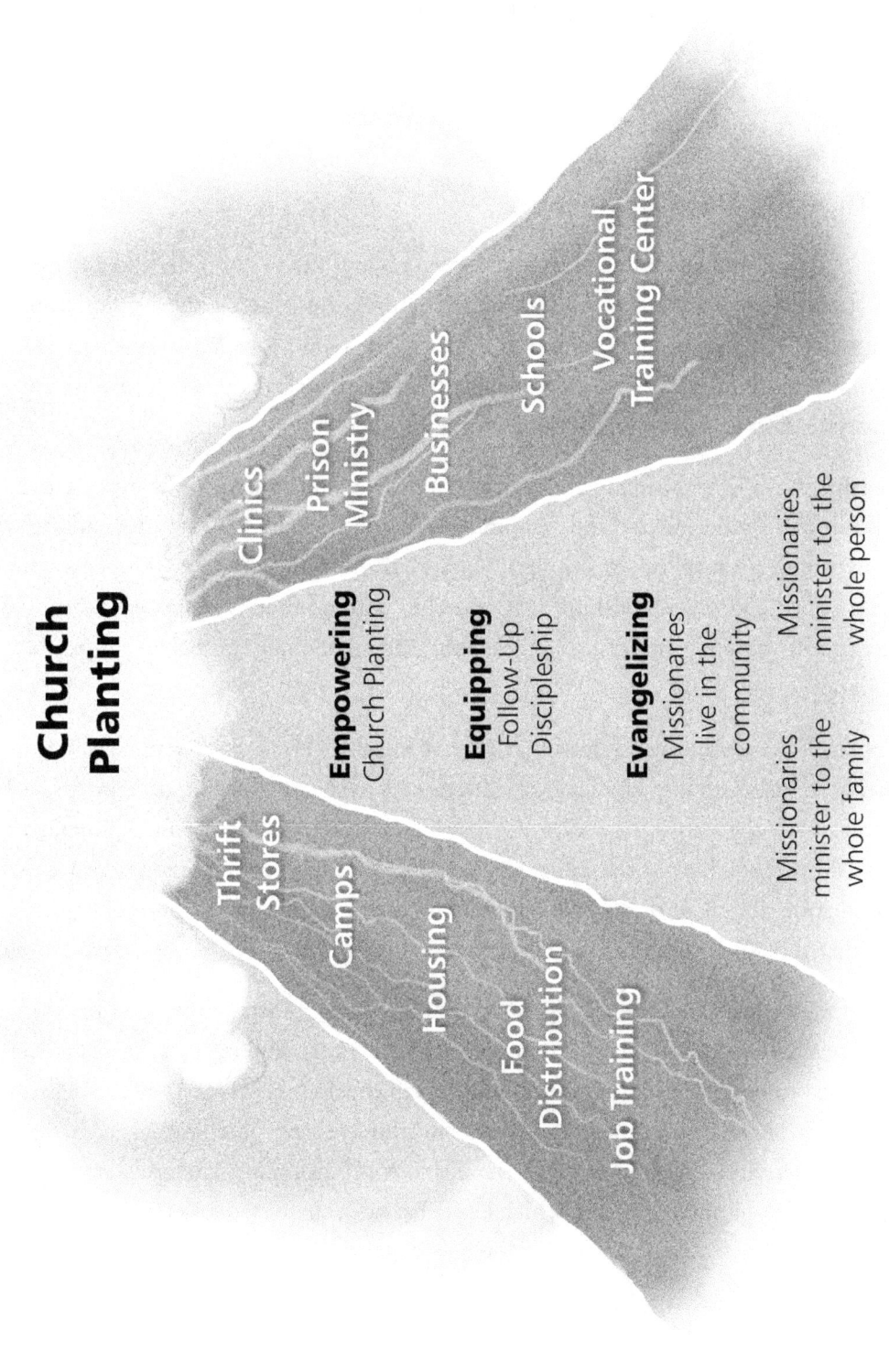

APPENDIX 28

Empowering People for Freedom, Wholeness, and Justice
Theological and Ethical Foundations for World Impact's Development Ministries
Don Davis and Terry Cornett

A Theology of Development

Love of God and love of neighbor have been pivotal themes of both Old and New Testament theology from their inception. From the time of the early Church forward, there has been a concern to demonstrate God's love and character to the world in word and deed, through faith and works, by both evangelistic proclamation and acts of justice and mercy.

Starting with its forerunners in Puritan, Pietistic, Moravian, and Wesleyan reform and revival movements, and extending into the modern Protestant missions movement, evangelical missionaries have combined a strong emphasis on evangelism and the establishment of churches with a serious attempt to engage in action that would foster justice and righteousness, especially on behalf of the poor and oppressed.

Evangelical reformers and missionaries have started schools and hospitals aimed at being accessible to the least advantaged segments of society, formed orphanages and worked for the reform of child labor laws, established businesses and cooperative ventures among the poor, supported legislation to abolish slavery and to ensure the protection of human rights, worked to upgrade the status of women in society, and mediated conflicts between warring groups and nations.[1]

Although Christians generally agree that evangelism and social action are important responsibilities of the Church, there is considerable variation in both the terms that are used to designate these responsibilities, and the way in which they are defined and placed in relation to one another. As a missions agency which is engaged in both of these activities, it is important to establish our definition of terms and a statement of the theological relationship which exists between these two tasks.

Prologue

[1] See Paul E. Pierson's article, "Missions and Community Development: A Historical Perspective," (Elliston 1989, 1-22) for an introduction to the history of development work in evangelical missions and Donald W. Dayton's book "Discovering an Evangelical Heritage" (Dayton, 1988) for a helpful look at evangelical reform movements.

Empowering People for Freedom, Wholeness, and Justice (continued)

1. The Kingdom of God as the Basis of Evangelism, Church Planting and Development

1.1 The Kingdom of God as the Basis for Mission

"Missiology is more and more coming to see the kingdom of God as the hub around which all of mission work revolves" (Verkuyl 1978, 203). Evangelism, church-planting and development work are not based on a few isolated "proof-texts," but are an abiding response to the theme of the Kingdom which is woven throughout the scriptural record. The Kingdom of God embodies the essence of what God's mission (*Missio Dei*) in the world is and provides a basis for seeing how our own activities are intended to fit into God's overall plan.[2]

[2] See George Eldon Ladd (1974, 45-134), for an introduction to a biblical theology of the Kingdom.

1.2 The Kingdom as Restoration

The Scriptures assert what human experience everywhere reveals; something has gone dramatically wrong with the world. The Bible teaches that the basis of this problem is humanity's rejection of God's rulership. The Genesis account of the Fall shows humanity repudiating God's right to give direction and boundaries to their decisions. From that time forward, evil filled the void left by the absence of God's loving rule. The world ceased to function correctly; death replaced life; disease replaced health; enmity replaced friendship; domination replaced cooperation; and scarcity replaced abundance. All human relationships with God and with each other were poisoned by the inner desire of each individual and social group to replace God's authority with their own rule.

In a response of grace to this situation, God decided not to reject and destroy the world, but to redeem it. He set in motion a plan to liberate the world from its bondage to evil powers, and to restore all things to perfection under his Kingly rule. Throughout the Scriptures this plan of reclamation is described as the "*Kingdom of God*," and insight into its nature and means of coming are progressively revealed.

Johannes Verkuyl summarizes the message of the Kingdom in this fashion:

> *The heart of the message of the Old and New Testament is that God . . . is actively engaged in the reestablishment of His liberating dominion over the cosmos and all of humankind. In seeking out Israel, He sought all of us and our entire world, and in Jesus Christ He laid the foundation of the Kingdom. Jesus Christ the Messiah "promised to the fathers," is the **auto basileia**[3]: in Him the Kingdom has both come, and is coming in an absolutely unique way and with exceptional clarity. In His preaching Jesus divulges the riches, the **thesaurus** of that Kingdom: reconciliation,*

[3] That is, the One who in his own person fully embodies the rule of God.

Empowering People for Freedom, Wholeness, and Justice (continued)

the forgiveness of sins, victory over demonic powers. Standing within the tradition of the Mosaic law, He expounds the core message of . . . the prophets; He accomplishes the reconciliation of the world to God; He opens the way to the present and future Kingdom which demands decisions of us in all aspects of life (Verkuyl 1993, 72).

1.3 Responsibilities for Those Who Seek God's Kingdom

The implications of the Kingdom of God for mission can be delineated in three central truths. A Kingdom-centered theology and missiology will be concerned for:

- Evangelizing so that people are converted to Christ as Lord.
- Creating churches where people are discipled and bear fruit.
- Helping the Church live out its commitment to bring freedom, wholeness, and justice in the world.

Thus:

A truly Kingdom-centered theology . . . can never neglect the call for the conversion of persons among all peoples and religious communities. To everyone of whatever religious persuasion the message must be repeated: "The Kingdom of God is at hand; repent, and believe in the Gospel." . . . Kingdom-centered theology entails a call to recognition of the lordship of the King and new orientation to the constitution of His Kingdom. In the absence of this aspect, proclamation of the good news of the Gospel is impossible. A theology and missiology informed by the biblical notion of the rule of Christ will never fail to identify personal conversion as one of the inclusive goals of God's Kingdom . . .

The Church . . . is raised up by God among all nations to share in the salvation and suffering service of the Kingdom . . . The Church constitutes the firstling, the early harvest of the Kingdom. Thus, although not limited to the Church, the Kingdom is unthinkable without the Church. Conversely, growth and expansion of the Church should not be viewed as ends but rather as means to be used in the service of the Kingdom. . . . The keys of the Kingdom have been given to the Church. It does not fulfill its mandate by relinquishing those keys but rather by using them to open up the avenues of approach to the Kingdom for all peoples and all population groups at every level of human society . . .

Empowering People for Freedom, Wholeness, and Justice (continued)

> *Finally, the gospel of the Kingdom addresses itself to all immediate human need, both physical and mental. It aims to right what is wrong on earth. It enjoins engagement in the struggle for racial, social, cultural, economic, and political justice. . . . The good news of the Kingdom has to do with all of these things. For this reason missiology must bend its efforts to the erection of a multiplicity of visible signs of God's Kingdom throughout the length and breadth of this planet (Verkuyl 1993, 72-73).*

Evangelism, church planting and development spring from a common theological base: a desire to live out the implications of the Kingdom of God which has broken into this present age in the person of Jesus Christ, the King of kings. This Kingdom is both *already* and *not yet*. It is currently *forcefully advancing* and *spreading like yeast through dough*, but also awaiting the return of Christ *when every knee will bow* and there will be a *new heaven and a new earth*. Our evangelism and our development work acknowledge God's kingly rule, now, during a time when the world, as a whole, does not. We announce the good news of the in-breaking Kingdom of peace and justice, call people to repentance and salvation through faith in its King, hope in its inevitable complete triumph, and live out obedience to its commands and values in the present moment.

2. Kingdom Work

Since evangelism/church planting and development work are intimately related, those who engage in them often find that their roles and projects overlap. While this is both normal and good, a clear beginning definition of each role may help to minimize the confusion which can sometimes result from this process.

2.1 Missionaries

Missionaries are called to pioneer new outreaches that focus on the evangelization of peoples in unreached (or under-reached) areas, social classes, or cultural groups.

Therefore, we assert that:

> *Missionaries cross class and cultural barriers to evangelize and disciple unreached groups so that reproducing churches are formed among them and placed at the service of God's kingdom rule.*

Empowering People for Freedom, Wholeness, and Justice (continued)

2.2 Development Workers

Development workers are called to confront conditions and structures in the world that do not submit themselves to the rule of God.

Therefore, we assert that:

> *Development workers enable individuals, churches and communities to experience movement toward the freedom, wholeness, and justice of the Kingdom of God.*

2.3 The Common Link

Both missionaries and Christian development workers are united in their common commitment to further God's kingdom rule in all areas of life.

Missionary activity is centered around the proclamation of "good news" that calls people into the Kingdom of God through an experience of salvation and regeneration. It focuses on bringing unreached peoples, cultures, and subcultures into the community of the redeemed (i.e., "bringing the world into the Church"). All of this is done with an eye toward creating churches which can disciple their members to acknowledge God's rulership and live out the values of his Kingdom in their individual and corporate life.

Missionary activity also encompasses development that seeks to call every area of life into conformity with God's kingdom rule. It evaluates every concrete life-situation in light of the Lord's Prayer ("thy Kingdom come, thy will be done, on earth as it is in heaven") and engages in deeds of compassion, love, and justice that demonstrate the nature of God's divine plan for all peoples. It focuses on bringing God's rule to bear on every human relationship and structure (i.e., "bringing the Church into the world").

3. Theological Relationship between Evangelism and Development

3.1 A Partnership Relationship

Missionary evangelism and church-planting and Christian development work are partners in the process of proclaiming, demonstrating, and extending the rule of the King. Both are responses to the fact that God has announced his desire to reconcile the world to himself through the gift of his Son. Although each is a legitimate response to God's plan for the world, neither is a sufficient response in and of itself.

Empowering People for Freedom, Wholeness, and Justice (continued)

Both word and deed are necessary components of the Church's announcement of, and faithfulness to, the Kingdom of God.

3.2 Interdependence and Interconnectedness

The relationship between Missions and Development is not a simple one. Their interconnectedness has many facets.

- *They are connected by a common goal.*

    Neither missionaries nor development workers are satisfied until God's reconciliation with man and man's reconciliation with man is completely realized. We believe that this makes both missions and development work Christocentric in orientation, since it is "in Christ" that God is reconciling the world to himself. Christ is the King. It is his sacrificial, reconciling death that provides the objective basis for reconciliation between humanity and God, and within human relationships and structures. It is his kingly authority and presence that allows the Kingdom to break into this present age destroying the works of darkness and creating authentic communities gathered under God's rule.

- *They retain a degree of independence from each other.*

    Evangelism and church-planting can sometimes be done without any immediate focus on development work. Conversely, development work can be sometimes be done without accompanying church-planting activity. Because both are authentic responses to God's activity in the world, they can, when appropriate, operate independently from each other. While each is a legitimate activity in its own right, it will obviously be healthier and more normal to find them occurring together.

- *They need each other for lasting effectiveness.*

    Without evangelism, there are no changed lives, no reconcilers who understand God's plan for man and society, and who undertake change in the power of the Spirit. Without development, the churches established by mission become withdrawn, and do not function as "salt and light" within their local and national communities. Missionary efforts are undermined when the existing church does not make visible in its life the effects of God's

Empowering People for Freedom, Wholeness, and Justice (continued)

> kingdom rule. The integration of the two is aptly expressed in Ephesians 2:8-10 which states, "For by grace you have been saved through faith. And this is not your own doing; it is the gift of God, [9] not a result of works, so that no one may boast. [10] For we are his workmanship, created in Christ Jesus for good works, which God prepared beforehand, that we should walk in them."

These facets may be summarized as "a threefold relationship between evangelism and social activity. First, Christian social activity [development] is a *consequence* of evangelism, since it is the evangelized who engage in it. Second it is a *bridge* to evangelism, since it expresses God's love and so both overcomes prejudice and opens closed doors. Third, it is a *partner* of evangelism, so that they are 'like two blades of a pair of scissors or the two wings of a bird'" (Stott 1995, 52).

3.3 The Need for Specialization

Modern missions have seen the rise of both mission and development agencies. This occurs as organizations specialize in one component of the overall task God has given. This recognition of the need for specialization arose early on in the life of the Church.

J. Chongham Cho comments:

> *In Acts 6 . . . a distinction between evangelism and social action was made. This was not a division in essence but for the sake of practical efficacy of the church's mission and as the solution to a problem which arose in the church. This is a necessary deduction from the nature of the church as Christ's body. Although we should resist polarization between evangelism and social action, we should not resist specialization (Cho 1985, 229).*

As a missions agency, our primary focus is evangelism and discipleship which results in the planting of indigenous churches. The fact that evangelism, church-planting and development are interconnected means that missions agencies, especially those who focus on the poor and oppressed, will engage in some form of development work. However, the mission agency must be careful to structure its development work so that it encourages the central task of evangelism and church-planting rather than detracts from it.[4] We should engage in development work which fosters the formation, health, growth, and reproducibility of indigenous churches among the poor.

[4] *See Appendix A for a variety of perspectives on how improperly implemented development work can adversely affect missionary work.*

Empowering People for Freedom, Wholeness, and Justice (continued)

Specialization allows organizations to maximize the training and resources that can be committed to a specific part of the overall task of mission. The development agency may engage in many good and necessary projects that have no immediate connection to evangelism and the planting and nurturing of emerging churches. The missions agency appreciates the many development agencies that engage in this type of work. Although the mission agency will want to network with them (and pray that God will vastly increase their number and effectiveness), the mission agency itself will focus on development projects that assist the task of evangelism, discipleship, and the establishment of indigenous churches. Without this commitment to specialization, the mission agency will lose its ability to accomplish its part of the larger task.

4. Development Work within Our Mission Agency

4.1 Statement of Purpose

While we recognize the legitimacy of engaging in development work for its own sake as a direct godly response to human need, we believe that we are called to specialize in development work that specifically supports and contributes to the task of evangelism, discipleship and church-planting. In light of this, we affirm the following statement.

The aim of World Impact's development ministries is to support the evangelism, discipleship, and church-planting goals of World Impact by:

- *Demonstrating the Love of Christ*

    Many oppressed people have little basis for understanding God's love for them and the essential justice and compassion of his character. Development work can provide a living witness to the love of Christ and his concern for justice and peace in urban neighborhoods. Holistic ministry can come alongside the verbal proclamation of the Gospel, verifying its credibility and enriching the depth of understanding among its hearers. Development work can function pre-evangelistically to prepare people to genuinely listen to the claims of Christ and his message of salvation.

- *Empowering Emerging Churches*

    Emerging urban churches often have few physical resources with which to face the enormous needs of the city. Development work can partner with the pastors of planted-churches, giving access to resources and programs

Empowering People for Freedom, Wholeness, and Justice (continued)

> that can meet immediate needs within their congregation, encourage leadership development, and help their congregations engage in effective holistic outreach to their community.

- *Modeling the Implications of the Gospel*

  We cannot hope to reproduce churches committed to engage in a task they have never seen lived out in practice. We engage in development work because we expect newly planted churches to do likewise. We want to provide a living example that the Gospel will necessarily move from belief to action, from word to deed.

4.2 An Important Reminder

One cautionary note is in order. We cannot, through our own efforts, bring the Kingdom of God. As Paul Hiebert reminds us, "Our paradigms are flawed if we begin missions with human activity. Mission is not primarily what we do. It is what God does" (Hiebert 1993, 158). Evangelism, church-planting and development work all function, first and foremost, at the disposal of the Spirit of God. Knowing what should be done, and how we should do it, is never primarily determined through strategic diagrams or well-thought-out organizational approaches. Our first duty is to be faithful to the King, to listen to his instructions, and to respond to his initiatives.

An Ethic of Development

We have stated that:

> *Development workers enable individuals, churches and communities to experience movement toward the freedom, wholeness, and justice of the Kingdom of God.*

The process by which we move toward this goal, and the decisions we make to achieve these ends must be guided by an ethic which is consistent with God's standard for human relationships.

Ethics has to do with human conduct and character. It is the systematic study of the principles and methods for distinguishing right from wrong and good from bad. A Christian ethic of development helps us make decisions about development issues in

5. Introduction

Empowering People for Freedom, Wholeness, and Justice (continued)

light of biblical revelation and theology. It enables us to think and act clearly so that we can discern what is right to do and how it should be done.

Ethics is concerned that our theology be applied to our behaviors and attitudes. It is not content to simply understand the truth. Instead, it continually seeks to help us discover how to apply the truth (and attempts to motivate us to do so). True ethical behavior means that ethical principles are understood, internalized, and applied to the situation through the development of specific strategies and practices. In an organization, true ethical behavior also requires that strategies and practices undergo regular testing, evaluation and refinement. This ensures that the organization is accomplishing in practice what it affirms in principle.

Finally, it should be noted that our experiences always confront us with paradoxes, anomalies and competing priorities. An ethic of development does not attempt to condense life into a neatly packaged system. Rather, it provides principles that will help us to clarify what is most important in the particular situation that are facing. Each ethical decision must involve discussion about how the various principles outlined below interrelate and about which are the most significant values for a given decision. Only in dialogue and in prayer can the correct decision be discerned.

The ethical principles of the Kingdom of God can be expressed in the values of freedom, wholeness, and justice. These values are the root and the fruit of doing development from a kingdom perspective.

6. World Impact's Development Work is Committed to Freedom

Freedom is the ability to exercise our God-given capacity to make choices that express love. Therefore, development should engender freedom by helping individuals:

- Gain dignity and respect.
- Be empowered to make wise choices.
- Take responsibility for themselves and others.

This process involves helping individuals *understand* and *achieve* what they need to live freely in community as biblically responsible, self-directing, maturing servants of God's Kingdom. It implies the development of relationships characterized neither by dependence nor independence, but by loving *interdependence* that results in partnership, mutuality, and increased freedom.

Empowering People for Freedom, Wholeness, and Justice (continued)

6.1 *Development affirms human beings as precious and unique in the sight of God, and believes that they have been granted unique capacities and potentials by God.*

Explanation

As beings made in the image of God, every person regardless of station or place, is worthy of dignity and respect. People are to be cherished, nurtured, and provided for according to their intrinsic value and preciousness to God. Biblically based development will never exploit people for the sake of economic purposes or treat people as instruments, but instead will value them as ends-in-themselves, to be loved and respected for their worth before God.

Implications

- *People are to be given priority in every dimension of development.*

    Development should contribute to the potential for self-sufficiency, should enhance the quality of life, and should encourage good stewardship among those participating in the programs.

- *Mutual respect is foundational to authentic development.*

    For the poor, life in the urban community is full of inconvenience, difficulty, and shame. The needy daily experience the indignities of being poor in an affluent society. Oftentimes they are accused of moral laxity, subjected to stifling bureaucracies, and pre-judged as causing their own poverty through incompetence or lack of motivation. Development is sensitive to these messages which are given to the needy in our society. It recognizes that the poor are the objects of God's compassion and good news, chosen to be rich in faith and heirs to the Kingdom of God (James 2.5). Development seeks to demonstrate God's righteous cherishing of the poor through its specific actions and relationships.

    Aid not founded on genuine respect can easily humiliate the poor. Therefore, assistance offered to those in need must affirm their dignity and self-respect. Anything that diminishes the worth and significance of the poor in the development process is sinful and injurious to the well-being of all, both those offering the aid and those receiving it.

Empowering People for Freedom, Wholeness, and Justice (continued)

- *The workplace should operate as a caring community.*

    While an impersonal atmosphere characterizes many business environments, Christian development strives to create a relational framework for trainees and employees. Development workers and those participating in the development project must develop habit patterns of caring for each other beyond the constraints of the project at hand.

6.2 Development should empower people to take full responsibility for their own lives and to care for the needs of others.

Explanation

Development emerges from the conviction that all work is honorable. God has mandated that human beings earn their living with integrity and excellence. This mandate for individual work is grounded in God's initial command given to humankind at creation, and continues on and is reaffirmed in the teachings of the Apostles. While God demands that his people be generous and hospitable to the needy and the stranger (2 Cor. 9), God likewise commands all to work honestly with their own hands (1 Thess. 4), and further charges that those who refuse to work ought to correspondingly be denied benevolent aid, that is, "if anyone will not work, neither let him eat," (cf. 2 Thess. 3.10).

Development rejects the notion that the creation of wealth is intrinsically evil. Such a view is simplistic and fails to grapple with the biblical notion of Christian stewardship. Development aims to create abundance, but never for the sake of selfish gain or lustful greed. Rather, development takes seriously the biblical requirement that we work, not merely to meet our own needs, but so that from the abundance God has provided we may use our goods and resources to meet the needs of others, especially those who are our brothers and sisters in the body of Christ (cf. Eph. 4; 2 Cor. 8; Gal. 6). The biblical standard is that those who stole before they entered the Kingdom are to steal no more, but to work honorably in quietness and integrity, in order that they may have sufficient resources to meet their own needs, and have sufficient wealth to care for others. Development not only seeks to honor the needy by ensuring they can participate in the basic human right to work, it also challenges them to trust God to supply their needs through honorable labor that allows them to be providers for themselves and others.

Empowering People for Freedom, Wholeness, and Justice (continued)

Implications

- *Nothing can excuse a worker, leader, or professional from the perils and potentials of personal responsibility.*

    Christian workers are not exempt from the vices of laziness, slothfulness, mismanagement, and greed, and they will not be spared from the consequences of such habits and conduct.

- *It is a primary aim of development to increase the maturity of everyone involved in the process.*

    It is assumed that the maturing individual will be increasingly characterized by vision (establishing and owning life-long purposes, aspirations and priorities), responsibility (acting on those purposes, aspirations and priorities with motivation, perseverance and integrity), and wisdom (increasing in skill, understanding and the ability to discern and do what is right for themselves and others).

    Maturing individuals should move from dependence toward autonomy, from passivity toward activity, from small abilities to large abilities, from narrow interests to broad interests, from egocentricity to altruism, from ignorance toward enlightenment, from self-rejection toward self-acceptance, from compartmentability toward integration, from imitation toward originality and from a need for rigidity toward a tolerance for ambiguity (Klopfenstein 1993, 95-96).

- *Decisions are best handled at the closest point to those affected.*

    National policies and procedures exist to:

    » Provide a framework for effective decision making.

    » Express the values and purposes that are corporately shared.

    » Ensure equity between peoples and projects at many different sites.

    » Provide accountability which safeguards integrity.

    Responsible decision making within a community assumes that there are mature individuals with a commitment to these common purposes and that open communication exists between the people involved. When these elements are present, most decision making should be done by the people

Empowering People for Freedom, Wholeness, and Justice (continued)

who are responsible to implement the decisions. All decisions must take into consideration the local context and the unique people, relationships, and project conditions that are present.

- *Wages should be fair.*

    When development work involves employment, the employee should be compensated equitably in relation to their contribution toward the success or profitability of the project.

- *Training programs should include teaching on the importance of stewardship and giving.*

    The need for people to give to God, to others and to their community should be made explicit in the development process. Each person's self-identity as a contributor should be reinforced and the intrinsic connection between receiving and giving (Luke 6.38) should be established.

6.3 Development work must discourage the inclination toward dependency.

Explanation

Development emphasizes that each person should be trained and equipped to achieve their potential to be self-sustaining and self-directing. Creating or nurturing dependency undercuts the deep human need to be a co-creator with God in using our gifts to honor him, and finding our significance and place in the world. Dependency can occur from either end of the people-helping relationship; the developer can create a sense of his or her own indispensability which leads to dependency, or the trainee can easily refuse to progress and grow on to interdependence and depth. Dependency pollutes the process of authentic development by creating unhealthy relationships which damage the trainee's initiative and self-motivation.

Implications

- *Trainees must be required to demonstrated initiative.*

    The basic rule of thumb is "Don't do for people what they can do for themselves-even if it means that the project (or training) will go slowly" (Hoke and Voorhies 1989, 224). When too much is done for the people who

Empowering People for Freedom, Wholeness, and Justice (continued)

are being assisted, the developer has taken from the trainees the opportunity to learn from their mistakes. Dependency, even when resulting from a spirit of benevolence and sympathy, inevitably stunts the growth of those who are so affected.

- *Development should avoid the extremes of authoritarian paternalism, on the one hand, and non-directive laissez-faire(ism) on the other.*

    Developers, by definition, are leaders, and cannot avoid their responsibility to mentor, train, teach, and provide direction to those they serve. Maintaining complete decision-making control, however, does not foster interdependent relationships. While close accountability is essential in the earliest stages of training, development workers must recognize the need to modify strategies and involvement based on the competency and ongoing progress of the learners.[5]

- *Projects should help trainees gain control of their own destiny.*

    Projects must be regularly evaluated to insure that they are not keeping people dependent on long-term employment by WIS. Projects which equip people to gain employment with existing businesses or start businesses of their own are the goal.

[5] *For a discussion of the Hersey-Blanchard training model that tailors leadership style to the competencies and attitudes of the trainee see* **Leadership Research** *(Klopfenstein, 1995)*

Wholeness (*Shalom*) is the personal and communal experience of peace, abundance, goodness, soundness, well-being, and belonging. Wholeness is founded on *righteousness* (right relationships with God and man), *truth* (right beliefs about God and man), and *holiness* (right actions before God and man). Shalom is a gift of God and a sign of his Kingdom's presence.

7. World Impact's Development Work Is Committed to Wholeness.

7.1 Development should create an environment where cooperative relationships can flourish.

Explanation

Development that leads to wholeness acknowledges that human activity takes place in community. The web of relationships that occurs in the work environment (e.g. trainer to trainee, co-worker to co-worker,etc.), must reflect our values of Christian community.

Empowering People for Freedom, Wholeness, and Justice (continued)

Implications

- *People are not means to an end.*

    Development seeks, first of all, to develop people. This will necessarily involve equipping them (and holding them accountable to) accomplishing tasks. However, it is the maturing of the person, not the completion of the task that is always the primary end of development work.

- *All people in the development process should work for each other as if they are working for Christ himself.*

    Colossians 3.23-24 reminds us that our work is ultimately directed toward and rewarded by Christ. Development projects must operationalize this principle. This suggests that our work must be done with excellence, integrity, diligence, meekness, love and whatever other virtues are necessary for proper service to God.

- *Relational dynamics must be taken seriously.*

    A development project which produces an excellent product and equips people with marketable skills, but which is characterized by disharmony or disunity among its employees has not achieved its goal. The developer must seek to develop genuine community within the workplace.

7.2 Development activities should demonstrate the truth of the Gospel.

Explanation

1 John 3:18 exhorts us to love not merely with words or tongue, "but with actions and in truth." The love of Christ is given not to "souls" but to whole persons. Development activities should minister unashamedly to the whole person and should serve as evangelism by example. Development work functions as a sign of the Kingdom by enabling people, families, and\or communities to experience the love and care of Christ. This suggests that development workers must know Christ intimately and be able to communicate his love to others.

Empowering People for Freedom, Wholeness, and Justice (continued)

Implications

- *Development projects may emphasize mental, physical, social, or economic development.*

   All aspects of human need are of concern to the development worker. As the development worker's love for people takes shape in concrete actions, it should be their intent that people "may see your good deeds and praise your Father in heaven." (Matt. 5.16).

- *Development workers should be maturing disciples of Christ who are actively engaged in ongoing spiritual growth.*

   Who we are is more important than what we do. Only as development workers are actively seeking to live in Christ's love and listen to his Spirit, will they effectively communicate his love to those they work with.

- *Development workers must receive care for their own physical, mental, emotional, and spiritual health and development.*

   Development workers face unique pressures in dealing with human need. They often feel particular stress from standing in between, and identifying with, both the interests of the particular people they serve and the organization they represent (See Hiebert 1989, 83). Physical, emotional or spiritual burn-out is an ever present possibility. Therefore, it is important that development workers give adequate time and attention to maintaining their own health so that they can continue to effectively minister to the needs of others.

- *Development workers need to be specifically equipped in evangelism and an understanding of missions.*

   Christian development workers usually understand that development and evangelism should work in partnership, but are often undertrained in evangelism (See Hoke and Voorhies 1989). Development workers also need to receive general training in missions and management in addition to being trained for their specific task of development (See Pickett and Hawthorne 1992, D218-19) since many of their daily tasks require an understanding of these disciplines.

Empowering People for Freedom, Wholeness, and Justice (continued)

7.3 Development activities should be above reproach.

Explanation

Wholeness and holiness are inseparable concepts. The way in which development work is conducted will have a profound impact on its ability to effect transformation. For development work to contribute to the wholeness, soundness, and well-being of people it must take special care to sustain integrity in word and deed.

Implications

- *Development projects should maintain high ethical standards.*

    Lack of adequate funds or personnel and the pressures of immediate human need can tempt us to "cut corners" in the way we develop and administrate projects. This temptation must be resisted. Our product cannot be artificially separated from our process. Development projects must serve as a witness to the government, society at large, and the people they train through adherence to high ethical standards of business conduct.

- *Development projects must work within the framework of our 501(c)(3) non-profit status.*

    State and Federal laws limit the ability of non-profits to create situations where individuals directly receive wealth and resources from the corporation. (This prevents individuals inside and outside of the organization from abusing the non-profit status for personal gain). As programs are created to empower people and share resources, the development workers must make sure that they are structured in such a way that they fall within the legal guidelines.

- *Appeals to donors must not motivate by guilt, overstate the need, promise unrealistic results, or demean the dignity of aid recipients.*

    Compressing the complexity of human need and relationships into an appeal to donors is a difficult and complicated task. It is, however, necessary and important work. Development workers in the field should take personal responsibility for relaying needs and vision in an accurate manner to those involved in publishing printed materials about a project.

Empowering People for Freedom, Wholeness, and Justice (continued)

Justice results from a recognition that all things belong to God and should be shared in accordance with his liberality and impartiality. Biblical justice is concerned both with equitable treatment and with the restoration of right relationship. It abhors oppression, prejudice and inequality because it understands that these separate people from each other and from God. Development which is based on justice is an important step toward repairing damaged relationships between individuals, classes and cultures which may harbor suspicion and ill-will toward one another. Development work seeks to engender right actions which lead to right relationships.

8. World Impact's Development Work Is Committed to Justice

8.1 Development is rooted in a biblical understanding of God as Creator and Ruler of the universe which demands that all things be reconciled in him.

Explanation

God has delegated to humanity the responsibility to be stewards of his world. This understanding manifests itself in concern for three broad categories of relationship: relations with God, relations with others, and relations with the environment (See Elliston 1989, *Transformation*, 176). Although these relationships were broken by the entrance of sin in the world, God's kingdom rule now demands their restoration.

Development recognizes that until the fullness of the Kingdom of Christ is manifested, there will inevitably be poverty, exploitation, and misery caused by sin's perversion of these three areas of relationship. This realization, neither paralyzes nor discourages authentic Christian development. While understanding the nature of moral evil in the world, authentic development seeks to demonstrate models of justice and reconciliation which reflect the justice of Christ's Kingdom.

Implications

- *Development intends to move people toward right relationship with God.*

    Authentic reconciliation between people is based on their mutual reconciliation with God. Although "common grace" and the "image of God" provide a ground for some degree of reconciliation between all people, it is ultimately in right relationship with God through Christ that the most profound and lasting form of reconciliation can occur. Therefore,

Empowering People for Freedom, Wholeness, and Justice (continued)

development work is eager to assist in preparing people for hearing the Gospel by witnessing to its truth and living out its implications.

- *Reconciliation between individuals, classes, and cultures is a key value.*

    Development will inevitably involve new ways of power-sharing, using resources, making decisions, enforcing policy, and relating to others. There is a need to innovate rather than simply imitate existing models. It is extremely important that the viewpoints of peoples from different classes and cultures be represented in the planning of any development project.

- *Development projects must not be wasteful of resources or harmful to the physical environment.*

    God's command to humankind is to recognize his ownership, and neither exploit nor destroy his earth, but to tend and care for it. Stewardship involves using the earth's resources to glorify him and meet the needs of our neighbors while keeping in mind our responsibility to future generations. Development must be sustainable, i.e., it must not simply consume resources but cultivate them as well.

8.2 Development recognizes the systemic and institutional foundations of producing wealth and experiencing poverty.

Explanation

The Bible delineates various moral vices that can lead to poverty in the lives of individuals (e.g., laziness, sloth, neglect of responsibility, cf. Prov. 6; Prov. 24, etc.), However, it is also clear that poverty can be caused by large scale societal and economic factors that create conditions of need, oppression, and want (cf. Isa. 1; Isa. 54, Amos 4, 5, etc.). Even a cursory reading of Scripture reveals that throughout biblical history the prophets condemned certain practices of business, politics, law, industry, and even religion that contributed to the imbalances among various groups within society, and led to the oppression of the poor. Development seeks to be prophetic by affirming that God is committed to the poor and the needy, and will not tolerate their oppression indefinitely. Development is not naive. It does not attribute all poverty in society to individual moral vice. On the contrary, struggling against injustice demands that people recognize the ever-present possibility of demonic influence in human structures (1 John 5.19).

Empowering People for Freedom, Wholeness, and Justice (continued)

Implications

- *Spiritual warfare is a key component of the development process.*

    Ephesians 6.12 reminds us that "we do not wrestle against flesh and blood, but against the rulers, against the authorities, against the cosmic powers over this present darkness, against the spiritual forces of evil in the heavenly places." Development work that does not intentionally and regularly set aside time for prayer and other spiritual disciplines is unlikely to effect lasting change. Development workers should have a plan for spiritual warfare that is as significant a focus as the plan for the development work itself.

    Development workers should also realize that their projects will experience spiritual attack. The accumulation of money or power within a project can be entry points for the perversion of that project despite its best intentions. Relationships between development project leaders, or between development workers and those they are training, can be twisted through the stress of conflict, jealousy, miscommunication, and cultural differences. Both personal relationships and institutional programs need to be protected from spiritual forces that would corrupt or destroy them. This requires an ongoing commitment to spiritual warfare, and to personal and corporate holiness.[6]

- *Development work should challenge unjust practices.*

    Development workers must prepare people to speak out against unjust practices in ways which demonstrate both the love and justice of God. While the non-profit organization is not itself a forum for political advocacy, it is responsible to train people to value justice and to make decisions in a moral context. In the marketplace, workers will be confronted by individual and systemic injustices and should be trained to respond to them in a manner which honors Christ and the values of his Kingdom.

- *The role of the Church in development must not be neglected.*

    Ephesians 2.14 records that it is "Christ himself" who is our peace and who has "destroyed the barrier, the dividing wall of hostility" between Jew and Gentiles. Reconciliation is rooted in the person and work of Christ and thus

---

[6] *See Thomas McAlpine,* **Facing the Powers** *(McAlpine, 1991) for a helpful discussion of ways in which Reformed, Anabaptist, Charismatic, and Social Science perspectives share both differing perspectives and common ground in understanding and confronting spiritual powers.*

Empowering People for Freedom, Wholeness, and Justice (continued)

the importance of Christ's body, the Church, cannot be overlooked. Missionary development projects should both flow out of and result in dynamic churches.

8.3 Development does not seek to guarantee equality of outcome, but equality of opportunity.

Explanation

Development concentrates on providing an environment in which people can learn the importance and disciplines of work, gain skills which enhance the value of their work, and apply the disciplines and skills they acquire. However, no human endeavor is exempt from the moral force of our ability to choose, i.e., to decide whether or not to fully use the gifts, opportunities, and potentials we have been given. Because of variations of motivation, effort and preparation, differences in incomes are inevitable, and ought to be expected. Development programs should both teach and reward initiative.

Implications

- *Each trainee plays a critical role in their own success.*

    While the developers can offer a vast amount of expertise and aid in creating wealth for the trainees, many of the most important attributes necessary for prolonged success are controlled by the trainees. Without the requisite vision, energy, and commitment to do the work for long enough time so profits can be seen, success will not occur. These qualities arise from the drive and conviction of the trainees, not merely from the availability of the developers. Because of this, development cannot guarantee the success of all those involved in the project.

- *Faithful stewardship should lead to increased responsibility.*

    All development projects should have a plan for rewarding faithfulness, skill development, and diligence. Justice demands that increased effort lead to increased reward.

Empowering People for Freedom, Wholeness, and Justice (continued)

8.4 Development workers should respect cultural differences and strive to create a training style that is culturally conducive to those being empowered.

Explanation

Every human culture is "a blueprint that gives the individuals of a society a way of explaining and coping with life. It teaches people how to think, act and respond appropriately in any given situation. It allows people to work together based on a common understanding of reality. It organizes ways of thinking and acting into forms that can be passed on to others" (Cornett 1991, 2). Culture shapes every form of human activity from the observable behaviors (language, dress, food, etc.) to the internal thoughts and attitudes (thinking styles, definitions of beauty and worth, etc.). Understanding how a culture perceives reality, what it values, and how it functions is fundamental information for the development worker.

Although all human cultures are affected by sinful perspectives, attitudes and behaviors which must be confronted by the Gospel, human cultures themselves are celebrated by the Scriptures. The Apostles confirmed that becoming a Christian did not entail having to change one's original culture (Acts 15). The vision of God's Kingdom from Old Testament (Micah 4) to New (Rev. 7.9) involves people from every nation, language and ethnicity. Missionaries from Paul onward have contextualized the Gospel, putting eternal truth in forms that could be understood and practiced by people of diverse cultures (See Cornett 1991, 6-9). Development workers, likewise, must respect cultural differences and seek to contextualize their instruction and resources (See Elliston, Hoke and Voorhies 1989).

Development workers have a unique interest in empowering groups that have been marginalized, oppressed or neglected by the larger society. This will frequently involve working with groups or individuals that are distinct from the dominant culture. Development work will effectively empower immigrants, unassimilated people groups, or people who have been victimized by race or class discrimination, only if it understands and respects the cultural distinctives of these groups.

Finally, development workers must prepare people to live and work in a pluralistic society. Learning how to successfully relate to customers and co-workers from other cultures has become a key component of job training. Although development work must start with the cultural context of those being assisted, it must also enable those workers to respect other cultures and to successfully work in the larger society.

Empowering People for Freedom, Wholeness, and Justice (continued)

Implications

- *Development workers should understand the culture(s) and sub-culture(s) of the people they work with.*

    Development workers should, first of all, gain a basic understanding of the nature of human culture and of strategies for developing effective cross-cultural training relationships.[7] They should gain the fundamental skills necessary for working in the cross-cultural environment (language acquisition, etc.). It is highly desirable for the development worker to have a mentor either from the culture or who is an experienced observer of the culture to assist in the training process.

- *The work environment should be functionally appropriate and aesthetically pleasing when viewed from the perspective of the culture(s) that work or do business there.*

    All human cultures desire environments that combine functionality with beauty. There is significant variation, however, in how beauty and functionality are defined, prioritized and applied from one culture to another. The physical environment in which the development project occurs should take cultural concerns into account.

- *Development workers should be sensitive to how conflict is handled by the culture of the people they work among.*

    Conflict is an inevitable part of working together. It can be a healthy opportunity for growth if handled correctly. Cultural differences, however, can sabotage the process of conflict management. The development worker must take cultural attitudes toward directness/indirectness, shame/guilt, individualism/collectivism, etc. seriously and adapt their conflict management style to reflect those concerns. They must also take seriously their responsibility to prepare people from sub-cultures to work within the dominant culture.

- *Development workers should be sensitive to roles or work that is considered degrading by the culture.*

    Although all honest work carries dignity before God, cultural perceptions of role and status have tremendous power to shape attitudes. Whenever possible, work should be chosen that is not repugnant to the culture. If this

---

[7] Basic resources for gaining an understanding of culture include *The Missionary and Culture* (Cornett 1991), *Beyond Culture* (Hall 1976), *Christianity Confronts Culture* (Mayers 1974), *Ministering Cross-Culturally* (Lingenfelter and Mayers 1986) and *Cross-Cultural Conflicts: Building Relationships for Effective Ministry* (Elmer 1993).

Empowering People for Freedom, Wholeness, and Justice (continued)

is not possible, careful preparation and training should be done to ensure that each person understands the necessity and dignity of the work involved. In some cases it may be necessary to challenge the cultural value system (see Miller, 1989) but this should be done sensitively and with adequate preparation and involvement of the trainees.

- *Developers should prepare trainees for situations that they are likely to encounter in the workplace.*

People from event-oriented cultures, for example, need to understand the time-oriented culture that defines American business practices. Helping workers learn skills and disciplines for success in the larger society is an important part of the training process.

8.5 *The goal of development is to glorify God through excellence and service, not merely to make a profit.*

Explanation

In the ethics of the corporate world, the highest indicator of success is usually the profitability of the business. However, development work that is informed by kingdom values involves a broader vision. Development seeks to emphasize the importance of people-nurturing and training and the production of a quality product that meets human need.

Since producing quality Christian and professional leadership models is a high aim of our development efforts, we must unashamedly emphasize both external profits as well as internal gains. On the one hand, a business, if it is to survive, must be profitable and able to stand on its on. On the other hand, we must strive to produce men and women who are spiritually mature as well as professionally oriented and technically competent. The creation of wealth is not an end in itself; it is a by-product of engaging in business with an eye toward excellence, in the name of Christ.

Empowering People for Freedom, Wholeness, and Justice (continued)

Implications

- *No skill will be taught or product produced simply because it is valued by society or likely to produce a profit.*

  All skills and products must be consistent with the aims of justice, peace and wholeness that characterize the kingdom rule of Christ. Skills and modes of production that degrade human dignity and products that promote injustice, inequity, or human misery are not to be considered fitting for development regardless of their acceptance by the society at large.

- *The aim of development work must not only be to help people obtain and generate resources but also to help them commit to using those resources on behalf of the Kingdom of God.*

  Helping people to obtain education, skills or wealth is ultimately unproductive if these things are not placed at God's service and the service of others. Good development projects will offer people the opportunity to serve God not only with the profits from their labor but through the work itself. Developers must teach and model that work is an opportunity for service to God (Col. 3.23-24).

9. The Need for Application

Each of the points listed above has a section titled "Explanation" and a section titled "Implications." However, for the paper to be complete one more step is necessary. Every implication must be accompanied by a series of *applications*. These applications should be created by development workers in the field, and structured for the unique needs of the local situation.

In creating these applications, the following guidelines should be followed:

- Each local ministry should thoroughly review the "Implications" sections and decide on specific steps which will enable them to apply these principles to their particular development project.

- These steps should be developed in a way that involves the people most affected by each development project.

- Once finalized, the application steps should be committed to writing.

- These applications should be regularly taught and reviewed.

Empowering People for Freedom, Wholeness, and Justice (continued)

- These applications should be included in each regularly scheduled evaluation done by the project.

- Following each scheduled evaluation, there should be a revising and updating of these applications based on what has been learned in experience.

Appendix A

Selected Quotes on the Role of Development Work within the Mission Agency

Christian social transformation differs from secular relief and development in that it serves in an integrated, symbiotic relationship with other ministries of the Church, including evangelism and church planting (Elliston 1989, 172).

My experience with scores of ministries among the poor has taught me that economic projects, when used as entrees into communities, do not facilitate church planting or growth. . . . the two goals—relief and church planting—are different. They are both Christian, and at times compatible. But many times they do not support each other well at all. . . . It appears that where workers enter a community with a priority to proclaim, many deeds of mercy, acts of justice and signs of power will occur. From these the church will be established. But when workers enter with a priority of dealing with economic need, they may assist the people economically very well, but they rarely establish as church. There is a time for both, and there are life callings to do both, but they must be distinguished (Grigg 1992, 163-64).

Avoid institutions if possible at the beachhead stage (community development programs unrelated to church planting, schools, clinics, etc.); they will come later. In Honduras we developed community development work but it grew out of the churches, not vice versa. We taught obedience to the great commandment of loving our neighbor in a practical way. A poverty program can aid church planting if the two are integrated by the Holy Spirit. But churches dependant on charitable institutions are almost always dominated by the foreign missionary and seldom reproduce (Patterson 1992, D-80).

Empowering People for Freedom, Wholeness, and Justice (continued)

All too often native pastors and churches have become preoccupied with ministries that attract Western dollars (such as orphan work) while neglecting more basic pastoral care and evangelism. Even development work, if not wisely administered, can hinder church growth (Ott 1993, 289).

There is a very real danger of recruiting missionary-evangelists primarily on the basis of their abilities and expertise. "Whatever your special interest is, we can use it in our mission"— this is an all-too-common approach to recruitment. As a result, many workers become frustrated when their special ability is not fully utilized; they react by simply "doing their thing" and contributing only indirectly to the task of planting growing churches. Consequently, the so-called secondary or supporting ministries have a way of becoming primary and actually eclipsing the central task! (Hesselgrave 1980, 112).

It is unfortunate that Christian service and witness often seem to be competing concerns in Christian outreach when, in fact, both are biblical and complementary. . . . One reason for this tension is that service enterprises such as hospitals and educational institutions have a way of preempting finances and energies so that evangelism and witness tend to get crowded out (Hesselgrave 1980 p. 328).

Since we believe in the unity of the Bible, we must say that 'The Great Commission is not an isolated command, (but) a natural outflow of the character of God. . . The missionary purpose and thrust of God. . .' Thus, we should not take the Great Commandment and the Great Commission as though they are mutually exclusive. We should take the Great Commandment—to love others—and the Great Commission—to preach—together, integrated in the mission of Jesus Christ, for it is the same Lord, who commanded and commissioned the same disciples and his followers. Therefore, as Di Gangi says, 'to communicate the gospel effectively we must obey the great commandment as well as the great commission' (Cho 1985, 229).

Empowering People for Freedom, Wholeness, and Justice (continued)

Works Cited

Cho, J. Chongham. "The Mission of the Church." See Nicholls, 1985.

Cornett, Terry G., ed. "The Missionary and Culture." *World Impact Ministry Resources*. Los Angeles: World Impact Mission Studies Training Paper, 1991.

Dayton, Donald W. *Discovering an Evangelical Heritage*. 1976. Peabody, MA: Hendrickson, 1988.

Elliston, Edgar J., ed. *Christian Relief and Development: Developing Workers for Effective Ministry*. Dallas: Word Publishing, 1989.

------. "Christian Social Transformation Distinctives." See Elliston, 1989.

Elliston, Edgar J., Stephen J. Hoke, and Samuel Voorhies. "Issues in Contextualizing Christian Leadership." See Elliston, 1989.

Grigg, Viv. "Church of the Poor." *Discipling the City*. 2nd ed. Ed. Roger S. Greenway. Grand Rapids: Baker Book House, 1992.

Hall, Edward T. *Beyond Culture*. Garden City, NY: Anchor Books, 1976.

Hesselgrave, David. *Planting Churches Cross-Culturally: A Guide for Home and Foreign Missions*. Grand Rapids: Baker Book House, 1980.

Hiebert, Paul G. "Evangelism, Church, and Kingdom." See Van Engen, et. al., 1993.

------. "Anthropological Insights for Whole Ministries." See Elliston, 1989.

Hoke, Stephen J. and Samuel J. Voorhies. "Training Relief and Development Workers in the Two-Thirds World." See Elliston, 1989.

Klopfenstein, David E. and Dorothy A. Klopfenstein. "Leadership Research." CityGates. 1 (1995): 21-26.

Klopfenstein, David, Dotty Klopfenstein and Bud Williams. *Come Yourselves Apart: Christian Leadership in the Temporary Community*. Azusa, CA: Holysm Publishing, 1993.

Ladd, George Eldon. *A Theology of the New Testament*. Grand Rapids: Wm. B. Eerdmans, 1974.

Empowering People for Freedom, Wholeness, and Justice (continued)

McAlpine, Thomas H. *Facing the Powers: What are the Options?* Monrovia, CA: MARC-World Vision, 1991.

Miller, Darrow L. "The Development Ethic: Hope for a Culture of Poverty." See Elliston, 1989.

Nicholls, Bruce J., ed. *In Word and Deed: Evangelism and Social Responsibility*. Grand Rapids: Wm. B. Eerdmans, 1985.

Ott, Craig. "Let the Buyer Beware." *Evangelical Missions Quarterly*, 29 (1993): 286-291.

Patterson, George. "The Spontaneous Multiplication of Churches." See Winter and Hawthorne, 1992.

Pickett, Robert C. and Steven C. Hawthorne. "Helping Others Help Themselves: Christian Community Development." See Winter and Hawthorne, 1992.

Stott, John. "Twenty Years After Lausanne: Some Personal Reflections." *International Bulletin of Missionary Research*. 19 (1995): 50-55.

Van Engen, Charles, et. al., eds. *The Good News of the Kingdom: Mission Theology for the Third Millennium*. Maryknoll: Orbis Books, 1993.

Verkuyl, Johannes. *Contemporary Missiology: An Introduction*. Grand Rapids: Wm. B. Eerdmans, 1978.

------. "The Biblical Notion of Kingdom: Test of Validity for Theology of Religion." See Van Engen, et. al., 1993.

Winter, Ralph D. and Steven C. Hawthorne, eds. *Perspectives on the World Christian Movement: A Reader*. Rev. ed. Pasadena: William Carey Library, 1992.

APPENDIX 29
Documenting Your Work
A Guide to Help You Give Credit Where Credit Is Due
The Urban Ministry Institute

Plagiarism is using another person's ideas as if they belonged to you without giving them proper credit. In academic work it is just as wrong to steal a person's ideas as it is to steal a person's property. These ideas may come from the author of a book, an article you have read, or from a fellow student. The way to avoid plagiarism is to carefully use "notes" (textnotes, footnotes, endnotes, etc.) and a "Works Cited" section to help people who read your work know when an idea is one you thought of, and when you are borrowing an idea from another person.

Avoiding Plagiarism

A citation reference is required in a paper whenever you use ideas or information that came from another person's work.

All citation references involve two parts:

- Notes in the body of your paper placed next to each quotation which came from an outside source.

- A "Works Cited" page at the end of your paper or project which gives information about the sources you have used

Using Citation References

There are three basic kinds of notes: parenthetical notes, footnotes, and endnotes. At The Urban Ministry Institute, we recommend that students use parenthetical notes. These notes give the author's last name(s), the date the book was published, and the page number(s) on which you found the information. Example:

Using Notes in Your Paper

> In trying to understand the meaning of Genesis 14.1-24, it is important to recognize that in biblical stories "the place where dialogue is first introduced will be an important moment in revealing the character of the speaker . . ." (Kaiser and Silva 1994, 73). This is certainly true of the character of Melchizedek who speaks words of blessing. This identification of Melchizedek as a positive spiritual influence is reinforced by the fact that he is the King of Salem, since Salem means "safe, at peace" (Wiseman 1996, 1045).

Documenting Your Work (continued)

Creating a Works Cited Page

A "Works Cited" page should be placed at the end of your paper. This page:

- lists every source you quoted in your paper
- is in alphabetical order by author's last name
- includes the date of publication and information about the publisher

The following formatting rules should be followed:

1. Title

The title "Works Cited" should be used and centered on the first line of the page following the top margin.

2. Content

Each reference should list:

- the author's full name (last name first)
- the date of publication
- the title and any special information (Revised edition, 2nd edition, reprint) taken from the cover or title page should be noted
- the city where the publisher is headquartered followed by a colon and the name of the publisher

3. Basic form

- Each piece of information should be separated by a period.
- The second line of a reference (and all following lines) should be indented.
- Book titles should be underlined (or italicized).
- Article titles should be placed in quotes.

Example:

Fee, Gordon D. 1991. *Gospel and Spirit: Issues in New Testament Hermeneutics.* Peabody, MA: Hendrickson Publishers.

Documenting Your Work (continued)

4. Special Forms

A book with multiple authors:

> Kaiser, Walter C., and Moisés Silva. 1994. *An Introduction to Biblical Hermeneutics: The Search for Meaning.* Grand Rapids: Zondervan Publishing House.

An edited book:

> Greenway, Roger S., ed. 1992. *Discipling the City: A Comprehensive Approach to Urban Mission.* 2nd ed. Grand Rapids: Baker Book House.

A book that is part of a series:

> Morris, Leon. 1971. *The Gospel According to John.* Grand Rapids: Wm. B. Eerdmans Publishing Co. The New International Commentary on the New Testament. Gen. ed. F. F. Bruce.

An article in a reference book:

> Wiseman, D. J. "Salem." 1982. In *New Bible Dictionary.* Leicester, England - Downers Grove, IL: InterVarsity Press. Eds. I. H. Marshall and others.

(An example of a "Works Cited" page is located on the next page.)

For Further Research

Standard guides to documenting academic work in the areas of philosophy, religion, theology, and ethics include:

> Atchert, Walter S., and Joseph Gibaldi. 1985. *The MLA Style Manual.* New York: Modern Language Association.

> *The Chicago Manual of Style.* 1993. 14th ed. Chicago: The University of Chicago Press.

> Turabian, Kate L. 1987. *A Manual for Writers of Term Papers, Theses, and Dissertations.* 5th edition. Bonnie Bertwistle Honigsblum, ed. Chicago: The University of Chicago Press.

Documenting Your Work (continued)

Works Cited

Fee, Gordon D. 1991. *Gospel and Spirit: Issues in New Testament Hermeneutics*. Peabody, MA: Hendrickson Publishers.

Greenway, Roger S., ed. 1992. *Discipling the City: A Comprehensive Approach to Urban Mission*. 2nd ed. Grand Rapids: Baker Book House.

Kaiser, Walter C., and Moisés Silva. 1994. *An Introduction to Biblical Hermeneutics: The Search for Meaning*. Grand Rapids: Zondervan Publishing House.

Morris, Leon. 1971. *The Gospel According to John*. Grand Rapids: Wm. B. Eerdmans Publishing Co. *The New International Commentary on the New Testament*. Gen. ed. F. F. Bruce.

Wiseman, D. J. "Salem." 1982. In *New Bible Dictionary*. Leicester, England-Downers Grove, IL: InterVarsity Press. Eds. I. H. Marshall and others.

Mentoring
The Capstone Curriculum

Before the Course Begins

- First, read carefully the Introduction of the Module found on page 5, and browse through the Mentor's Guide in order to gain an understanding of the content that will be covered in the course. The Student's Workbook is identical to your Mentor's Guide. Your guide, however, also contains a section of additional material and resources for each lesson, called *Mentor's Notes*. References to these instructions are indicated by a symbol in the margin: 📖. The Quizzes, Final Exam, and Answer Keys can all be found on the TUMI Satellite Gateway. (This is available to all approved satellites.)

- Second, you are strongly encouraged to view the teaching on both DVDs prior to the beginning of the course.

- Third, you should read any assigned readings associated with the curriculum, whether textbooks, articles or appendices.

- Fourth, it may be helpful to review the key theological themes associated with the course by using Bible dictionaries, theological dictionaries, and commentaries to refresh your familiarity with major topics covered in the curriculum.

- Fifth, please know that the students *are not tested on the reading assignments*. These are given to help the students get a fuller understanding of what the module is teaching, but it is not required that your students be excellent readers to understand what is being taught. For those of you who are receiving this module in any translation other than English, the required reading might not be available in your language. Please select a book or two that is available in your language - one that you think best represents what is being taught in this module - and assign that to your students instead.

- Finally, begin to think about key questions and areas of ministry training that you would like to explore with students in light of the content that is being covered.

Before Each Lesson

Prior to each lesson, you should once again watch the teaching content that is found on the DVD for that class session, and then create a *Contact* and *Connection* section for this lesson.

Preparing the Contact Section

Review the Mentor's Guide to understand the lesson objectives and gather ideas for possible Contact activities. (Two to three Contacts are provided which you may use, or feel free to create your own, if that is more appropriate.)

Then, create a Contact section that introduces the students to the lesson content and captures their interest. As a rule, Contact methods fall into three general categories.

Attention Focusers capture student attention and introduce them to the lesson topic. Attention focusers can be used by themselves with motivated learners or combined with one of the other methods described below. Examples:

- Singing an opening song related to the lesson theme.

- Showing a cartoon or telling a joke that relates to an issue addressed by the lesson.

- Asking students to stand on the left side of the room if they believe that it is easier to teach people how to be saved from the Gospels and to stand on the right side if they believe it is easier to teach people from the Epistles.

Story-telling methods either have the instructor tell a story that illustrates the importance of the lesson content or ask students to share their experiences (stories) about the topic that will be discussed. Examples:

- In a lesson on the role of the pastor, a Mentor may tell the story of conducting a funeral and share the questions and challenges that were part of the experience.

- In a lesson about evangelism, the Mentor may ask students to describe an experience they have had of sharing the Gospel.

Problem-posing activities raise challenging questions for students to answer and lead them toward the lesson content as a source for answering those questions, or they may ask students to list the unanswered questions that they have about the topic that will be discussed. Examples:

- Presenting case studies from ministry situations that call for a leadership decision and having students discuss what the best response would be.

- Problems framed as questions such as "When preaching at a funeral, is it more important for a minister to be truthful or compassionate? Why?"

Regardless of what method is chosen, the key to a successful Contact section is making a transition from the Contact to the Content of the lesson. When planning the Contact section, Mentors should write out a transition statement that builds a bridge from the Contact to the lesson content. For example, if the lesson content was on the truth that the Holy Spirit is a divine Person who is a full member of the Godhead, the Contact activity might be to have students quickly draw a symbol that best represents the Holy Spirit to them. After having them share their drawings and discuss why they chose what they did, the Mentor might make a transition statement along the following lines:

> *Because the Holy Spirit is often represented by symbols like fire or oil in Scripture rather than with a human image like the Father or the Son, it is sometimes difficult to help people understand that the Spirit is a full person within the Godhead who thinks, acts, and speaks as personally as God the Father or Jesus Christ. In this lesson, we want to establish the scriptural basis for understanding that the Spirit is more than just a symbol for "God's power" and think about ways that we can make this plain to people in our congregations.*

This is a helpful transition statement because it directs the students to what they can expect from the lesson content and also prepares them for some of the things that might be discussed in the Connection section that comes later. Although you may adapt your transition statement based on student responses during the Contact section, it is important, during the planning time, to think about what will be said.

Three useful questions for evaluating the Contact section you have created are:

- Is it creative and interesting?

- Does it take into account the needs and interests of this particular group?

- Does it focus people toward the lesson content and arouse their interest in it?

Again, review the Mentor's Guide to understand the lesson objectives and gather ideas for possible Connection activities.

Preparing the Connection Section

Then, create a Connection section that helps students form new associations between truth and their lives (implications) and discuss specific changes in their beliefs, attitudes, or actions that should occur as a result (applications). As you plan, be a little wary of making the Connection section overly specific. Generally this lesson section should come to students as an invitation to discover, rather than as a finished product with all the specific outcomes predetermined.

At the heart of every good Connection section is a question (or series of questions) that asks students how knowing the truth will change their thinking, attitudes, and behaviors. (We have included some Connection questions in order to "prime the pump" of your students, to spur their thinking, and help them generate their own questions arising from their life experience.) Because this is theological and ministry training, the changes we are most concerned with are those associated with the way in which the students train and lead others in their ministry context. Try and focus in on helping students think about this area of application in the questions you develop.

The Connection section can utilize a number of different formats. Students can discuss the implications and applications together in a large Mentor-led group or in small groups with other students (either open discussion or following a pre-written set of questions). Case studies, also, are often good discussion starters. Regardless of the method, in this section both the Mentor and the learning group itself should be seen as a source of wisdom. Since your students are themselves already Christian leaders, there is often a wealth of experience and knowledge that can be drawn on from the students themselves. Students should be encouraged to learn from each other as well as from the Mentor.

Several principles should guide the Connection discussions that you lead:

- First, the primary goal in this section is to bring to the surface the questions that students have. In other words, the questions that occur to students during the lesson take priority over any questions that the Mentor prepares in advance–although the questions raised by an experienced Mentor will still be a useful learning tool. A corollary to this is to assume that the question raised by one student is very often the unspoken question present among the entire group.

- Second, try and focus the discussion on the concrete and the specific rather than the purely theoretical or hypothetical. This part of the lesson is meant to focus on the actual situations that are being faced by the specific students in your classroom.

- Third, do not be afraid to share the wisdom that you have gained through your own ministry experience. You are a key resource to students and they should expect that you will make lessons you have learned available to them. However, always keep in mind that variables of culture, context, and personality may mean that what has worked for you may not always work for everyone. Make suggestions, but dialogue with students about whether your experience seems workable in their context, and if not, what adaptations might be made to make it so.

Three useful questions for evaluating the Connection section you have created are:

- Have I anticipated in advance what the general areas of implication and application are likely to be for the teaching that is given in the lesson?

- Have I created a way to bring student questions to the surface and give them priority?

- Will this help a student leave the classroom knowing what to do with the truth they have learned?

Finally, because the Ministry Project is the structured application project for the entire course, it will be helpful to set aside part of the Connection section to have students discuss what they might choose for their project and to evaluate progress and/or report to the class following completion of the assignment.

Steps in Leading a Lesson

- Take attendance.
- Lead the devotion.
- Say or sing the Nicene Creed and pray.
- Administer the quiz.
- Check Scripture memorization assignment.
- Collect any assignments that are due.

Opening Activities

- Use a Contact provided in the Mentor's Guide, or create your own.

Teach the Contact Section

- Present the Content of the lesson using the video teaching.

Oversee the Content Section

Using the Video Segments
Each lesson has two video teaching segments, each approximately 25 minutes in length. After teaching the Contact section (including the transition statement), play the first video segment for the students. Students can follow this presentation using their Student Workbook which contains a general outline of the material presented and Scripture references and other supplementary materials referenced by the speaker. Once the first segment is viewed, work with the students to confirm that the content was understood.

Ensuring that the Content is Understood
Segue
Using the Mentor's Guide, check for comprehension by asking the questions listed in the "Student Questions and Response" section. Clarify any incomplete understandings that students may demonstrate in their answers.

Ask students if there are any questions that they have about the content and discuss them together as a class. NOTE - The questions here should focus on understanding the content itself rather than on how to apply the learning. Application questions will be the focus of the upcoming Connection section.

Take a short class break and then repeat this process with the second video segment.

Teach the Connection Section

- Summary of Key Concepts
- Student Application and Implications
- Case Studies
- Restatement of Lesson's Thesis
- Resources and Bibliographies
- Ministry Connections
- Counseling and Prayer

Remind Students of Upcoming Assignments

- Scripture Memorization
- Assigned Readings
- Other Assignments

Close Lesson

- Close with prayer
- Be available for any individual student's questions or needs following the class

Please see the next page for an actual "Module Lesson Outline."

The quizzes, the final exam, and their answer keys are located at the back of this book.

Module Lesson Outline

    Lesson Title — Introduction
    Lesson Objectives
    Devotion
    Nicene Creed and Prayer
    Quiz
    Scripture Memorization Review
    Assignments Due

    Contact (1-3) — Contact

    Video Segment 1 Outline — Content
    Segue 1 (Student Questions and Response)
    Video Segment 2 Outline
    Segue 2 (Student Questions and Response)

    Summary of Key Concepts — Connection
    Student Application and Implications
    Case Studies
    Restatement of Lesson's Thesis
    Resources and Bibliographies
    Ministry Connections
    Counseling and Prayer

    Scripture Memorization — Assignments
    Reading Assignment
    Other Assignments
    Looking Forward to the Next Lesson

DOING JUSTICE AND LOVING MERCY: COMPASSION MINISTRIES Capstone Curriculum / 3 0 3

MENTOR'S NOTES 1

Let Justice Roll Down
The Vision and Theology of the Kingdom

📖 **1**
Page 13
Lesson Introduction

Welcome to the Mentor's Guide for Lesson 1, *Let Justice Roll Down: The Vision and Theology of the Kingdom*. The overall focus of the Doing Justice and Loving Mercy: Compassion Ministries module is to provide you with missional, theological, and strategic foundation to this important ministry in the life of the urban Christian leader. We are exposed to the issues of communities which have been historically subject to a litany of chronic social problems, spiritual oppressions, economic exploitation, and moral compromise. To be an urban Christian leaders is synonymous with being a messenger of the justice, mercy, and peace of Jesus Christ, and the church in which he or she serves is the literal outpost and embassy of the Kingdom of God, a rule known by its justice and mercy. In order to benefit from this module, you must embrace this vision as your own, that is, you must see that a critical element in your understanding and application of this material is your ability to visualize yourself as a leader for justice and peace, and the church where you worship and serve Christ as a center for that same justice and mercy. Without your own acceptance of this passion in your own life as mentor, you will be severely limited in your ability to help your students embrace this as their own vision.

As you discuss the various concepts, questions, and issues that arise from the material in this module, it will be important for you to stay cognizant of how central this theme of demonstrating justice and loving mercy truly is. In many ways this entire module is an attempt to understand and to flesh out the simple yet powerful admonition of Micah 6.6-8, an analysis and injunction which summarizes what God would have his person and people to become and to do.

> Mic. 6.6-8 - With what shall I come before the Lord, and bow myself before God on high? Shall I come before him with burnt offerings, with calves a year old? [7] Will the Lord be pleased with thousands of rams, with ten thousands of rivers of oil? Shall I give my firstborn for my transgression, the fruit of my body for the sin of my soul? [8] He has told you, O man, what is good; and what does the Lord require of you but to do justice, and to love kindness, and to walk humbly with your God?

This text is a summary judgment about the kind of service and worship that the Lord desires and demands. On the one hand, God is not interested in the wooden fulfillment of ritualistic obedience in an outward, formalistic manner. Rather, God wants the outward expression of an inward passion concerning his will and its fulfillment in our relationship with him and others. God asks that his people act justly, that is, that they express fairness and rightness in all of their dealings with others, that they love mercy, expressing authentic care and compassion in all facets of their relationships with others, and finally, walk humbly with their God, relating to God in gratitude and humility based upon his gracious covenant and care. God desires this throughout the Scriptures, so the demands here are neither novel nor scarce:

> Deut. 10.12-13 - And now, Israel, what does the Lord your God require of you, but to fear the Lord your God, to walk in all his ways, to love him, to serve the Lord your God with all your heart and with all your soul, [13] and to keep the commandments and statutes of the Lord, which I am commanding you today for your good?

> 1 Sam. 15.22 - And Samuel said, "Has the Lord as great delight in burnt offerings and sacrifices, as in obeying the voice of the Lord? Behold, to obey is better than sacrifice, and to listen than the fat of rams."

> Prov. 21.3 - To do righteousness and justice is more acceptable to the Lord than sacrifice.

> Isa. 1.16-19 - Wash yourselves; make yourselves clean; remove the evil of your deeds from before my eyes; cease to do evil, [17] learn to do good; seek justice, correct oppression; bring justice to the fatherless, plead the widow's cause. [18] "Come now, let us reason together," says the Lord: "though your sins are like scarlet, they shall be as white as snow; though they are red like crimson, they shall become like wool. [19] If you are willing and obedient, you shall eat the good of the land;"

> Isa. 58.6-11 - Is not this the fast that I choose: to loose the bonds of wickedness, to undo the straps of the yoke, to let the oppressed go free, and to break every yoke? [7] Is it not to share your bread with the hungry and bring the homeless poor into your house; when you see the naked, to cover him, and not to hide yourself from your own flesh? [8] Then shall your light break forth like the dawn, and your healing shall spring up speedily; your

righteousness shall go before you; the glory of the Lord shall be your rear guard. [9] Then you shall call, and the Lord will answer; you shall cry, and he will say, "Here I am." If you take away the yoke from your midst, the pointing of the finger, and speaking wickedness, [10] if you pour yourself out for the hungry and satisfy the desire of the afflicted, then shall your light rise in the darkness and your gloom be as the noonday. [11] And the Lord will guide you continually and satisfy your desire in scorched places and make your bones strong; and you shall be like a watered garden, like a spring of water, whose waters do not fail.

To do justice and to love mercy is the surest way we can offer acceptable worship to God, and prove in fact that we are actually walking humbly with him. Unfortunately, the history of God's leaders and his people are often littered with acts of injustice (cf. Mic. 2.1-2; 3.1-3; 6.11), being selfish and disloyal to our neighbors (Mic. 2.8-9; 3.10-11; 6.12), and walking in arrogance and haughtiness before God (2.3). Our aim in this module is to ground the students in the theology of these truths, and probe for implications of them for those living in the city.

The aims of this module are bold and important, so please pay careful attention to them. They are clearly stated, carefully integrated throughout the material, and designed for you to emphasize them throughout the lesson, especially during the discussions and interaction with the students. The more you can highlight the objectives throughout the class period, the better the chances are that they will understand and grasp the magnitude of these objectives.

2
Page 13
Lesson Objectives

The objectives above are designed to shape the entire learning experience of this lesson. Your philosophy must be to integrate all the various ideas, activities, and issues probed in this lesson around them. They represent, in fact, what we hope the students will retain, understand, recite, and embrace as a result of engaging the data in this lesson. They are critical for all you do, and should be referred to often and discussed throughout.

Do not hesitate, therefore, to discuss these objectives briefly before you enter into the class period. Draw the students attention to the objectives, for, in a real sense, this is the heart of your educational aim for the class period in this lesson. Everything discussed and done ought to point back to these objectives. Find ways to highlight these at every turn, to reinforce them and reiterate them as you go.

This devotion technically focuses upon the second commandment, Lev. 19.18, "You shall not take vengeance or bear a grudge against the sons of your own people, but you shall love your neighbor as yourself: I am the Lord." To live out and to experience a growing, intimate walk with God will demand that we do justice and love mercy, and express it in the lives of those with whom we come into contact. We express this neighbor love, this justice and mercy, in the context of specific, particular, and consistent acts of love and mercy to our brothers and sisters, our neighbors, and even our enemies. The idea of being our brother's keeper lies at the heart of what it means to be authentically God-related. To ignore one's brother (neighbor) is to be caught in the web of jealousy, smallness, and cruelty of Cain, who according to John's commentary on the story murdered his brother Abel because his own deeds were evil and his brother's deeds were righteous, 1 John 3.11-15.

To embrace this vision of human interaction as the heart of all true understanding of God is the way to understand John's recurrent refrain on the need to prove and display one's love for God through a love for others (cf. 1 John 4.7-21; John 13.34-35; 15.12; etc.).

As you discuss the truth of the Genesis story with your students, seek to help them understand the correlation of this ancient tale with the injustice and cruelty that is taking place in so many urban communities today. Our only way out of this fog of viciousness is to rediscover this fundamental characteristic of a truly God-conscious person: to be the keeper of one's neighbor and one's brother. At the heart of all true spiritual discernment, this is the central insight into living our lives as leaders who both act justly and demonstrate God's mercy.

*3
Page 13
Devotion*

📖 4
Page 17
Contact

The Contact sections in this lesson were designed to enable your students prepare for the hard intellectual work of considering the vision and theology underlying God's mandate to demonstrate justice and mercy in our lives and through our churches. To investigate the theological data dealing with this, you will need to help your students reflect intentionally on ideas that they normally either take for granted or do not consciously meditate upon very often. Use these questions and ideas to prompt your students to bring to the front of their attention and passions their central questions as they relate to loving others, being loved, and loving God, and how these loves relate to one another, and what the issues and consequences are for failing to demonstrate this justice and mercy to others.

📖 5
Page 28
Student Questions and Response

Review and discussion are important ways to enable your students to clarify the concepts covered on the video, as well as exploring the implications of these questions for their lives and ministries. The following questions are designed to ensure that you work with your students to properly recite and give evidence of their knowledge of the truths covered in the segment, as well as to provide you with an opportunity to rehearse again the critical aims and facts presented in the first video segment. Gauge your time well as you explore the questions here, especially if the questions strike chords in your students and they are intrigued with the concepts. Encourage feedback, reaction, and engagement with the ideas, but monitor your time well in light of the overall schedule you are keeping for this lesson. Additionally, please focus in on the main points considered, and ensure all around that you will have ample time for a break before the next video segment is started.

📖 6
Page 29
Summary of Segment 2

The Concept of the *Imago Dei*

As you explore the meanings of the *imago Dei* with your students, it may be helpful for you to read a nice and concise summary of its major meanings in Scripture from professor Ryken on this critical point:

Psalm 8 is a classic statement of comparison between God and people. In verse 4 the psalmist's question to God, "What are human beings" (RSV) was generated by his contemplation of the three realities of the inanimate creation, humanness and the divine. The reason the psalmist could even pose this question is that humans are image-bearers of God (Gen. 1.26–27) and are self-aware. Because of the imago Dei ("image of God"), the following comparisons can be discerned in Scripture.

At the heart of the imago Dei is personality. God and humans can communicate intelligently together (Ps. 8; Isa. 6.8–13). Both can receive information (Gen. 1.28–30; Heb. 1.1–2), conceive thoughts (Gen. 2.19; 2.23) and process information (Isa. 1.18–20). Although God's knowledge is limitless in accuracy and content (Rom. 11.33–34; Matt. 11.21–24), human knowledge is incomplete (1 Cor. 2.9; 13.12) at its best and twisted at its worst (Eph. 4.17–18). The affective dimension of God (Gen 6.6; Mt 25.21; 2 Cor 7.6) is always perfectly balanced and not dependent on anyone outside the triune Godhead for its completion (Hos. 11.8–9; Acts 17.25; John 17.24–26). God is the lover who never stops loving (Jer. 31.3; Hos. 11.1–9). Although humans can express noble emotions (Ps. 13.5–6; Mark 12.20–30; 2 Cor. 1.24–2.4; 2 John 4), their love often diminishes (Rev. 2.4), is prostituted by loving the evil (2 Tim. 3.2, 4) and rejoices in the wrong thing (Ps. 13.4; Mic. 3.2; 1 Cor. 13.6). They also give themselves to "degrading passions" (Rom. 1.26). God's choices are always wise and right (Gen. 18.25; Isa. 10.13; Rom. 16.27), whereas human choices are often perverse (Rom. 1.32).

Although there are some overlaps in the following, comparisons are also seen in such areas as character (Isa. 54.5; Hos. 3.1–3; Jer. 5.7, 8; 1 Pet. 1.14, 15), metaphors/similes (John 1.19; Isa. 1.6, 7; Luke 3.22; Matt. 10.16), familial relationships (Jer. 5.7, 8; 31.32; Eph. 5.28; Rev. 21.2) and occupational images (Ps. 23; Zech. 11.17; Matt. 13.55; John 10.11; 1 Cor. 3.5–17; Heb. 11.10; 1 Pet. 5.2). Although time- and space-bound image-bearers (Ps. 90.9–10; 139.7–9) do share some finite continuities with the eternal (Ps. 90.2), unlimited (Ps. 139.7–9), nondependent (Acts 17.25) God, they will always be dependent creatures (Gen. 1.27; Ps. 100.3) in need of other humans (Gen. 2.18), divine information (Matt. 4.4; 1 Cor. 2.6–9) and God himself (John 15.5, 11; 17.3; Ps. 16.5–11; 1 Cor. 6.17).

~ Leland Ryken. **Dictionary of Biblical Imagery**. (electronic ed.). Downers Grove, IL: InterVarsity Press, 2000. pp. 336-337.

📖 **7**
*Page 45
Summary of
Key Concepts*

The *Summary of Key Concepts* section allows for you to have quick scan of the central ideas, doctrines, and truths covered in the lesson. They represent the fundamental truths of the entire learning sessions written in declarative sentence form. These ideas are meant to be the residual messages of the lesson, that is, those insights which the lesson's study, interaction, and investigation were meant to unearth and make plain to the students. Rehearsing these statements is your way to cement the central ideas of the study sessions in the minds of the students, and provide them with a ready reference to the outline of the lesson. Make sure that these concepts are clearly defined and carefully considered, for their quiz work and exams will be taken from these items directly.

📖 **8**
*Page 47
Student Application
and Implications*

The *Student Application and Implications* section challenges the student to wrestle with the implications of the lesson for their own life and ministry. It is quite easy for students to forget that the point of our work is not merely to consider ideas, but to connect the content of the lesson to their actual *Sitz im Leben* (German for "situation in life"). Each student must be challenged to ponder the personal ramifications of the truths contained in the lesson for his or her own life, and explore the ideas as they might relate to their own ministry.

Your role, therefore, is to enable your students to think through the central truths with an eye toward their own situations. You may wish to design some questions or use those provided below as water to "prime the pump" of their interests, so to speak. What is significant here is not the questions written below, but for you, in conversation with your students, to settle on a cadre of issues, concerns, questions, and ideas that flow directly from their experience, and relate to their lives and ministries. Do not hesitate to spend the majority of time on some question that arose from the video, or some special concern that is especially relevant in their ministry context right now. The goal of this section is for you to enable them to think critically and theologically in regards to their own lives and ministry contexts. Again, the questions below are provided as guides and primers, and ought not to be seen as absolute necessities. Pick and choose among them, or come up with your own. The key is relevance now, to their context and to their questions.

The overall success of the students in a cohort learning situation is for them to learn as they peruse the material individually, as well as when they gather with their fellow students in dialogue, discussion, and prayer. Both individual and group study are significant. Emphasize the need for both individual and group preparation for an insightful and effective learning session.

You will want to make sure that you remind and challenge your students to set aside quality time to fulfill their assignment for next class lesson, and remind them to pay attention especially to their reading of the material, and the precis (summary) of the written assignment. This is not difficult; the goal is that they would read the material as best as they can and write a few sentences on what they take them to mean. This is a critical intellectual skill for your students to learn, so make sure that you encourage them in this process. Of course, for those students who might find this difficult, assure them of the intent behind this assignment, and emphasize their understanding of the material being the key, not their writing skills. We want to improve their skills, but not at the expense of their encouragement and edification. Nor, however, do we want to sell them short. Strike to find the midpoint between challenge and encouragement here.

 9
*Page 53
Assignments*

Doing Justice and Loving Mercy (1)
The Urban Congregation

MENTOR'S NOTES 2

📖 1
Page 57
Lesson Introduction

Welcome to the Mentor's Guide for Lesson 2, *Doing Justice and Loving Mercy: The Urban Congregation*. This lesson focuses on the congregation's role and responsibility to be a place where the justice and mercy of God are both experienced as well as expressed to others. Indeed, Christian love and charity were designed by the Lord to "begin at home," i.e., in the relationships of brothers and sisters in the church. Where a Christian leader ignores or bypasses his or her responsibility to be concerned *especially* with the welfare and edification of their brothers and sisters in the church, they will inevitably lose the moral authority to demonstrate that same care to others who are outside the faith. For us who believe, we are to do good, but especially to those of the household of faith.

A number of NT texts underwrite this important claim:

Gal. 6.10 - So then, as we have opportunity, let us do good to everyone, and especially to those who are of the household of faith.

Eph. 2.19 - So then you are no longer strangers and aliens, but you are fellow citizens with the saints and members of the household of God.

1 John 3.13-19 - Do not be surprised, brothers, that the world hates you. [14] We know that we have passed out of death into life, because we love the brothers. Whoever does not love abides in death. [15] Everyone who hates his brother is a murderer, and you know that no murderer has eternal life abiding in him. [16] By this we know love, that he laid down his life for us, and we ought to lay down our lives for the brothers. [17] But if anyone has the world's goods and sees his brother in need, yet closes his heart against him, how does God's love abide in him? [18] Little children, let us not love in word or talk but in deed and in truth. [19] By this we shall know that we are of the truth and reassure our heart before him.

1 John 5.1 - Everyone who believes that Jesus is the Christ has been born of God, and everyone who loves the Father loves whoever has been born of him.

John 13.34-35 - A new commandment I give to you, that you love one another: just as I have loved you, you also are to love one another. [35] By this all people will know that you are my disciples, if you have love for one another.

John 15.12-13 - This is my commandment, that you love one another as I have loved you. [13] Greater love has no one than this, that someone lays down his life for his friends.

Rom. 12.10 - Love one another with brotherly affection. Outdo one another in showing honor.

1 Cor. 12.26-27 - If one member suffers, all suffer together; if one member is honored, all rejoice together. [27] Now you are the body of Christ and individually members of it.

Gal. 5.6 - For in Christ Jesus neither circumcision nor uncircumcision counts for anything, but only faith working through love.

Gal. 5.13-14 - For you were called to freedom, brothers. Only do not use your freedom as an opportunity for the flesh, but through love serve one another. [14] For the whole law is fulfilled in one word: "You shall love your neighbor as yourself."

Eph. 5.2 - And walk in love, as Christ loved us and gave himself up for us, a fragrant offering and sacrifice to God.

Col. 3.12-13 - Put on then, as God's chosen ones, holy and beloved, compassion, kindness, humility, meekness, and patience, [13] bearing with one another and, if one has a complaint against another, forgiving each other; as the Lord has forgiven you, so you also must forgive.

Heb. 13.1 - Let brotherly love continue.

1 Pet. 3.8 - Finally, all of you, have unity of mind, sympathy, brotherly love, a tender heart, and a humble mind.

1 John 4.7-9 - Beloved, let us love one another, for love is from God, and whoever loves has been born of God and knows God. [8] Anyone who does not love does not know God, because God is love. [9] In this the love of God

was made manifest among us, that God sent his only Son into the world, so that we might live through him.

These and other texts remind us in Christian leadership that our primary role of demonstrating the love and justice of God must always begin at home.

As before, notice again the objectives below, and remember the role that they play in helping you direct the attention of the students to the truths you will want them to concentrate upon as they engage in the study. Your challenge again as Mentor and instructor is to emphasize the centrality of these concepts throughout the lesson, especially during the discussions and interaction with the students. The more you can highlight the objectives throughout the class period, the better the chances are that they will understand and grasp the magnitude of these objectives.

📖 2
Page 57
Devotion

This devotion focuses on God's intention that his people be abundant in good works, the natural and authenticating sign of those who truly worship God. What is significant here is that the most appropriate expression of a life that comprehends the grace of God will be fleshing out that awareness in tangible acts of kindness, care, and love shown first to members of the family of God, and then and also to those whom we encounter in need.

The concept of hospitality, of practicing good works of tangible care and concern for others, is a key NT concept. John Koenig's concise summary of hospitality may give you insight into the thoroughgoing nature of care for others in the Scriptures:

> Paul writes that "the kingdom of God is not food and drink but righteousness and peace and joy in the Holy Spirit" (Rom. 14.17). This statement appears to contradict the gospel traditions in which meals are seen as a primary locus for the appearance of the Kingdom. But the context in Romans shows that Paul does not intend to separate meals as such from the impact of the gospel. Instead, he is trying to reconcile two factions of believers who disagree over which foods may be consumed and are thus prevented from sharing the common meals of the Church. Presumably, these would include the Lord's Supper. Paul's hope is that all groups in Rome will "welcome one another . . . as Christ has welcomed [them] for the glory of God" (Rom. 15.7). This

reciprocal welcoming, preeminently at meals, becomes both an act of worship and a display of unity that will attract outsiders. A similar point is made when Paul writes to correct abuses of the Lord's Supper in Corinth which have the effect of excluding or dishonoring certain believers, especially the poor. Paul insists that there must be no second-class citizens in this ritual proclamation of the crucified Christ and his world-reversing gospel (1 Cor. 11.17–34). Much earlier in his ministry Paul had opposed Peter publicly in Antioch when the latter reneged on his practice of eating with gentile converts (Gal. 2.11ff.). For Paul, the meals of the Church have become a critical arena for the revealing of God's righteousness in Christ and humanity's response to it. It is not surprising that the Pauline disciple who wrote 1 Timothy considered the talent for hospitality much to be desired in one who occupied the office of bishop (3.2).

In the Fourth Gospel exchanges of food or drink also function as occasions for the revelation of God's love in Christ (4.7ff.; chaps. 6 and 13–17). But the distinctive character of John's concern for hospitality shows itself in his Christological statements. Jesus is not only the door to the sheepfold, the preparer of heavenly chambers, and the way to the Father (10.1ff.; 14.1–6), he is himself the place where believers worship (2.13–22) and dwell (14.20, 23; 15.1ff.). These images take on special meaning if members of the Johannine community have recently suffered expulsion from the synagogue. In the Johannine letters the presbyter-author urges his readers not to receive Christian travelers who do not abide in the doctrine of Christ (2 John 9-10). But he and his emissaries are themselves the objects of inhospitable treatment by a certain Diotrephes (3 John 9-10). Apparently the issue is one of conflict over authority.

Images of hospitality occur with some frequency in the general epistles. James exhorts the recipients of his epistle not to humiliate poor people by assigning them to inferior places in the public assemblies of the Church (2.1–7). The author of 1 Peter addresses his readers as aliens and exiles who were once "no people" but are now a "chosen race... built into a spiritual house to be a holy priesthood" (1.1; 2.4–10). As such, they are to "practice hospitality ungrudgingly to one another" (4.9). This terminology may reflect a real social-political situation in which the readers suffered from their status as resident aliens and transient strangers (Elliott 1981). Perhaps the most winsome of all reflections on hospitality by early Christian writers is found in Hebrews 13.2 where believers are urged to receive strangers graciously on the ground that "thereby some have entertained angels unawares." Clearly the allusion is to Abraham's enthusiastic reception of the three heavenly messengers. But Jesus too may come as a stranger. Matthew, Luke, and John all make this point (Matt. 25.31–46; Luke 24.13–35; John 20.11ff.; 21.1–14). And so does the author of Revelation when he records the words of the Risen One to the church in Laodicea: "Behold, I stand at the door and knock; if any one hears my voice and opens the door, I will come in to him and eat with him, and he with me" (3.20). The context indicates that this meal with Jesus, like many of those narrated in the gospels, will be one of repentance and reconciliation.

~ John Koenig. "Hospitality." **The Anchor Bible Dictionary**. Vol. 3. D. N. Freedman, ed. New York: Doubleday Press, 1996. pp. 299-301.

While Koenig's summary focuses on the meal and welcoming strangers aspect of hospitality, it clearly shows how central the idea of good works shown in basic, tangible ways to others is for us as believers. Challenge your students to recognize and seek to realize the importance of practical good works lived out daily in the midst of the Christian community.

3
Page 74
Student Questions and Response

All of the questions below highlight some aspect of these central ideas, and you will want to help your students both review their importance as well as explore the meaning of these claims. Seek to ensure that the students know the material, the basic claims, the Scriptures offered to support the points, and some of the critical issues they may have as they connect to the lesson aims of the first segment. Make certain that you watch the clock here, covering the questions below and those posed by your students, and watch for any tangents which may lead you from rehearsing the critical facts and main points.

4
Page 88
Student Questions and Response

In this segment you will want to explore the "2-4-6" principles of doing justice and loving mercy in the segment. Remember, we just covered two objects of justice and mercy (the Church and outsiders), four channels of God's divine justice (the family, the local assembly, the association, order, or mission society, and finally the state). We also listed the six principles of doing this kind of ministry in a local church setting. Your aim here ought to be to enable your students to get a bird's eye view of some of the central elements involved in a local church setting where issues of justice, mercy, love, peace, and good works are to be considered. This segment provided an overview of those elements, and the questions below are designed to help you both review and explore their meaning and ramifications.

The following case studies center upon dilemmas, problems, and questions related to the issue of fleshing out love and justice in the midst of our urban congregations today. These studies are meant to be discussed critically and carefully. One of the most important skills for emerging Christian leaders is their ability to wrestle with the details of a situation, see patterns, apply principles of Scripture, and suggest alternative approaches to resolve the dilemmas raised in the cases. Wrestle together with your students on these cases, explore trajectories that they want to consider, and probe beneath the surface for more tangible, basic solutions. Of course, you will have to gauge your time well, especially if your students are intrigued with the concepts, and want to discuss their implications at length.

📖 5
Page 93
Case Studies

Before we finish this lesson, you may find Ryken's summary excellent on the role of the Church as a "house of hospitality." It will provide you with much wisdom as you explore the final two lessons, which deal very specifically in how we may demonstrate this kind of love and justice in the urban community and beyond.

📖 6
Page 95
Restatement of the Lesson's Thesis

> *The NT likewise abounds in references to hospitality. The record of Jesus' life as an itinerant teacher and miracle worker is a virtual chronicle of hospitality received (Matt. 26.6; Mark 1.29; 7.24; 14.3; Luke 7.36; 14.1, 12; John 12.1-2). The most famous pictures of that hospitality are Mary and Martha's entertainment of Jesus (Luke 10.38-42) and the occasion when Jesus invited himself to the house of Zacchaeus (Luke 19.1-10). In his Olivet Discourse, Jesus made hospitality to himself and to his missionary "brothers" the key to entering the Kingdom of heaven in his statement, "For I was hungry and you gave me food, I was thirsty and you gave me*

something to drink, I was a stranger and you welcomed me" (Matt. 25.35 NRSV). When Jesus dispatched his followers, he sent them out on the assumption that they would depend on hospitality as they traveled (Matt. 10.9–14; Mark 6.7–10; Luke 9.1–4). Failure on the part of villagers to provide such hospitality was said by Jesus to seal their doom (Matt. 10.14–15; Mark 6.11; Luke 9.5).

Similar pictures of hospitality pervade NT glimpses of life in the early church (Acts 2.46). Hospitality was key to the missionary endeavor of the early church, as evidenced by the way the ministries of Peter (Acts 10.6, 18, 32, 48) and Paul (Acts 16.15; 18.7; 21.4, 8, 16; 28.7) relied on a supply of hospitable contacts as they traveled on their missionary ventures. Corresponding to these pictures of hospitality are NT injunctions to practice it: "Extend hospitality to strangers" (Rom. 12.13 NRSV); "Do not neglect to show hospitality to strangers, for by doing that some have entertained angels without knowing it" (Heb 13.2 NRSV); "Be hospitable to one another without complaining" (1 Pet. 4.9 NRSV). The qualifications for a bishop included the showing of hospitality (1 Tim. 3.2; Titus 1.8). The same qualification applied to widows who wished to be "put on the list" of Christian workers (1 Tim. 5.10).

The Kingdom of God and heaven are figured as places and times where God will fulfill the desire and promise of unspoiled ultimate hospitality-unending feasting in God's vast abode, heaven. The criterion for entering heaven is acceptance of the offer of salvation in Christ. In a surprising reversal early in the book of Revelation, the individual who accepts Christ is pictured as the host, with Christ as the self-invited guest who says, "Behold, I stand at the door and knock; if any one hears my voice and opens the door, I will come in to him and eat with him, and he with me" (Rev. 3.20 RSV). Later, those who enter heaven are pictured as guests at a marriage supper of the Lamb (Rev. 19.7–9). The Apocalypse ends with a final invitation: "The Spirit and the bride say, 'Come.' And let everyone who hears say, 'Come.' And let everyone who is thirsty come. Let anyone who wishes take the water of life as a gift" (Rev. 22.17 NRSV).

~ Leland Ryken. **The Dictionary of Biblical Imagery**. (electronic ed.) Downers Grove, IL: InterVarsity Press, 2000. p. 404.

It may be helpful for you to remind the students of the correlation between their own wrestling with the truth of God as soldiers of the Lord and prevailing prayer. E.M. Bounds provides a clear exposition of this connection in the following extended quote:

> *How can the strong soldier be made stronger still? How can the victorious battler be made still more victorious? Here are Paul's explicit directions to that end: "Praying always with all prayer and supplication in the Spirit, and watching thereunto with all perseverance and supplication for all saints." Prayer, and more prayer, adds to the fighting qualities and the more certain victories of God's good fighting-men. The power of prayer is most forceful on the battle-field amid the din and strife of the conflict. Paul was preeminently a soldier of the Cross. For him, life was no flowery bed of ease. He was no dress-parade, holiday soldier, whose only business was to don a uniform on set occasions. His was a life of intense conflict, the facing of many adversaries, the exercise of unsleeping vigilance and constant effort. And, at its close — in sight of the end — we hear him chanting his final song of victory, a "I have fought a good fight," and reading between the lines, we see that he is more than conqueror!*
>
> *In his Epistle to the Romans, Paul indicates the nature of his soldier-life, giving us some views of the kind of praying needed for such a career. He writes: "Now I beseech you, brethren, for the Lord Jesus Christ's sake, and for the love of the Spirit, that ye strive together with me in your prayers to God for me, that I may be delivered from them that do not believe in Judaea."*
>
> *Paul had foes in Judaea — foes who beset and opposed him in the form of "unbelieving men" and this, added to other weighty reasons, led him to urge the Roman Christians to "strive with him in prayer." That word "strive" indicated wrestling, the putting forth of great effort. This is the kind of effort, and this is the sort of spirit, which must possess the Christian soldier.*
>
> *Here is a great soldier, a captain-general, in the great struggle, faced by malignant forces who seek his ruin. His force is well-nigh spent. What reinforcements can he count on? What can give help and bring success to a warrior in such a pressing emergency? It is a critical moment in the conflict. What force can be added to the*

📖 7
Page 96
Counseling and Prayer

energy of his own prayers? The answer is — in the prayers of others, even the prayers of his brethren who were at Rome. These, he believes, will bring him additional aid, so that he can win his fight, overcome his adversaries, and, ultimately, prevail.

The Christian soldier is to pray at all seasons, and under all circumstances. His praying must be arranged so as to cover his times of peace as well as his hours of active conflict. It must be available in his marching and his fighting. Prayer must diffuse all effort, impregnate all ventures, decide all issues. The Christian soldier must be as intense in his praying as in his fighting, for his victories will depend very much more on his praying than on his fighting. Fervent supplication must be added to steady resolve, prayer and supplication must supplement the armour of God. The Holy Spirit must aid the supplication with his own strenuous plea. And the soldier must pray in the Spirit. In this, as in other forms of warfare, eternal vigilance is the price of victory; and thus, watchfulness and persistent perseverance, must mark the every activity of the Christian warrior.

~ E. M. Bounds. **The Necessity of Prayer**.
Oak Harbor, WA: Logos Research Systems, Inc., 1999.

Challenge your students in every way to make and keep prayer a priority in every aspect of their ministry, from study to life application to teaching others.

Doing Justice and Loving Mercy (2)
The Urban Community and Neighborhood

MENTOR'S NOTES 3

📖 1
Page 101
Lesson Introduction

Welcome to the Mentor's Guide for Lesson 3, *Doing Justice and Loving Mercy: The Urban Community and Neighborhood*. The overall focus of this lessons is to explore the kinds of ways the Church throughout history has come to understand their relationship to the world, and therefore, how it has determined what are the best ways to both do justice and love mercy in the world. As always, we will not take our cues from the latest fad or phase of teaching in current evangelical practice, but root our understandings in the doctrine of the Church revealed in Scripture and affirmed in the Nicene Creed. As we understand the role of God as Creator and Sovereign Controller of all things, and his appointment of the risen Jesus as Lord of all, we will then have a framework for understanding a *Christian* view of love and justice. Christian thinkers and practitioners throughout history have explored their conception of church/world relationships in a number of ways, and often their experimentation has led to compromise of the Word (on the one hand) as well as terrible persecution (on the other). Your role this lesson is to help your students gain a historical perspective on these issues, and once that is acquired, to help them develop their own personal ministry strategy that will allow them to pursue love and justice in the most effective, wise, and collaborative fashion possible.

One of the things you will emphasize throughout this study is the need for wisdom and simplicity as we explore models and ways to live out the implications of the Kingdom in our urban neighborhoods. As you explore the church and world relationships covered in this lesson, it may provide you with an adequate background to see how D. S. Lim describes the plan of action that the earliest followers of Jesus used as they considered how to fulfill the Great Commission throughout the world. Notice especially his emphasis on simplicity and responsiveness in their approaches to touching their world for Christ:

> *Was there a general plan of action to evangelize the world? In terms of geographical expansion, it was spontaneous via the existing networks of sea and land trade routes, perhaps even to India and Armenia. Like Paul, most evangelizers settled in cities of Roman governance, Greek culture, Jewish influence and commercial importance, such as Antioch, Philippi, Corinth, Paphos, Ephesus, Rome. Paul chose to set up churches in only a couple of urban centers in each province (cf. Acts 19.10; Rom. 15.19-23; see Centers of Christianity) to serve as outreach centers in their respective*

regions. The neat schema of outward expansion "to the ends of the earth" from Jerusalem (summed up in Acts 1.8) is most probably Lukan.

Total Mobilization. The prime agents in evangelism were the ordinary believers (Acts 8.4; 11.19–21), called "informal missionaries" (Harnack; Green). Wherever they lived or migrated, the good news spread by word of mouth through their natural relationships of families, friends and acquaintances (cf. 1 Pet. 3.15). As they "gossiped the gospel" with conviction and enthusiasm, people were converted and added to the church and its evangelistic force. Those who were gifted with special endowments to preach were encouraged to use them faithfully (1 Pet. 4.10–11; cf. 1 Cor. 12–14; Rom. 12.6–8).

These evangelizers were "equipped" (cf. Eph. 4.11–13) by two kinds of church leaders: the itinerant **apostoloi** ("apostles" or "missionaries") and the resident **presbyteroi** ("elders"). Besides the Twelve and Paul, there were "missionaries of the churches" commissioned and supported by the house churches (2 Cor. 8.23; Phil. 2.25; 3 John 6–7; Rev. 2.2; cf. 1 Cor. 9.4; 1 Thess. 2.7; etc.). They went from place to place, appointed local leaders and then proceeded to preach in other areas where people had yet to be evangelized (cf. Acts 14.23–28).

Though the main task of the elders (also called **episkopoi**, "overseers" or "bishops," and **diakonoi**, "deacons," as in Phil. 1.1) was to build up the Christian community so that all members discovered and used their spiritual gifts; they also served as exemplars in doing evangelism (2 Tim. 4.5; cf. 1 Pet. 5.3), just as Paul set this evangelistic concern as a model for the Ephesian elders (Acts 20.18–28). One of their qualifications for church "office" was a good reputation before unbelievers (1 Tim. 3.1–7).

Simple Structures. Total mobilization was maintained for a couple of centuries, because the early Christians met in homes and ministered "from house to house" (Acts 20.20; cf. 2.46; 5.42; Rom. 16). With no buildings to maintain, they used their limited resources to support the itinerant ministers and the poor among them. This was most probably done consciously, not just by force of circumstance (frequent poverty and persecution), for they were not without resources (cf. Acts 2.44–45;

4.34–5.11; 1 Cor. 16.1–4; 2 Cor. 8.1–5) and faced no prohibition against building temples, synagogues or shrines for religious purposes.

The conversion of a husband led usually to the baptism of the entire household, which included relatives, friends, slaves or freedmen, and even clients. Though the process was very difficult, converted wives were exhorted to win their husbands to Christ through godly behavior (1 Pet. 3.1–6; cf. 1 Cor. 7.14). Such homes then served as centers for prayer and worship (Acts 1.13–14; 2.46; 12.12), pastoral care and fellowship (Acts 16.40; 18.26; 20.20–21; 21.7), hospitality (Acts 16.15, 32–34; 17.5–7; 18.7; 21.8) and especially evangelism (Acts 5.42; 10.22; 16.32; 28.17–18).

~ D. S. Lim. "Evangelism in the Early Church."
Dictionary of the Later New Testament and its Developments
R. P. Martin, ed. (electronic ed.). Downers Grove, IL: InterVarsity Press, 2000.

Notice how the spreading of the Good News and good works was both *organic* and *spontaneous*. This does not undermine the need for a strategy, but shows *the spiritual nature of all genuine Christian care*. What is striking here is the mixture between a flexible responsiveness to their culture and an openness to the Holy Spirit's leading and guidance. This is still a good combination for change for urban leaders and congregations seeking to demonstrate the life of the Kingdom in their perspective neighborhoods.

The objectives listed will provide your students with the direction and insight they need to master the materials in the lesson. Ensure that they both understand them and rehearse them throughout the study.

Page 102 Devotion

This devotion focuses on the need to depend upon the Lord for wisdom. While this lesson will concentrate upon the need for us to exercise the shrewdest kind of judgment and foresight in approaching many of the difficult and intractable problems being faced in the city today, ultimately spreadsheets, research data, and logical plans can never do what the filling of the Holy Spirit can. In Christ Jesus all the treasures of wisdom and knowledge reside (cf. Col. 2.2-3); if we in fact desire to be wise in our endeavors of good works, we will inevitably have to entreat the direction and love of our Lord Jesus.

Does this mean that all forms of planning and strategizing are fundamentally ungodly and ineffective? Of course not! The Scriptures contain numerous examples of those who employed methods of planning, strategy, foresight, shrewdness, and ingenuity in carrying out the will and plan of God, including Noah, Moses, Joshua, Hezekiah, Jacob, and many others. What this lesson seeks to resolve is the old, and unconvincing dichotomy and disagreement between faith and strategy, between the filling of the Spirit and wise strategy from God. The goal here is to see how these concepts are *complimentary* rather than *contradictory*, and in fact *supplement* each other rather than *annul* one another. The devotion asserts what the Bible does without any equivocation: God Almighty is the source of all truth, wisdom, and knowledge. This being the case, we can seek him with all our hearts and come to experience his grace and mercy directly through the provision of his wisdom in our lives and ministries. We do not seek to do justice and mercy in either our own strength or wisdom. Rather, seeking the mind of the Lord and the goodness of God, we unashamedly affirm God as the Source of all wisdom, and refuse to go forward without his intervention, leading, and guidance. This kind of humility and approach, combined with a deep resolve to bring glory and honor to God in all that we do, can lead to new, innovative, and long lasting results and acts of compassion. We must begin, however, at the beginning–the goodness and wisdom of the God and Father of our Lord Jesus Christ.

As you begin to explore with your students the biblical and historical understandings of the relationship of the Church and world, you will find B. J. Dodd's summary of the concept of world helpful:

> *The most common usage of "world" in James, 2 Peter and 1 John is to identify people at enmity with God, those who oppose God's will and purpose: "Do you not know that friendship with the world is enmity with God" (James 4.4). Therefore a Christian is "to keep oneself unstained from the world" (James 1.27). 2 Peter describes the world as the place where antagonism toward God dwells, incurring "defilements" that need to be escaped (2 Pet. 2.20; cf. Pol. Phil. 5.3; Ign. Rom. 3.3; 7.1).*

3
*Page 106
Summary of
Segment 1*

*In 1 John (see John, Letters of) and John's Gospel, where more than half of the occurrences of **kosmos** in the NT occur, the focus is no longer on the world perceived as creation, but now the emphasis lies upon the world as people who have turned away from God to deceit and delusion. . . . 1 John depicts a sharp dichotomy between two sides, the world's and God's. The two are diametrically opposed, and his auditors must choose between the world and God. The world is considered apostate from God, and the whole point of John's rhetoric is to urge full loyalty to God: "We know that we are of God, and the whole world is in the power of the evil one" (1 John 5.19); "they are of the world, therefore what they say is of the world and the world listens to them" (1 John 4.5). The believer is not to "love the world or the things in the world. If anyone loves the world, love for the Father is not in him" (1 John 2.15). Because the things of God and the people of God are in sharp opposition with the world, believers are not to be perplexed that the world "hates" them (1 John 3.13). Sinfulness originates from and belongs to this world and is to be avoided (1 John 2.16–17; cf. 1 John 4.3–5, 9). Similarly Ignatius sharply exhorts, "Do not talk about Jesus Christ while you desire the world" (Ign. Rom. 7.1).*

Even though the world is characterized in so many negative ways in the Johannine writings, there is hope for it because Christ was sent "as the savior of the world" (1 John 4.14), and whoever has faith in him will be victorious in overcoming the opposition of the world (1 John 5.4–5). It is worthwhile to compare this distinctive emphasis with the Fourth Gospel's characterization of the world as a place under God's mercy (e.g., John 3.16–17; 12.47), though still in opposition to the truth (John 15.18–19), and Johannine believers are rescued "from the world" (John 17.6; cf. John 17.11) to which they are sent back (John 17.18). 1 John uses "world" sometimes in a sense that encompasses the entire sphere of people outside the church. This is how false teachers can be identified: they no longer side with the church but "have gone out into the world" (1 John 4.1). Since they are "of the world" they no longer should be heeded or trusted (1 John 4.5; cf. 2 John 7).

~ B. J. Dodd. "World." **Dictionary of the Later New Testament and its Developments.** R. P. Martin, ed. (electronic ed.). Downers Grove, IL: InterVarsity Press, 2000.

Because of this remarkably dialectical relationship between the world and the Church, believers have wrestled with how ought we to correctly view the Church's relationship to the world, as strictly antagonistic, as transformative, as completely separate, and so on. Pay careful attention to the various kinds of models that theologians and church men and women have viewed as the relationship between the two.

As you explore the various church and world models considered in the first video segment, seek to help your students view this relationship both *theologically* and *missionally*, that is, in light of the doctrines of the Word of God, and our responsibility to engage the word by proclaiming the good news of the Kingdom, as well as demonstrating the good works comprised of love, mercy, and justice. Concentrate on helping your students grapple with the difficulty these questions have given believers of conscience for centuries, and suggest ways in which they may begin to form their own theological judgments about these important theological and ministry issues.

📖 **4**
*Page 118
Student Questions
and Response*

The difficulty the Church has had in comprehending its precise relationship to the world has been solidly captured in the commentary of O. R. Barclay in an article of the biblical meaning of the world:

📖 **5**
*Page 118
Student Questions
and Response*

> *In few biblical passages the word 'world' (**kosmos**) is used in the sense of mankind. In John 3.16, for instance, we are told of God's love for 'the world' in this sense. When this is what is meant, then the Christian duty to love mankind is clear.*
>
> *It is in the other, and more usual, sense that there are problems. In this wider sense 'the world' usually means 'the environment of humanity'. That is to say, it includes not only the natural environment and all its varied resources, but also the cultural and social environment brought into being by sinful humanity. In this sense, the devil is described as the 'prince' or 'ruler of this world' who was condemned and cast out by the power and work of Christ (John 12.31; 16.11; Eph. 6.12). 'The whole world lies in the power of the evil one' (1 John 5.19).*
>
> *When these passages about the rule of the devil over the world are added to verses like 1 John 2.15-17, where we are warned to love neither 'the world nor the things in the*

> *world', there is a prima facie case for a negative attitude to both material goods and to man's cultural and other natural abilities such as marriage. On the other hand, 'everything created by God is good', even in a fallen world. We are to receive all these gifts with thanksgiving if we 'believe and know the truth'. A negative view of food and marriage, and even money and the things that it can buy, is roundly condemned by the NT, especially in the Pastoral Epistles (notably 1 Tim. 2.1-4; 4.1-10; 5.8-23; 6.17-19, and Titus 3.8-14). The church down the ages has wrestled with these two apparently competing emphases.*
>
> ~ O. R. Barclay. "World." **New Dictionary of Theology.** (electronic ed.) S. B. Ferguson, ed. Downers Grove, IL: InterVarsity Press, 2000. p. 279.

What we must help our students understand is that this relationship has been contested by sincere and godly Christian thinkers down through the centuries, producing different results depending on the times in which the views were formed, and the emphasis of the thinkers involved. As emerging Christian leaders, they must carefully and critically come to terms with their own belief about the role of the Church in the world, and their role as leaders of the Church. What we are arguing in this module is that as those "in the world but not of it," we must find ways to display the life of the Age to come *in the midst of this present age*. Jesus' commentary sums it up well:

> John 17.14-19 - I have given them your word, and the world has hated them because they are not of the world, just as I am not of the world. [15] I do not ask that you take them out of the world, but that you keep them from the evil one. [16] They are not of the world, just as I am not of the world. [17] Sanctify them in the truth; your word is truth. [18] As you sent me into the world, so I have sent them into the world. [19] And for their sake I consecrate myself, that they also may be sanctified in truth.

Page 143 Assignments

It is now important for you to attend some of the particulars dealing with the administration of the course, especially those dealing with the assignments that the students must shortly begin to complete.

By the end of the second class session, you ought to have emphasized with the students the need for them to have done the spadework and thought out precisely how they intend on carrying out their Ministry Project. Also, by this time, you should have emphasized their selection of the passage they will study for their Exegetical Project. Both will be done with far better thought and excellence the earlier the students begin to think through them and decide what they want to do. Do not fail to emphasize this, for, as in all study, at the end of the course many things become due, and the students will begin to feel the pressure of getting a number of assignments in at the same time. Any way that you can remind them of the need for advanced planning will be wonderfully helpful for them, whether they realize it immediately or not.

Because of this, we do advocate that you consider docking a modest amount of points for late papers, exams, and projects. While the amount may be nominal, your enforcement of your rules will help them to learn to be efficient and on time as they continue in their studies.

Doing Justice and Loving Mercy (3)
Society and World

MENTOR'S NOTES 4

📖 **1**
Page 147
Lesson Introduction

Welcome to the Mentor's Guide for Lesson 4, *Doing Justice and Loving Mercy: Society and World*. In the previous lessons we concentrated our attention on the theological framework underlying the doing of justice and mercy in the Scriptures, and explored its ramifications through the creed, through the local congregation, and through ministries of compassion. We have also looked at a variety of models of church/world relations, and explored what it means to embrace a strategy that allows us to efficiently and effectively minister under the constraints of limited time, money, and resources.

Now, in this final lesson, we zoom out to take a look at our responsibility to deal with some of the critical issues of our day and time, namely, poverty and oppression, the human environment, ethnocentrism and difference, and war and violence. As world Christians committed to displaying Christ and his Kingdom *throughout the entire earth*, we must labor to wrestle with the issues that shape our world today. Ultimately, if we are concerned about the Kingdom's advance in the earth, we must also wrestle with these issues as they are affecting the lives of untold millions of people who today live in conditions and societies where even the most basic needs and rights are unmet and eclipsed respectively. Your responsibility is to help your students feel the weight of their responsibility not just for those close by, but those far off. Indeed, our ultimate goal is that these leaders and students will develop burdens for justice that embrace all people wherever they live and whatever they face.

At the heart of the Christian prophetic burden is the responsibility to wrestle with the weightiest matters of the Law and the heart of the Gospel, even those described by our Lord in Matthew's Gospel. His indictment of the misplaced priorities of the religious leaders of his day ought to bring a sense of pause and sobriety to our lives today:

> Matthew 23:23 - "Woe to you, scribes and Pharisees, hypocrites! For you tithe mint and dill and cumin, and have neglected the weightier matters of the law: justice and mercy and faithfulness. These you ought to have done, without neglecting the others."

This text reveals that within the Law and its self-understanding, some things are weightier than others: *justice, mercy, and faithfulness* are considered by our Lord to be the things that matter most. This is confirmed in the fact that as early as the pre-exilic prophets, the will and word of God was plainly interpreted to show how certain national disasters occurred in Israel as a transparent sign of God's righteous judgment against his people, elementally for two distinct and interlocking reasons: for rank idolatry and for failure to do justice and love mercy among those most needy and vulnerable (e.g., Amos 4-8; Hos. 4-10; Jer. 2-8).

What we are seeking to establish now is a way in which we can expand our understanding of these concepts to include our responsibility not merely for our own families and congregations, not merely for our own neighborhoods and cities, or even our own regions or nations. To truly be a world Christian is to be concerned about the needs of the poor throughout the entire earth, to feel a sense of personal burden and responsibility for all who suffer wherever they are, and a desire to contribute to the advance of the Kingdom in all places needing to see and hear of the justice and righteousness of Jesus Christ in their own midst.

As in all previous lessons, your attention to the objectives will be strategically important. Because of the breadth of ideas and concepts covered in this lesson, you will want to clearly state and patiently cover these aims throughout the lesson, and especially remind the students of them during the discussions and interaction with them. The more you can highlight the objectives throughout the class period, the better the chances are that they will understand and grasp the magnitude of these objectives.

This devotion highlights one of the critical obligations and manifestations of authentic spirituality: overwhelming, hilarious generosity. One recurring flaw we can unfortunately fall prey too is equating ritualistic regularity with the kind of open-hearted, open-handed generosity and care that is characteristic of all true spiritual reality. Once the life and power of God has come into the hearts and lives of his people, so does an overwhelming impulse to give, to serve, to be hospitable.

📖 2
*Page 148
Devotion*

This tangible love as the sign and token of all legitimate salvation and spirituality seems to be less mentioned and emphasized as the sign of authentic faith, even in churches claiming unbroken allegiance to the Word of God.

Authentic righteousness which comes through faith in Jesus Christ also results in tangible works of righteousness and mercy that are visible, legitimate, and expressive of a redeemed heart. R. C. Sproul speaks poignantly about the inability for many professing Christians to interpret their religious lives in terms of the kind of righteous acts that are indicative of true spirituality:

> *In Old Testament Israel and among the New Testament Pharisees, liturgical righteousness was substituted for authentic righteousness. That is to say, men became satisfied with obeying the rituals of the religious community, rather than fulfilling the broader implications of the law. The Pharisees, for example, were rebuked by Jesus for tithing their mint and cumin while omitting the weightier matters of the law: justice and mercy. Jesus indicated that the Pharisees were correct in giving their tithes, but were incorrect in assuming that the liturgical exercises had completed the requirements of the law. Here liturgical righteousness had become a substitute for true and full obedience.*
>
> *Within the evangelical world, righteousness is a rare word indeed. We speak of morality, spirituality, and piety. Seldom, however, do we speak of righteousness. Yet the goal of our redemption is not piety or spirituality but righteousness. Spirituality in the New Testament sense is a means to the end of righteousness. Being spiritual means that we are exercising the spiritual graces given by God to mold us after the image of his Son. That is, the discipline of prayer, Bible study, church fellowship, witnessing, and the like are not ends in themselves, but are designed to assist us in living righteously. We are stunted in our growth if we assume that the end of the Christian life is spirituality.*
>
> *Spiritual concerns are but the beginning of our walk with God. We must beware of the subtle danger of thinking that spirituality completes the requirements of Christ. To fall into such a trap—the trap of the Pharisees—is to substitute liturgical or ritualistic practices for authentic righteousness. By all means we are to pray and to*

study the Bible; we are to bear witness in evangelism. But we must never, at any point in our lives, rest from our pursuit of righteousness.

~ R. C. Sproul. **Following Christ**. (electronic ed.). Wheaton, IL: Tyndale House Publishers, 1996.

For us to speak about the nature of spirituality absent from the tangible deeds of good works, generosity, and hospitality sterilizes our view of spiritual reality, and turns our faith into something abstract and unconvincing. God loves the cheerful giver. The focus is not on the amount, but the way in which the gifts are given. Cheerfully, joyfully, and hilariously. The grace of God produces such an impact that the one so touched by it is compelled to give–of their goods, of their time, and even their lives. This is both the standard and heart of what it truly means to be spiritual, righteous, and authentic. Paul's statement still resonates today as it did when he spoke our Lord's word to the Corinthians: "In all things I have shown you that by working hard in this way we must help the weak and remember the words of the Lord Jesus, how he himself said, 'It is more blessed to give than to receive.' " (Acts 20.35).

With this statement, the entire tenor of Scripture agrees. Here is a sampling of the same sentiment:

> Ps. 41.1-3 - Blessed is the one who considers the poor! In the day of trouble the Lord delivers him; [2] the Lord protects him and keeps him alive; he is called blessed in the land; you do not give him up to the will of his enemies. [3] The Lord sustains him on his sickbed; in his illness you restore him to full health.

> Ps. 112.5-9 - It is well with the man who deals generously and lends; who conducts his affairs with justice. [6] For the righteous will never be moved; he will be remembered forever. [7] He is not afraid of bad news; his heart is firm, trusting in the Lord. [8] His heart is steady; he will not be afraid, until he looks in triumph on his adversaries. [9] He has distributed freely; he has given to the poor; his righteousness endures forever; his horn is exalted in honor.

Prov. 19.17 - Whoever is generous to the poor lends to the Lord, and he will repay him for his deed.

Isa. 32.8 - But he who is noble plans noble things, and on noble things he stands.

Isa. 58.6-12 - Is not this the fast that I choose: to loose the bonds of wickedness, to undo the straps of the yoke, to let the oppressed go free, and to break every yoke? [7] Is it not to share your bread with the hungry and bring the homeless poor into your house; when you see the naked, to cover him, and not to hide yourself from your own flesh? [8] Then shall your light break forth like the dawn, and your healing shall spring up speedily; your righteousness shall go before you; the glory of the Lord shall be your rear guard. [9] Then you shall call, and the Lord will answer; you shall cry, and he will say, 'Here I am.' If you take away the yoke from your midst, the pointing of the finger, and speaking wickedness, [10] if you pour yourself out for the hungry and satisfy the desire of the afflicted, then shall your light rise in the darkness and your gloom be as the noonday. [11] And the Lord will guide you continually and satisfy your desire in scorched places and make your bones strong; and you shall be like a watered garden, like a spring of water, whose waters do not fail. [12] And your ancient ruins shall be rebuilt; you shall raise up the foundations of many generations; you shall be called the repairer of the breach, the restorer of streets to dwell in.

Luke 14.12-14 - He said also to the man who had invited him, "When you give a dinner or a banquet, do not invite your friends or your brothers or your relatives or rich neighbors, lest they also invite you in return and you be repaid. [13] But when you give a feast, invite the poor, the crippled, the lame, the blind, [14] and you will be blessed, because they cannot repay you. You will be repaid at the resurrection of the just."

2 Cor. 8.9 - For you know the grace of our Lord Jesus Christ, that though he was rich, yet for your sake he became poor, so that you by his poverty might become rich.

Heb. 13.16 - Do not neglect to do good and to share what you have, for such sacrifices are pleasing to God.

Cheerful giving of oneself is the heart of the Gospel, and the key to urban ministry and missions.

What is significant in covering the broad scope of the concepts covered in the first video segment is that you scan all the pertinent issues associated with them. The questions below are meant to help you give a kind of "at-a-glance" approach to this material. It is unrealistic and undesirable to think that you can cover the specific details of all the things associated with poverty and oppression and the environment in your review time. Rather, focus on the general notions of what it means to be a world Christian, and help them understand how such a person might then interpret the pressing issues of poverty and the environment thinking and acting in the most Christian way possible, in other words, to behave *Christianly*.

📖 3
Page 165
Student Questions and Response

The issues covered in this segment all have to do with the question of difference, conflict, and peace. How do we resolve our Lord's insight of Matthew 5.9 "Blessed are the peacemakers, for they shall be called sons of God" and "Do not think that I have come to bring peace to the earth. I have not come to bring peace, but a sword" (cf. Matt. 10.34)?

📖 4
Page 167
Summary of Segment 2

To understand the role of peace as a fundamental and underlying predisposition of the Church and the Christian is to resolve these apparently different statements.

The authors of Hard Sayings of the Bible provide us with a concise and compelling interpretation of the relationship between the two. In speaking of the Matthew 10.34, the authors suggest:

> *This is a hard saying for all who recall the message of the angels on the night of Jesus' birth: "Glory to God in high heaven, and peace on earth among human beings, the objects of God's favor" (as the message seems to mean). True, the angels' message appears only in Luke (Luke 2.14) and the hard saying comes from Matthew. But Luke records the same hard saying, except that he replaces the metaphorical "sword" by the nonmetaphorical "division" (Luke 12.51). Both Evangelists then go on to report Jesus as saying, "For I have come to turn 'a man against his father, a daughter against her*

mother, a daughter-in-law against her mother-in-law'" (Matt. 10.35; Luke 12.53), while Matthew rounds the saying off with a quotation from the Old Testament: "a man's enemies will be the members of his own household" (Mic. 7.6).

One thing is certain: Jesus did not advocate conflict. He taught his followers to offer no resistance or retaliation when they were attacked or ill-treated. "Blessed are the peacemakers," he said, "for they will be called sons of God" (Matt. 5.9), meaning that God is the God of peace, so that those who seek peace and pursue it reflect his character. When he paid his last visit to Jerusalem, the message which he brought it concerned "what would bring you peace," and he wept because the city refused his message and was bent on a course that was bound to lead to destruction (Luke 19.41–44). The message that his followers proclaimed in his name after his departure was called the "gospel of peace" (Eph. 6.15) or the "message of reconciliation" (2 Cor. 5.19 RSV). It was called this not merely as a matter of doctrine but as a fact of experience. Individuals and groups formerly estranged from one another found themselves reconciled through their common devotion to Christ. Something of this sort must have been experienced even earlier, in the course of the Galilean ministry: if Simon the Zealot and Matthew the tax collector were able to live together as two of the twelve apostles, the rest of the company must have looked on this as a miracle of grace.

But when Jesus spoke of tension and conflict within a family, he probably spoke from personal experience. There are indications in the gospel story that some members of his own family had no sympathy with his ministry; the people who on one occasion tried to restrain him by force because people were saying, "He is out of his mind" are called "his friends" in the KJV but more accurately "his family" in the NIV (Mark 3.21). "Even his own brothers did not believe in him," we are told in John 7.5. (If it is asked why, in that case, they attained positions of leadership alongside the apostles in the early church, the answer is no doubt to be found in the statement of 1 Corinthians 15.7 that Jesus, risen from the dead, appeared to his brother James.)

*So, when Jesus said that he had come to bring "not peace but a sword" he meant that this would be the **effect** of his coming, not that it was the **purpose** of his coming. His words came true in the life of the early church, and they have verified themselves subsequently in the history of Christian missions. . . . In [the words of Matthew 10.34]* *then, Jesus was warning his followers that their allegiance to him might cause conflict at home and even expulsion from the family circle. It was well that they should be forewarned, for then they could not say, "We never expected that we should have to pay this price for following him!"*

~ Walter C. Kaiser, Jr., and Peter H. Davids, F. F. Bruce and Manfred T. Brauch, eds. **Hard Sayings of the Bible**. Downers Grove, IL: InterVarsity, 1996. pp. 378-379.

Congratulations, you have completed your class session for this module. Now, your attention must shift to your role as grader in collecting the assignments of the students, and providing them final instructions regarding their work.

Your primary role now is the clear communication of your expectations, and careful recording keeping of what has been turned in to you, by whom, and according to what deadline you have given them. Please make certain that you have commitments for the ministry projects, exegetical projects, and any other assignments that you have given to the students. Careful recording of what each student has given you is central to an accurate assessment of each of your student's overall grades. Again, your discretion regarding late work can easily determine whether you dock students of points, resulting in letter grade changes, or give students an "Incomplete" until the work is finished. However you adopt your standard regarding their work, remember that our courses are not primarily about the grades that students receive, but the spiritual nourishment and training these courses provide. Also, however, remember that helping our students strive for excellence is an integral part of our instruction.

📖 **5**
*Page 189
Assignments*